The Perfect Fit

The Perfect Fit

CREATIVE WORK

in the GLOBAL

SHOE INDUSTRY

CLAUDIO E. BENZECRY

The University of Chicago Press • *Chicago and London*

The University of Chicago Press, Chicago 60637
The University of Chicago Press, Ltd., London
© 2022 by The University of Chicago
Published 2022
Printed in the United States of America

31 30 29 28 27 26 25 24 23 22   1 2 3 4 5

ISBN-13: 978-0-226-81588-6 (cloth)
ISBN-13: 978-0-226-81590-9 (paper)
ISBN-13: 978-0-226-81589-3 (e-book)
DOI: https://doi.org/10.7208/chicago/9780226815893.001.0001

Library of Congress Cataloging-in-Publication Data

Names: Benzecry, Claudio E., author.
Title: The perfect fit : creative work in the global shoe industry /
Claudio E. Benzecry.
Description: Chicago : University of Chicago Press, 2022. |
Includes bibliographical references and index.
Identifiers: LCCN 2021031025 | ISBN 9780226815886 (cloth) |
ISBN 9780226815909 (paperback) | ISBN 9780226815893 (ebook)
Subjects: LCSH: Shoe industry. | Women's shoes—Design. |
Fashion and globalization.
Classification: LCC HD9787.A2 B45 2022 | DDC 338.4/768531—dc23
LC record available at https://lccn.loc.gov/2021031025

Marco Polo imagined answering (or Kublai Khan imagined his answer) that the more one was lost in unfamiliar quarters of distant cities, the more one understood the other cities he had crossed to arrive there; and he retraced the stages of his journeys, and he came to know the Port from which he had set sail, and the familiar places of his youth, and the surroundings of home, and a little square of Venice where he gamboled as a child.

Italo Calvino, *The Invisible Cities*

CONTENTS

PREFACE

The Frailty of Commodity Chains

If you are reading this, it means that humanity has survived the COVID scare of 2020, the virus did not mutate, vaccination worked, and the event is remembered not as a cataclysm but as a great interruption; an interruption in our daily routines, rhythms, relationships, practices. We saw how toilet paper went missing from the supermarket, and we desperately bought brands we had never heard of before. We also switched our consumption patterns, hoping for Amazon and other digital merchants to get us what we needed without the inconvenience of human contact. But the convenience we were used to just wasn't available; packages were delivered much later than usual, if at all; items were not restocked, regardless of whether at a giant chain or a mom and pop shop. We had gotten used to the idea of a frictionless and seamless world, a world that was fully global, with no space not covered in some way by the planetary dream of total connection. This interruption directed our attention to the fact that the global world we inhabit(ed) wasn't exactly as we imagined it. Its stop did not signal that an automated process had come to a halt. Rather, it pointed us toward the fine-tuned work of making sure it never stopped again by paying more attention to the personnel, techniques, and devices that sustained and made the world "global" daily. It wasn't necessarily a world made anew, but it was certainly one that—paraphrasing Dominguez Rubio (2020)—depended on Sisyphean activities, the kind of work that has an end that only signals the beginning of a similar cycle to yield a similar result in the near projected future. The things we are used to having all have to be produced, developed, and distributed, and each of those points in a circuit involves a myriad of people, tasks, and objects that have to be assembled into something relatively coherent to operate in a seamless fashion.

This COVID-19 moment helps us see just how frail commodity chains are on a global scale. And while this vulnerability is easy to notice when it comes to a *détente*, it invites the opposite question about the felicity conditions of commodity chains: How is it that the world of global commodities is built, made to work without breaking points, and kept at such constant pace that we have taken it for granted and accepted it as the condition of our contemporary consumer life? What would it look like to make the work behind the scenes visible?

There are a few candidates to answer this question. Some would point to the political economy and talk about tariffs; other scholars would argue for the role of regulations at the level of world commerce, or of the geopolitical struggle between the US and China for international dominance. In this book I want to suggest a different route, looking instead at the kind of infrastructural work necessary to make sure products (novelty goods in this case) are put together despite geographical distance. And I do this by exploring the work of designers, developers, production managers, fit models, trade agents, and "office girls" in the shoe industry, making sure South Brazil, South China, and New York City are in a contiguous plane.

Female footwear is distinctively individualized, yet at the same time widespread. Fashion supposes—by definition—the supply of constant novelty to consumers. It is a privileged arena to see how commodity chains are sustained, since it combines patterns of repetition and innovation, the monotonous and cheap labor of the factory with the expertise involved in the care of making craft-like products, highlighting a whole series of challenging disjunctures that need to be bridged. Shoe companies have privileged the just-in-time model of work, storage, and product turnover—a model that relies on flexible specialized contractors, which adds an extra layer of complexity in comparison to industries that depend on vertical integration.

Seeing the work of expert care, in situ and unraveling in real time, is a powerful reminder of how the world—as we learned during the COVID pandemic—is not globalized in any final or set way. For five years I followed the women's shoe industry at key clusters of ideation, development, and production. I was able to witness the work of doing globalization, as much as the work of undoing and unraveling it; every attempt to generate stable linkages can be erased or can break down. The work of design is a unique entry point, since shoemaking implies a kind of collective object-creation—with its seasonal emphasis on new products, only for those products to mutate and be consumed in the production process, and for the process to start again—that resembles the Sisyphean labor of keeping "the global" going each and every day.

The pages that follow untangle what techniques, devices, and personnel were behind the scenes making sure shoes made it to consumers in the US, and in the process unravel another puzzle: what are the dynamics of cultural creation on a global scale? If we can think of infrastructures as ties that bind different locales, how are those relationships forged, maintained, and socially lubricated? What are the stories behind the technicians, designers, fit girls, agents, and managers who are usually made into the black box of commodity development, just a blip into the input-output chart? In answering these questions and making these stories visible, the book aims to specify how microempirical situations can give force or substance to a comprehensive account of global production. By the end of the journey, I hope I will have managed to understand not just the unfamiliar quarters that Khan and Marco Polo referred to, but also—more importantly—how much they are linked to the familiar comforts of our home.

Chapter 1

FROM HEAD
TO TOE

GLOBALIZATION, PERIOD

"My friend Herb McGinnis was talking."

This is how Raymond Carver opens his renowned short story "What We Talk about When We Talk about Love." Carver started many of his critically acclaimed short stories this way: we arrive at a stage that is already set, we must guess who these characters are, what their story is, what is actually going on. This suggestive rhetorical device drops us in the middle of the action, immediately forcing us to ask: what was there before? Is that imagined past the same for everyone?

So I wish to start this book by writing: globalization, period.

This is not a book about the beginning of globalization—when would that be, anyway? In the Mediterranean World of AD 1200? At the dawn of the Mongol Empire in the thirteenth century, or during the Islamic expansion into the Iberian Peninsula? At the European basin in the sixteenth century? During the imperial expansion of the nineteenth century? By the migration explosion before the First World War? Or after the recent transformation of the world of production and communication that has led to many books like this one? Who can possibly say? What we do know is that the stage has been set, the story has already started, and in no way have the players involved been invented anew for the occasion.

The players constitute a large ensemble, one in which there are multiple agents, both human and nonhuman, collaborating to generate the global as a scale, not only by producing it but also working on maintaining it—and even repairing it when necessary.

And though this globalization story is not a linear narrative but one made out of multiple intersecting storylines and characters, it can be told through one particular cultural object, one that has historically served as a signifier for gender and class. This one object embodies a world of mobility, with materials and people circulating in multiple ways; it tells a story of labor markets and how it affects their movements; and it shows what it means to produce "original" objects in a fast-moving industry that relies heavily on copying and altering preexisting objects and ideas. It's also about the secondary actors behind this object: the infrastructural workers who support the creators' "heroic" work. This book shows how the creation of a cultural object intertwines capital and its movement, personal careers, the processes of coordination that come from producing a craft at a distance, and complementary and competing types of knowledge. In other words, this is a book on shoes.

This book can also be read as an *anatomy of a scale*, which reveals all the agents, processes, and forms of labor that craft the global from the bottom up. In that sense, it is most certainly about how a global craft (shoemaking) is developed, but it is also about how *the global itself is crafted*. Differently put, it is not just about *a* global craft, but about the craft of *the* global, its idiosyncrasies and the details of scale-making. What kinds of material and social processes put globalities together? What kinds of cultural and personal commitments?

Our characters here are designers in Manhattan preoccupied by trends, what young women wear on the streets of Brooklyn, the quality of sketches, or by how to best imitate a shoe from an expensive brand; a Brazilian technician in South China pissed off at the designer who doesn't know the difference between an Italian shoe size 37 and an American size 6; a Taiwanese developer trying to reproduce in cheaper materials the work he has just done for an American brand for their own designs; a Chinese pattern-maker who has to reproduce the measurements given to him for the upper part of a shoe and make it into a paper pattern by hand; or a Chinese fit model who has been trained by an expat technician to best understand how her foot can be used to standardize production for all women's shoes, anywhere they are sold. What all these people share is a viewpoint in which they know themselves to be complementary to other agents whom they need to coordinate with.

And yet, each in his or her corner of the world, they all imagine themselves as "the" key player in developing a shoe, from beginning to end.

Like many scholars before me, I followed one of the *dicta* of global ethnographies over the last quarter century: to follow the object (Marcus 1995; Clifford 1997). Of course, if we take an infrastructural understanding of what an object is, we need to go beyond the object qua thing, and think also of the knowledges, discourses, forms, templates, tools, and people attached to and stored in them. My threefold strategy was (1) to follow how shoe development for the US market moved from Novo Hamburgo in Brazil to Dongguan in South China; (2) to trace the detailed and widespread knowledge contained in making a shoe; and (3) to follow the careers of the agents who aim to produce an ecology of taste.

WHY SHOES?

Studies of globalization have divided themselves rather neatly. For instance, there are a lot of studies about labor regimes. Thanks to them we know a lot about the gendered character of factory production in the third world, the role of managers in surveillance and control, the search for cheap and docile bodies to occupy places in the factory line, the role that gender and racial stereotypes play in the production of those bodies to begin with, the daily work rhythms and routines in such factories, the exploitative character and low pay that explain the cheap cost of clothing in the US, and the variation of the organization of work depending on whether the commodities involved are state-produced or private.[1] There are also plenty of studies about the role of screens, forms, templates, and some face-to face-interaction in coordinating the generation of knowledge at a distance, whether studying high-end finance, the production of cars, the creation of video games, the work of engineers, or the support networks of scholars in the physical and social sciences.[2]

There is, on the one hand, a robust scholarship on commodities with added value, one that mobilizes ideas and concepts from the sociology of knowledge and from social studies of science and technologies. On the other hand, though, there are very few studies that have explored how knowledge is generated in commodities with relatively low value added to them, such as shoes. This conception of shoes as products without much elaboration is not only a scholarly misconception; world agencies such as the United Nations also classify shoes as a low commodity chain, with light manufacture and low wages, considered only above animal products and byproducts. Studying shoe development and design for the export market for mid-tier women's shoes beyond—or before—the factory is a unique opportunity to show how these two scholarships can be combined to scrutinize knowledge generation in low-value-added commodities. Leather shoes are a particularly fruitful case in which to observe this, as they combine the search for cheap labor throughout the globe with the need for a particular kind of expert knowledge: embodied, tacit, informal, localized.

SPEED AND GEOGRAPHY

Shoes are not only the result of cheap labor; rather, they result from the encounter of relatively unskilled work with clusters of expert knowledge. And the geography of that encounter is disjunctured. The two kinds of work coincide in the same place usually for a few years, requiring different strategies to match the work of design and sample rooms and the work of factories, and the coordination, control, and supervision of the former over the latter. Thus, to the coexistence of these two kinds of work—one highly qualified, the other with very little expertise—we need to add a second dimension that contributes to the disjuncture and to the issues of coordination and knowledge transfer I explore in this book: the speed with which factories move, and the changing geographies of control and supervision that result from this.

To wit: much of the shoe production for the US moved from South Brazil to South China in the mid-1990s after a currency readjustment in Brazil made the cheaper part of the labor too expensive. Chinese shoe labor reached its apex in 2004—when almost 80 percent of leather shoes for the women's market were produced in Dongguan, in comparison to the 30 percent still being made there when I finished fieldwork in early 2017. Shoe production has receded to other parts of China and into Southeast Asia. This abrupt movement resulted in all kinds of problems of delegation and control at a distance, and it provides us with a unique case that looks at expertise networks and coordination issues within the production of a low-added-value commodity.

The Perfect Fit studies the design and development of leather shoes for the US women's market, focusing on the multiple coordination issues that result when shoes are designed and developed in between New York and Dongguan (China); on the intimacies that develop between workers with very different backgrounds and skills (US designers, Brazilian and Taiwanese technicians, Chinese and Taiwanese managers, and Chinese and Brazilian fit models); and on the diverse paths that materials and careers follow until they meet on the sample-room floor. Instead of another study of global exploitation—be it on the labor regimes of the workers or on the transnational elite networks of owners and managers—I look at another type of work: people in charge of design and development. These people are of course exploited and contribute to the creation of value as well, but a focus on them allows us to explore dimensions of the global production process that are usually occluded by the dichotomies organizing the scholarship.

This ecological view—in the sense that the Chicago School and later scholars of science, technology, and society (STS) have given to the term—is at the service of one important question: how is it that mass-produced shoes are developed as a "global" craft even before they enter the factory? That inquiry is at the service of a larger warrant: to understand the design component that makes relatively inexpensive, beautiful objects and results in customers in the US knowingly buying products from countries with inhumane labor conditions. To paraphrase Walter Benjamin (1974), while it is true that there has never been a document of culture that is not simultaneously one of barbarism, we know—when it comes to mass fashion—a lot about the latter and little about the former. To be blunt, we know why shoes are cheap but very little about how they are made beautiful.

In exploring the global craft of making inexpensive but compelling shoes, I show how knowledge is generated and mobilized. I do so by discussing the processes of apprenticeship of designers, technicians, and fit models; the tension between embodied and disembodied forms of knowledge; the possibilities of codifying and formalizing embodied and tacit knowledge; and the traffic in objects, forms, and people necessary to make correction and approval possible. What are the coordination mechanisms? How is it that things move? And how do they stay the same while being moved from one place to the next?

Answering these questions goes to the heart of an issue that has interested social scientists studying how social and spatial proximity have been able to substitute for vertical integration in production.[3] Some of these sociologists and geographers have looked at the process of regionalization and how it relates to the outsourcing of production to the poorer areas of the world. While the regionalization process points at how the cluster of services, workers, and infrastructure generates a spillover effect in which firms learn how to coordinate with one another, outsourcing, on the other hand, refers to how the less elaborated and expensive parts of the process can be shipped to the periphery. Looking at these processes has been a proxy for interrogating the differential rates and speeds at which capital and labor are movable. Key to

this literature has been the kinds of knowledge that can be moved or mobilized from one context to another. What some scholars have called "sticky"
knowledge, which is costly to acquire, transfer, and use in a new location, is
in this project a fruitful avenue to study how and when work can be moved
from one location to the next (Von Hippel 1994). Part of what I'll be discussing
in detail here is how this kind of knowledge—embodied, informal, tacit—can
be reproduced, and by which procedures, in lower nodes of the value chain.

OF FETISHES AND COMMODITIES

Objects like shoes have been conceptualized and studied under two different overarching frameworks. Scholars of capitalism—following Marx—have
decried the tension between the material and the immaterial character of
production, the homogenizing effect of producing for a mass market, and
how much procedures like branding (i.e., the signature on the produced object by a singular creator) generate alienation and hide the actual relations
of production behind the commodity, underlining its abstract nature. The
exchangeable quality of production for profit is presented as the actual reality
behind a secondary ghostly presence, one made out of presenting the object
as unique and, as such, potentially capable of attachment and identification.[4]

Yet some anthropologists (Kopitoff, 1986; Appadurai, 1986; Lee and Li-
Puma, 2002), by bringing together the Marxist theories of production and the
work of anthropologists like Marcel Mauss or Brosinslaw Malinowski, have
instead focused on the meanings produced as objects circulate, and how even
things produced under capitalism can still generate singularization—the personalized attribution of value beyond what it costs to produce something,
instead of the homogeneity that one would expect from the production of
commodities. While shoes are mass-produced, they still act as fetishes, in
most cases as personalized markers of identity, and—as multiple documents
of popular culture have shown—as sources of fantasy. (See the whole *Sex and
the City* series, for instance, and its obsession with shoes at large and *Manolo
Blahniks* in particular.) Designers know this, as they systematically go to
shops in New York to observe the routines of friends who shop together—and
sometimes of mothers and daughters, who have ingrained shopping in their
everyday practices of satisfaction.

So instead of thinking of shoes either as commodities or as fetishes,
this book focuses on those who work in producing the logic of difference—
designers and developers—which bridges the two ways of conceptualizing

shoes. In lieu of decrying and denouncing the reality of one as substituted by the other, the two bodies of the ghostly presence of production and potential consumption inhabit the shoe together. Rather than analyzing commodities to unveil the exploitation that is hidden in them, I want to unpack the commodity to reveal other relationships between people that the object, seen as dull and inert, is not revealing. I scrutinize the commodity to show the relationships between people—without assuming from the get-go that we will *only* find exploitative relationships, but keeping that assumption at bay or in suspense, to illuminate other relationships that remain hidden if we only look at the commodity as a container of exploited labor and not much else. It is not, in other words, that a schematic Marxist view gets it wrong, but rather that it takes a part (commodities' exploitative and alienating aspect) for the whole (the commodity as the crystallization of human relationships), in what it could be called a misplaced or misleading synecdoche.

There is of course an economic story to be considered when studying object design and development; it goes hand in hand with one about the realization of desires, and the story can't be exhausted just by the explanation of the relationships of production (on this see Stallybrass 1998). The history accumulated in the object—as I unpack it from its inception to its production—is one in which both people *and* objects are social beings. Looking at design and development allows us to think of production and identification in a different way, one that underscores the strategies for creating singularization (making objects unique or special, and as such not immediately substitutable for any and every other) *within* the process of commodity-making itself.

That cohabitation gives us a good entry point into what historian William Sewell, Jr. (2010) has called the subsumption of desire under capitalism. In his work on the textile industry in Lyon in the late eighteenth and the nineteenth centuries, the historian shows how the success of the early capitalist entrepreneurs in that industry depended both on their ability to coordinate production spatially and temporally, as well as on their providing goods that had consumer appeal in Paris—where the word for fashion was coined, after all.[5] Moreover, his article exploring the beginning of design-oriented capitalism highlights a second dimension central to the kind of work undertaken in this book: how design adds value to the capitalist process without adding hours of labor for input. It did so through the work of Lyonnaise designers who would go to Paris to see what was in fashion and then adapt it a bit and put together their new materials. The parallelisms with the story I narrate here—at a different scale—are staggering.

Looking at designers allows us to see a key agent in the lash-up between the already existing fashion objects and those only projected by trend fore-casters, as well as between the taste of consumers in New York and the pro-ductive capacities of sample rooms and factories in Dongguan. Unlike most studies focused either on consumption or on labor at the factories, entering through the sample room allows us to complement the more traditional Marx-ist view of the political economy of commodity creation with the wondrous interpretation of the accomplishments of capitalism qua modernity and mod-ernism. As advanced by Marshall Berman's (1982) reading of *The Communist Manifesto*, the idea here is that capitalism can thrive in crisis and catastrophe, that it has been an engine for both reinvention and self-destruction, and that within it tragedy and beauty go hand-in-hand. The last empirical chapter of the book focuses on the tragic dimension of the development of capitalism, as it explores the ruin-like character of what was left behind in Novo Hamburgo, Brazil, and the personal and collective consequences for those living there, as production for export to the US moved mostly to South China.

If the story of globalization is usually presented as one of progress and endless expansion, the last two sections of the book show the unfolding of the global narrative. Novo Hamburgo is the flip side of South China and of the mundane, yet extraordinary, activities of maintenance that make that region what it is. Thanks to that juxtaposition we get to see that (a) there is nothing set or teleological about how globalization unfolds; (b) the projects of order and classification that we associate with globalization are always on the verge of breakdown, almost like a monster storm blowing in on the horizon. In doing this research, I was able to witness the work of doing glob-alization as much as the work of undoing, unraveling, and disconnecting it—understanding how every attempt at generating stable linkages can be erased or break down.

AN ECOLOGY OF TASTE

I can imagine a lot of scholarly readers most likely don't care about shoes—or at least they like to pretend that is the case. And yet, if you are reading this book, there is a strong chance you have owned or currently own shoes from one of the these brands, which all produce their lines through procedures similar to the ones described here: Aldo, Nine West, Kenneth Cole, Tory Burch, and Michael Kors, among plenty of others. Shoes are ubiquitous ev-eryday objects, all around us.

The paradox about people who are not interested in fashion is that the less they care about it, the more dependent they are on fashion's expert systems. To put it bluntly, if you do not care about what you wear, there is a strong chance a lot of your choices are shaped by experts who make things closer and easier for you. You are more likely to look to the selections made by designers, trend forecasters, salespeople, and others who compete and coordinate to put together what I've called an "ecology of taste": the relatively finite number of items that are made available after an intense process of curation, selection, and decanting out of all the information available from trends, shopping trips, sales teams. Fashion is not about the management of scarcity but rather about the management of excess (see Abbott 2014) and the different procedures for deciding what to weed out and how to provide stability to an endless set of possibilities.

This process of soaking in can be best seen in a scene from the movie *The Devil Wears Prada*, in which Meryl Streep plays a fictionalized version of legendary *Vogue* editor Anna Wintour. Streep is shown two belts, which to the untrained eye look the same, by an assistant who says, "It's a tough call. They are so different." A second assistant chuckles at the comment, and—after being reprimanded—says, "They look the same to me. I'm still learning about this stuff." Streep's answer—which has been the source of multiple memes and videos online—highlights, synthesizes, and underscores the relationship between detachment towards fashion, expert curation, and choice. Referring to the sweater worn in that scene by the second assistant, she retorts,

> This "stuff?" Oh. Okay. I see. You think this has nothing to do with
> you. You go to your closet and you select, I don't know, that lumpy
> blue sweater, for instance, because you're trying to tell the world
> that you take yourself too seriously to care about what you put on
> your back. . . . However, that blue represents millions of dollars and
> countless jobs and it's sort of comical how you think that you've
> made a choice that exempts you from the fashion industry when,
> in fact, you're wearing the sweater that was selected for you by the
> people in this room from a pile of "stuff."

The ecological approach (Dominguez Rubio 2015) I'm using to organize analysis and narrative takes into account the kind of knowledge that knowing "this stuff" generates. It does so via the observation of people in "this room" across time and space, looking at the work of people in charge of design but observing also *how* that backstage work happens.

In addition to the most obvious actors like designers and trend forecasters, the book shows at the empirical level all the nonmanagerial material care—as Leigh Star (1995) called it—that takes place within the craft itself, via the work of sourcing agents, leather and shoe technicians, fit models, and other usually minor and unobserved players (see, for instance, Entwistle 2009; Mears 2011; Wissinger 2015; Lantz 2016). We can then see how knowledge is coordinated, enacted, learned, and contested. We can also make sure we are reconceptualizing fashion not just as an immaterial practice but as a practice heavily dependent on the intimate knowledge of how materials (leather, lace, cow suede) behave.

Taking an ecological view means thinking of the particular and deliberate ways in which all the things that have to be placed to be able to produce shoes get there, as well as how they are arranged together. I take an infrastructural standpoint and pay attention to both human and nonhuman actors because this approach allows us to see how both object and subject participate in a particular kind of career pattern that ties them to particular assemblages. We get to see how materials arrive at the sample room in Dongguan, as well as the different kind of subjects that navigate their way there. This approach has the double advantage of allowing us to see firsthand the power of the little routines, standards, technologies, devices, and infrastructure that take time to set up. It also explains why capital cannot move somewhere with cheaper labor immediately, as it needs the supervision of these expert clusters of infrastructural knowledge.[6] The second advantage is that the interconnection I conceptualized comes from how participants in these overlapping social worlds think about their own craft: over and over during fieldwork, designers, technicians, sourcing agents, and fit models said—in the words of Joao and Rose, two Brazilian developers—"Shoes are made by lots and lots of people!"

HOW DO YOU LIVE IN A WORLD OF SALIERIS?

The movie *Amadeus* presented Mozart as the pinnacle of an irreverent version of how culture is created in which novelty, creativity, inspiration, and originality go hand-in-hand. The movie used as a dramatic counterpart to his genius the figure of another composer, Italian Habsburg court *kappelmeister* Antonio Salieri, who was presented not only as envious of Wolfgang Amadeus

Mozart but, more importantly for us, as derivative: a formalist who reproduced the same music over and over and over. These tropes are easy to find in
different worlds of symbolic production, and its study has resulted in a robust
scholarship within sociology. (To mention a few, see the work of authors as
disparate as Elias 1993; DeNora 1997; Becker 2013; Bourdieu 1988; Heinich
1996.) What matters to this book is less the debunking of the genius theory of
creativity than seeing how people who inhabit an industry that has since its
inception organized itself around the idea of novelty, beauty, distinction, and
originality cope with the incessant demand for new products to make it to
the shops, as well as with the intricate structure of the shoe-producing world.

In transitioning from questions about ecology and its constraints and
affordances, I explore in the first part of the book the interactions between
the complexity of infrastructural work; how designers, technicians, and others organize their experience; and through which categories of attachment
they do so.

Despite the recognition of working interdependence and the ensuing
distributed cognition, agents participate in this world called into action by
categories of uniqueness. Though authorship of shoes actually does not exist in the way we think of it (there is no signature, no outside recognition of
the work of the many under the name of one), practices and careers are still
organized by the passion for producing originality and novelty, even if under
a different guise. It was common during my fieldwork to see designers and
technicians excited as final samples and finalized shoes actually came back
from the factory. Designers would claim particular shoes while walking with
me on the streets of New York, letting me know, "That shoe is mine!" Technicians and developers—even though their work always came after the work
of others—were excited about how some of their proposed solutions altered
a shoe as to make it work.

This attachment at the level of craft-making is predicated on two relatively
contradictory but related phenomena. First, while copying is a backbone of
the industry, people in it are very secretive about their own work, design,
sketches, and procedures. I had people ask me to please erase identifying
details as much as possible as to not be recognized in interviews; office managers authorized me to take notes but not to take pictures of their facilities;
designers asked me not to publish the sketch for a particular shoe (even after
I explained to them the pace of scholarly publication), or the names of shops
where they go to chase after the shoes they base their designs after, which
they call "originals." To honor these requests, I have modified the names of

specific companies and people in the book to ensure anonymity, although I use the real names of cities, provinces, regions, and public figures.

Second, that restricted version of originality goes hand-in-hand with this: the better the shoe, the more significant the brand, and the more successful the line, the more its authorship is hidden. Only insiders in the industry—who systematically poach designers from one company to the next, which makes the issue of protecting oneself against copying via secrecy more absurd for an outsider—know the head designer behind a particular brand within a particular company. As Roma, one of the many designers I met through fieldwork, explained: "Folks who buy shoes believe behind all this there is an older Italian gentleman who draws inspiration from thin air and just sketches."

GLOBAL INTIMACIES

The connection between the collective process of self-selection and originality, and the way both are sustained by knowledge distributed across multiple actors and locales, results in the recognition of that interdependence as seen in the gratitude and intimacy between designers and support personnel in China. The category of intimacy has been used to map out the interrelated yet distant geographies of how the liberal ideal of citizenship, indentured servitude, colonialism, and slavery were connected in the eighteenth and nineteenth centuries (Lowe 2015), as well as to show the face-to-face ethnic links that sustain the fashion industry behind the scenes (Moon 2014). Little has been made of the fact that intimacy is built both face-to-face and at a distance, and that it crosses over geographical and ethnic lines. Intimacy is sometimes easier to sustain than when constantly in the same location; and it is of a more intense kind than intimacy between coworkers in the same location. This intensity derives from designers arriving in China looking forward to hanging out after working hours with their temporary coworkers—Brazilian and Taiwanese technicians, Chinese office girls—as well as looking for former coworkers who may also be in town. They also travel especially for weddings, and attend end-of-the-year company parties together. Kin, friendship, and intimate relations work as "the connective tissue" that makes globalization possible.

Putting a bigger spotlight on kin, friendship, and intimate relations supposes a shift from narratives treating globalization as the byproduct of just organizational and politicoeconomic arrangements. As the book shows, scale-making is not just a matter of standards, networks of expertise, infrastructures, and the like, but also a process that takes place through the intimate lines and vectors created by kin and affective relations.

Intimacy and distributed cognition are closely related, which points to another dimension explored in this book: knowledge is distributed across multiple individuals, forms, templates, devices, and objects at a *global* scale. Most classic studies of how knowledge operates through multiple means and human and nonhuman actors looks at a relatively self-enclosed ecology of how this happens, so there are numerous studies of airplane cockpits (Hutchins and Klausen 1996), engineers solving working problems (Leonardi 2010; Vaughan 1996), or naval ships' maneuvering operations (Hutchins 1995).

One of the warrants for writing this book is to show the collaborative and social production of knowledge on a different scale, extending the classical "worlds/conventions" (Strauss 1978; Becker 1982; Star 1990) approach at a different scale. This necessitates showing both the labor of microcoordination at the level of work practices, as well as the practices that allow for the flattening of the world, the production of the global scale as coming from micro, everyday practices. We see this especially in chapters 4 and 5, where I show the work of generating standards for the shoe industry and how they stem from the interaction between a fit model's actual foot and technicians' careful craft. There are multiple problems of translation between differential rhythms of production and geographies. Some of these are about enrolling actors so they think of the task at hand as the same; some are about producing scalability and translatability, via the stability of the object that gets circulated and moved between locales. In elaborating these challenges, I underscore how *The Perfect Fit's* analytical purchase is not just about putting shoes together but rather about how the global scale itself is put together and maps out what is at stake: understanding the constant, expert care and coordination work at the micro level that allow for the global scale to actually function, even for a lower-value-added commodity like shoes.

This relationship has, of course, a historical dimension. As hinted earlier, global shoemaking was actually geographically segregated until the mid-1990s, with two clear-cut circuits: one for US mid-tier markets, which used expert labor from Spain, Portugal, Italy, Mexico, and Brazil; and another circuit for cheaper shoes that was put together by Taiwanese entrepreneurs (on this see Hamilton and Kao 2017) and united mainland China with Hong Kong and Taiwan. While US buyers made sure Elche, León, Novo Hamburgo, Veneto, and Estoril were all part of the same map, all of them existed as part of a different world than Dongguan.

The currency crisis of Brazil in 1994, which ended up revaluing the local currency against the dollar and consequently made the cost of labor "too expensive," gave impetus to US buyers and Brazilian factory owners to explore what would it be like to produce shoes in South China. This relationship was further cemented in 2005, when a second currency crisis killed large-scale production from Brazil for the US market, resulting in the migration to Guangdong province of technicians, developers, fit models, and other kinds of expert work (Kuhn Jr. and Nunes 2012). New York, Novo Hamburgo, and Dongguan all coexist in the same space (as Law 1986 and Hetherington and Law 2000 would have put it); space is not a given, an empty container, but it is rather made and includes problems of distance, coordination, the stability of objects, and the passage points they have to go through.

Exploring the interrelation between scale, knowledge, coordination, and intimacy results in a few important sociological lessons—which I develop more in detail in the conclusion. This allows us to disentangle and re-entangle major taken-for-granted categories usually thought of *a priori* in binary terms, like global and local; the difference between design and production; and how the geographical division of labor has been thought about after the distinction between industrial districts and outsourcing. I am interested in looking at scale-making projects within the development process itself and how this examination results in a different understanding of those binaries.

A LABORATORY OF COMMODITIES

At the theoretical level, this book puts the framework of laboratory ethnography developed by sociologists of knowledge and STS scholars in dialogue with commodity-chain literature and the "follow the thing" approach. Ultimately, I aim to show that globalization is a patterned and unequal process, but it does not happen unidirectionally (on this see Carrillo 2017), nor in neatly divided geographical locations. Although these approaches are by no means entirely compatible, I rely on them to steer me in certain directions of importance.

Like historians of the commodity chain, I emphasize how production and circulation happen in multiple contingent ways, rather than by executive fiat or managerial omniscience. Whether studying the attempt to replicate rubber production in Amazonia (Grandin 2009); how different strains of plantain became the bananas we consume in our supermarkets (Soluri 2005); the interrelations between slavery, sugar plantations in the Caribbean, and middle class consumption in Britain (Mintz 1985); the interdependence of cotton, slavery, war, and state-formation in the US (Beckert 2015); the unexpected changes in gender roles in rural Mexico because of the closure of an Illinois appliance factory, and its relocation on the other side of the border (Broughton 2015); or the multiple ways in which coca became cocaine (Gootenberg 2008), this scholarship has emphasized the work of intermediaries in building transnational connections, and how objects are used to trace deeper, hidden relational stories and meanings.

Like anthropologists who study value chains and cycles, I take as an orientation how to think of the production of an object as a career, and the different valuation regimes under which a good can be qualified. When and how are objects commodities (Kopytoff 1986)? When are they decommodified (Appadurai 1986)? When does a thing become an object (Gell 1998; Dominguez Rubio 2016; Gordillo 2014)? When is its value predicated on uniqueness (Velthuis 2005; Karpik 2010; Callon et al. 2002)? When is it predicated on personalization (Kopytoff 1986)? How do particular agents coproduce the object as a multiplicity able to be different things in different contexts (Tsing 2013; Bestor 2004)?

From materiality-centered cultural sociology I've been inspired by work that has explored objects' role in affording and constraining particular lines of action (Molotch 2003; Zubrzycki 2011); the extent to which objects are docile or unruly in their interaction with the infrastructure they generate (Dominguez Rubio 2014); the intersection of multiple—expert and nonexpert—accumulated kinds of material knowledges necessary for the construction of infrastructure (Mukerji 2009, 2010); and my own previous work on how selfhood and particular versions of an object become intertwined over time (Benzecry 2015).

From laboratory studies and the scholarship on science and technology studies, I take their interest in mapping out the connections between multiple sites, not as something taken for granted but as something that has to be empirically traced and unraveled (Latour 2005). Sometimes this happens by looking at the role of virtual microstructures and scenes that produce connections between the sites (as in the work of Knorr-Cetina and her collaborators). The literature on standards and commensuration that has developed from this scholarship has looked at how standards are produced, and yet they are constraining, generating infrastructures and patterns of action attached to them (Bowker and Star 1999; Lampland and Star 2009; Timmermans and Epstein 2010).

While I know these literatures are disparate and do not cohere into one body of scholarship or a tradition, I would like to highlight how much they all share the emphasis on practice, on the role of routines, and on the centrality of understanding the material world both as a source of resistance and as a processual accomplishment. I believe this choral take on theories in the plural matches well with the multiple agents and geographies presented in the manuscript.

Ultimately, this book aims to bring into the sociology of (global) cultural production insights from the pragmatist-inspired sociology of work (Blumer 1969; Garfinkel 1967; Hughes 1971; Strauss 2001) that have since been developed and turned into common knowledge within the sociology of knowledge and Science and Technology Studies (STS). I'm thinking here of concepts like *translation, inscription, invisible work, immutable mobiles, infrastructure*, or *boundary objects*.[7] Low-level commodity production is not usually thought of as a place where knowledge is produced; rather, it is studied either through a global value-chain approach or an attention to shop-floor politics. In this unexpected match between case and theory, I aim to defamiliarize the work of coordinating tacit and embodied forms of knowing.

IN THEIR SHOES

Hasta que choque China con Africa, te voy a perseguir
Hasta que choque China con Africa, te voy a preguntar

Sumo, *Lo Quiero Ya*

Much as the verses in the epigraph for this section, to understand the movement of commodities around the world (until China and Africa collide, the lyrics on the epigraph say) I developed a strategy in which I could both chase the process of shoemaking (*te voy a perseguir*) and inquire into it (*a preguntar*). When studying globalization, the theory-method nexus has usually favored macrolevel approaches. Even those that focus on the micro have emphasized it as an *explanandum* of the macro. Some scholars have worked to generate large-scale accounts of commodity production or network formation (as in the work of Manuel Castells or Gary Gereffi and his collaborators, most noticeably Bair 2009), whereas others have used the ethnographic yet "localized" study of how global forces act in particular locales (mostly Michael Burawoy and his students; see Sallaz 2009, 2019; Hanser 2006; Thayer 2001). A few recent studies have focused on the "production of" culture, knowledge, and subjects—or their contestation—by looking at the role of state and market actors in changing colonial and postcolonial contexts.[8] Less attention has been given in sociology to "friction" (Tsing 2005), the contingency lurking within every link of the large-scale chains, and the notion that each step along a commodity chain is an arena of its own, with actors *in micro* competing and collaborating in real time. So my methodological choices for this book have been anchored in one organizing question: What happens when we look at "the global" as something that needs to be maintained by actors worried in the quotidian about its potential breakdown? What are the routines, techniques, and practices that sustain the scale day to day? And what happens when they do not work?

To trace this, I put myself in the shoes of multiple agents, sometimes for long periods. For instance, I "shadowed" designers for over a year, going with them to shopping and development trips, attended review meetings, sharing their working days. On the other hand, I spent two or three days with sourcing agents trying to figure out their daily routines and understand how they established the worth of one piece of lace over another. I also put myself on the other side of the counter and traveled with an Italian team trying to sell leather to Chinese wholesalers for their domestic market. In between, I spent several days with technicians, sometimes on-site looking at their work, be it with the fit models or at factories supervising that final samples and the shoes to be dispatched look and feel the same; other times I was off-site, usually talking with them over a meal for a few hours—usually in their homes—about their life stories and work routines.

Doing this kind of ethnographic research meant working on- and off-site. It also meant that—while always privileging firsthand observation of routines and interactions—some of the data I produced was the result of "being there" and seeing, hearing, and touching with my own body. When I could not be there, I relied on multiple accounts of work routines as communicated by different agents. And by "different" I mean that I tried not only to corroborate how work happened via other agents from the same team (if the designer said something, I checked with the technician, the fit model, and the developers and managers when available) but also to ask other designers, technicians, and fit models if they worked in the same way.

Lastly, I was shown a lot of routines and spaces. When producing data in that way I adopted what sociologist Margaret Kusenbach (2003) called "going along," focusing mostly on the cognitive, perceptual, and mnemonic evocations generated by the agents walking me along their daily routine, still in what naturalist ethnographers call their "natural setting," but organizing the experience of it so as to help me make sense of "what was going on."

Research for this project began in 2012, when I started looking at images from a trend-forecasting site, in a category it called "Global Streets"—where people from different parts of the world posed and served as a resource for designers looking for inspiration for designs and sketches. I collected 3,827 pictures ranging from May 2009 to May 2012. Later in 2013—as I described above—I started "shadowing" a New York design team, visiting their offices weekly, attending some review meetings, and accompanying them on shopping trips, first within New York and then to Miami, Los Angeles, and later—twice in 2014—Europe. In some cases—following the back-and-forth of approval process of three shoe styles—I had access to email communication between designers and their Dongguan office. I also attended two corporate meetings on the West Coast, as well as trade fairs in New York, Miami, and Milan, seeing how designers looked at materials to use in their designs.

My first trip to Dongguan took place in January 2014. I went there with the design team to see their development process. I returned in December 2014, and then twice a year in 2015 and 2016. I spent a total of 107 days in Dongguan during those three years, moving slowly away from the design team into the work of trading offices, sample rooms, and showrooms. I later interviewed technicians, managers, developers, and fit models as well—seventy-nine in total. When possible, I interviewed the designers from the team I followed later, as they were working for other companies. This follow-up enabled me to see how much the work routines I had observed and learned applied in other contexts. I also interviewed designers from other companies as to better compare.

As I encountered the work of Brazilian technicians in South China, I slowly started focusing one part of the research there on their life stories and on the process of how they transferred their knowledge between contexts. Encouraged by them, I pursued a third geographical site, and during the summer of 2016, I conducted research in Novo Hamburgo, in Rio Grande do Sul, and surrounding areas, where the export shoe industry had its heyday during the 1980s and 1990s. In total, I conducted fifty-two semistructured interviews with Brazilian technicians, fit models, and agents at both sites. I also undertook archival and visual research in the Vale dos Sinos region, mainly at the Sindicato dos Trabalhadores do Calçado, and used secondary sources from a local specialized journal, *Jornal NH*. At that site I enlisted the help of a local research assistant, Francieli Ruppenthal, who continued the archival research.

Much like the dean of global ethnography Ulf Hannerz (Hannerz 2003, 2004) has discussed, this kind of ethnographic work constitutes a polymorphous engagement, where not only the ethnographer has to be in multiple locales and show the linkages among them, but also in which the classic character of long-term immersive work in one site gets transformed into something else: the constant in and out of sites; the multiplicity of activities—observation, conversation, reenactment—and forms—face-to-face, text message, Skype, communication via research assistant—used for staying in touch with people in the field; as well as augmentation of something that is intrinsic to the practice of qualitative work itself, its iterative character. The complexity of studying a site that has porous borders and gets drawn and redrawn as questions get established and then refined is magnified by the lack of *one* actual site where things happen. As I've hinted already, they happen in parallel in multiple sites, but also on screens and sometimes between the same group of people (designers, for instance) throughout multiple contexts: a shopping trip to Los Angeles, an email exchange with developers in Dongguan, a meeting in New York to decide on the sketches to become prototypes, or physically on China or Brazil to work with local teams of developers and technicians.

The modesty of this kind of exploration (Hannerz 2004, 10) or ethnology (Holmes and Marcus 2006, 23) and its relatively limited character from the get-go is also the result of the fact that unlike the more traditional ethnographies of global work, this one studies up (Nader 1972; Gusterson 1997; Ho 2009; Ortner 2010). *The Perfect Fit* focuses on actors with a certain amount of power and expertise, who in a lot of cases granted me only indirect and absolutely anonymous access to the experiences of their social worlds. Doing this kind of fieldwork was odd at first for those of us trained in the classic techniques of naturalistic observation; it felt like being deployed and constantly waiting. Some days I saw three people and ended up with six hours' worth of tape; some others had a twenty-minute morning conversation and a bunch of missed appointments. Sundays were particularly fruitful days, as most people had the day off and wanted to meet for lunch or breakfast (Brazilians, usually at a German place owned by a Brazilian), visit Starbucks (Chinese fit models), hang out at the hotel (US designers relaxing from work), or visiting them for a whole day with other co-nationals while enjoying a barbecue (Brazilians again).

My access was also intermittent and dependent on intermediaries. This was especially true with some of the Chinese fit models. While the industry operates on "work" English—a relatively limited and task-oriented version of the language—and most other people within the industry operate fully within that language in work contexts—that wasn't the case for a lot of the fit models.[9] Whenever I saw them outside work, it was together with an intermediary, either a technician they had worked with or a Chinese expert worker with better English skills who served as a translator and third participant in the conversation. Those interviews became more like long unfolding polyphonic conversations than the classic one-on-one conversation going through a questionnaire.

WRITING AN ETHNOGRAPHY; BUILDING A STUDY OBJECT

There's doors and . . . more doors.
And behind all the doors, there's another inside, and another outside.
And things happen, happen, HAPPENING. It never stops.

Emma Donoghue, *Room*

This epigraph captures the sheer sense of exhilaration that comes from doing this kind of ethnographic work. Every scene opens up a potential new path for research, and with it a whole series of questions: Shall I learn how to do technical work on a shoe, like one of the senior technicians suggested? Should I follow the sourcing agents to the markets? Once in the markets was it smart to try to understand how leathers make it there? And if I did that, should I have accepted an invitation from an Italian tannery, the showroom of which I visited in Houjie, to go back to Arzignano and see how they process the material? And once there, should I have taken advantage of my Argentinean contacts, and gone to Luján to see where the leather carcasses that are treated in Italy and then used in Dongguan come from?

Every new contact, every new observation—each long and engaging conversation with someone from the industry—opened up a new avenue for exploration that led to one important question for ethnography: where does one stop? Why? How? One of the challenges that accompanies this kind of qualitative scholarship is how to best capture and reveal the bewildering childlike excitement of what happens without resulting in an incomprehensible collection of details without an order or a conceptual story to tell.

The key to understand how to confront this issue, as advocated by my colleague Andrew Deener (2018), might be to explain not the *process of empirical inclusion* (as we see in appendixes where we read about the heroic character of the incredible amount of fieldwork we've done, resulting in thousands of pages of notes and transcriptions) as the only way to demonstrate the reliability of our data, but rather to focus on the *process of narrowing down the case*. Doing so allows us to better understand the research process as a collective and institutional project that involves colleagues, students, reviewers, mentors, and editors.

And I want to quote Deener (2018) verbatim here:

> How researchers learn to exclude certain subjects, points of data, and alternative analytic themes is difficult to recount and assess, but it is of equal importance to constructing cases. Empirical errors occur when ethnographers misstate or misidentify basic facts as they relate to subjects, situations, events and locations. Empirical errors are different than the observational and interpretive omissions necessary to narrow down and hold constant the units and levels of analysis. Ethnographers should be very concerned about getting the facts right, but they should be equally concerned about getting the case right.

I started with a perspective that combined the literatures on global value chains, outsourcing, and creative industries. I ended up with a laboratory-studies and materiality-friendly account of how global collaboration happens. Following an object meant following also the translation and diffusion of ideas, capital, and work. The focus on designers and office workers slowly produced a different picture of globalization than if I had followed—as other scholars have already done with great gusto and success—the transnational elite or the sufferings of factory or domestic workers. While some of the key ideas were there from the outset (questions about originality and replicability, about how to disembody and recodify informal types of knowledge), they gained definition, logic, and coherence as I encountered the right kinds of questions and the conceptual apparatus to make sense of them. Much as when developing photographs, time adds definition and contrast, adding much clarity to a phenomenon that has been there since the beginning of the project.

In terms of writing, this means that sometimes the book provides copious detail, but that in others it presents the process abstracted instead. Some of these choices have to do with the tension between opening up the description too much versus using the material to advance an argument; sometimes it was about the dullness and opacity of doing ethnographic work on these settings and how little some of the scenes "communicate" on their own. In fact, this is what happened at the beginning of the project, as I was trying to make meaning in traditional ethnographic ways of designers sitting in a room, looking at their screens while listening to podcasts and music on headphones. Without access to their exchanges, there was little to do; without being present in their meetings, there was little to communicate. The same thing happens—albeit differently—in the scenes where shoes are being fitted by technicians on fit models: there is nothing paradigmatic, revealing, or "charismatic" about those moments; it's only the accumulation of scenes and their construction as a process that helps the reader understand how fitting works and why it matters to projects of scale-making. Thinking both thick and thin means that sometimes the aim is not the richness of data but rather what Brekhus (2005) calls "thin description," aiming analytically to extract general forms from particular contents, committing the ethnographer to focused observation and developing analytic aims on the available data.[10]

OUTLINE OF THE BOOK

The Perfect Fit evokes a journey that starts at a mall in Los Angeles and ends in Dongguan, with stopovers in New York, Hong Kong, northern Italy, Ho Chi Minh City, and southern Brazil. The book is divided in three parts; it has six chapters, a preface, a conclusion, an interlude, and a coda. In the first part I focus on the work of designers, highlighting in chapter 2 all the information they assess and evaluate when finding disparate materials to put together a collection, as well as the noneconomic ways they are rewarded for their work. Chapter 3 focuses on how a shoe goes from sketch to finalized object, to demonstrate the work designers perform and to highlight all the background work by other actors designers have to take for granted to do their work seamlessly, along with the myriad procedures to make sure distance is not a deterrent to craft-making. The book's second part focuses on the work that has been "black-boxed" in the first part, concentrating on opening up what kind of knowledge disputes exist in shoe making, highlighting the work of inside competitors and collaborators (technicians, who build and measure lasts and molds) and the negotiations between different groups about what a shoe is.

As *The Perfect Fit* continues, chapter 4 focuses on fit models and how—as the a priori less-important part of the infrastructure—a female foot is at the center of a worldwide assemblage of standardization. Chapter 5 expands on the centrality of fit models by looking at their jurisdictional struggles with technicians, and all the work necessary to "translate" their "ideal" foot to the world of consumers.

The third and last part is preceded by an interlude that presents us with four life stories to show the loss of centrality of Taiwanese entrepreneurs and specialized workers in South China, and their replacement by Brazilian managers and technicians, who moved as US women's shoe production left Novo Hamburgo in Brazil for Dongguan. Chapter 6 explores what happened to Brazil's industry once US production left, scrutinizing the variegated relationship between the active process of ruination and its memorialization.

If chapters 2 to 5 are about sustaining and maintaining, chapter 6 is about the coming-apart of the hard work of keeping a location "global"; looking at what the erosion, decay, and breakdown of globalization looks like. Moving from Dongguan and New York to Novo Hamburgo offered an opportunity to see the material and personal traces that the undoing of the global leaves behind. And the two stories go better together, when we want to highlight—paraphrasing Stephen Jackson (2014)—the hidden history of repair, maintenance, and sometimes breakdown that have always sustained scale-making projects like globalization. The coda takes stock of that history, wondering whether Dongguan will soon become an ex-global cluster, replaced as such by Ho Chi Minh City, and suffer the destructive fate unleashed on the Vale dos Sinos.

Chapter 7 wraps up by bringing back some of the themes from chapter 1, revealing what can be learned about globalization when looking at knowledge generation in a product as quotidian—and with as low aggregate value—as a shoe.

PART 1

From the Designer's Point of View

Chapter 2

FROM "THE GLOBAL" TO "THE GIRL"

INTRODUCTION: PERFORMING OM

This photograph comes from a "Meet the Designers" event organized in Los Angeles by Nordstrom, which specializes in high-end shoes and fashion at large. The performance was supposed to give consumers an exclusive behind-the-scenes look at how shoes are imagined, designed, and produced. The head designer of shoe brand OM, her assistant, and an associate designer were flown in from New York to chat with female customers, talk to the store sales staff about the styles, and take pictures with consumers, both for their personal collections and for the brand and store Facebook pages.

The atmosphere was festive as a DJ entertained the crowd, and a special area of the store had been designated for this performance. Surrounded by stalls with shoes from higher-end brands like Salvatore Ferragamo, Dolce & Gabbana, and Prada—among others—there was a big cut-out board that imitated the "mood boards" designers use to make sense of trends and translate them into design patterns, as well as three smaller signs atop the merchandise tables indicated the name of the brand (OMA!), the collection that was being promoted (OM, the diffusion line of the shoe company), and the particular styles that

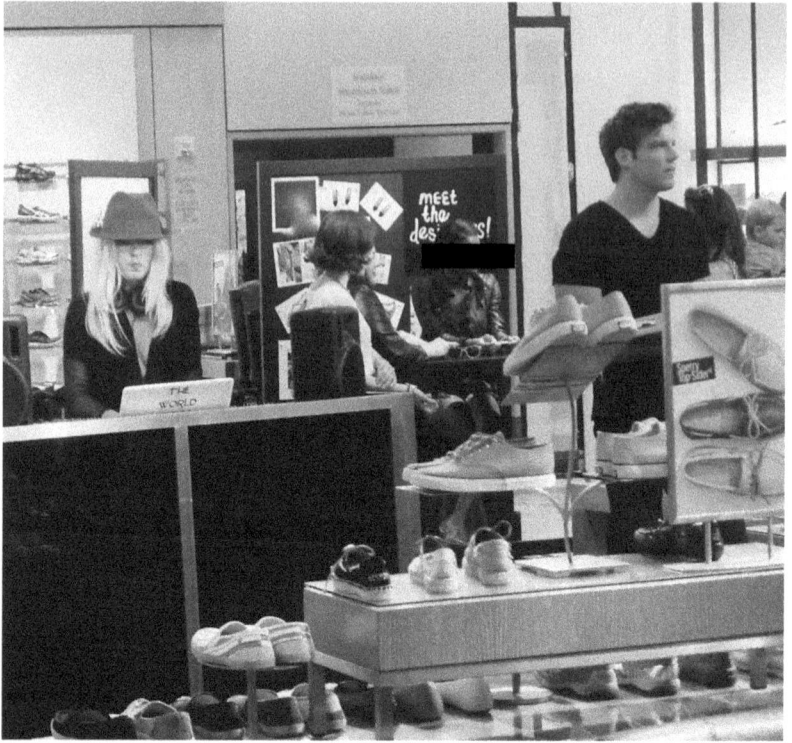

Figure 2.1. "Meet the Designers" event, West Hollywood, June 2013.

were on sale because of the event. The sellers worked on special commission that day and wore the shoes from the brand, mostly the ones on sale. Two male models, wearing tight dark T-shirts, distributed gifts—sunglasses and water bottles—emblazoned with the OM name. A female shoe model, in a short skirt that showed off her long legs, walked around, showing how the shoes fit, and engaged in banter and conversation with the customers, complementing the designers' socializing. The event was closely monitored by three people from the promotional department of the mall, who, on top of taking pictures, wrote down how many shoes were sold, which styles people went for, and compared this event sales-wise to other events they had put together at the Chicago and Miami stores.

From this starting scene (actually the end point of the commodity chain), I aim to trace back the role designers play in shoe production. The stylized idea of what they do behind the scenes, the "creative" impulses, the exciting "aha!" moments of discovery and reverie, give us a good excuse to explore how designers operate and serve to anticipate some of the guiding questions for this chapter: How are shoes imagined, conceived, designed, and produced? Who coordinates the apparently seamless work from thinking of a product to its finalized production? How does the global scale of shoe production transform said coordination?

The focus of this chapter is less on the many actors who actually comprise the chain, but rather on how to see them from the vantage point of designers. Pushing designers to the foreground highlights all the support systems that have to be in place for them to do their work. This means that for the purposes of the argument presented in this chapter, the other actors (fit models, technicians, office managers, line builders, sketchers, source and quality control people) are all backgrounded—though they will reappear in the second part of this book, with a vengeance.

Based on shadow ethnography, interviews with insiders, and digital archival work, this chapter follows a group of designers from a US shoe company to show the taken-for-granted work of deciding when, how, and where fashion patterns are generated and produced. Looking at designers put me in a great position to describe how all the networks are pulled together in the process of assembling one finalized product, in a way that would be impossible to observe from the endpoint of a factory worker. We can witness the "scalar work" of designers when entangling different locales and scales (situations, interactions, interfirm linkages, entrepreneurial cities, agglomeration economies, global networks) involved in the making of the global shoe. The designer's vantage point allows also us to take stock of the difficulties of coordinating actions in those many different locales, as their daily lives highlight the weight not only of place but also of time. Much as other professions like arbitrage trading or architecture, the assemblage of products results in temporal incongruity, with designers working in more than one time zone at a time.

At the theoretical level this chapter engages with the commodity chain literature and the "follow the thing" approach to show that globalization is not a process that happens in unidirectional flows, nor in neatly divided geographical locations. This chapter shows that the coordination of design is a simultaneous process; it takes place through a negotiation of interlocking practical competencies of shaping ideas into materials. In each step I aim to show how different parts of the globe are connected through imagination, execution, decision-making, and production itself. Rather than emphasizing the meso- and macro levels of networks, regional states, or Trans National Corporations, this chapter aims to show how globalization is a practical accomplishment of interlocking agents dependent on other components—both near and distant—to shape a material outcome.

In showing the global process by which a shoe is put together, this chapter aims to advance three distinct yet related arguments. The first one is to show the paradoxical production of originality in a creative industry through mimetic repetition and the accumulation of competing similar objects. The second one is to restore objects' multifaceted and sensory textures before they become quantifiable or homogeneous abstractions to be sold and bought. To quote Adorno (1973, 163): "Cognition of the object in its constellation is cognition of the process stored in the object." The third is to show that some comparative advantages of agglomeration economies—what scholars have called its sticky character, because of the intersection between face-to-face, tacit, kinesthetic, and informal kinds of knowledge—can be replicated in other places, unlike what most scholarship (especially that studying low-grade manufacture) would predict.

This chapter continues by showing what kinds of information designers collect before the drawing process begins. In the next section, I discuss the use of trend-forecasting sites and then move on to the shopping trips designers undertake to gather ideas and materials to use as resources for design. Ultimately, I show how all the information gets synthesized in mood boards that provide a narrative organization to patterns, colors, and materials before these get translated into proper designs. The section after that compares the work of design as mediated via electronic communication and the work of design in the company's China office, in which there are daily face-to-face exchanges with sample-room managers and the agents involved in placing production in factories. The chapter ends with a conclusion that aims to go beyond this case; in it I offer some methodological and theoretical implications for the study of the global production of culture.

WHERE DO IDEAS COME FROM? OR, HOW IS THE GLOBAL BOTH IMAGINED AND A SOURCE OF IMAGINATION?

I start by showing what kinds of information designers collect before the sketching process begins. In doing so, I want to emphasize the practices of assessment they engage to classify and qualify all the information they receive.

I'm going to pay special attention to two processes: (a) how the "global" is sourced and indexed in the shoe in gradients of co-presence; and (b) the competing ways prospective fashion futures are forecasted.

Though designers travel between four and six times a year, foreign places appear daily on their screens courtesy of the photographic services provided by the trend-forecasting company hired by OM. Access to a database like this, which updates almost daily, can cost clients up to US$30,000 per year. Working through the site provides us with an interesting window to observe how trend services perceive the world as a stratified network of cities, as well as to understand how information on "everyday" clothing use is presented to professional fashion producers.

Designers peruse the site regularly, looking at what competitors are doing, what the latest images coming from runway and trade shows are, and what colors and materials are in vogue, even if they are presented not on shoes but rather on accessories and general clothing. While the site is divided into many sections—it presents information on the speed of trends to make it into the market, images from fashion runaways, specialized reports on fabric and materials, and almost-weekly reports on accessories, shoes, intimate apparel, and swimwear—I'm focusing here on the site's Global Street service, which provides pictures of people taken from a variety of cities around the globe. The trend category, which is called Global Streets, appears monthly and comes organized and catalogued in four different categories: everyday wear, shoes, sneakers, and accessories. Observing how images taken in a previous month can be used to design for future collections helps complicate theories about cultural circulation in which fashion is presented either as a top-down imposition or the result of organic use by consumers.

The next two figures come from the Global Street section of a trend forecasting site. In them we see "cool" people on the street flaunting what they are wearing.

I want to call attention to two things:

1. how something called the *global*, embodied in a few current people around the world, makes it to the screens of designers, from the cities noted on the photos as well as places like Fortaleza, Medellin, Adelaide, Istanbul, and Buenos Aires; and
2. how forecasting in this case is not about predicting or imagining the unseen future but rather about consumers in the present who

have bought finalized goods and are somehow embodying future tendencies, and, as such, worthy of emulation.

This is what Global Street pictures look like. Although the lower corner of each picture provides information on where the snapshot was taken, images on the site are actually organized not by city but by trend.

I looked at Global Street pictures from May 2009 until May 2012 (3,827 pictures) to organize the information at hand and to obtain a clearer sense of which cities are privileged as data and made available to designers. Bear in mind that most of the other categories are organized by brand—or, in the case of fashion weeks, by the city in which they take place and by brand[1]—so the trend site is one of the main indexes to see how something called "the global" is presented to and used by designers as a source. Pictures are taken by freelance photographers who either scout people in particular "fashionable" areas within cities (in New York City, for example, they hang out in Nolita or on the Lower East Side) or take advantage of festivals and fashion shows where young people concentrate to take pictures to sell to trend services (though at first they sometimes do it for free to establish themselves

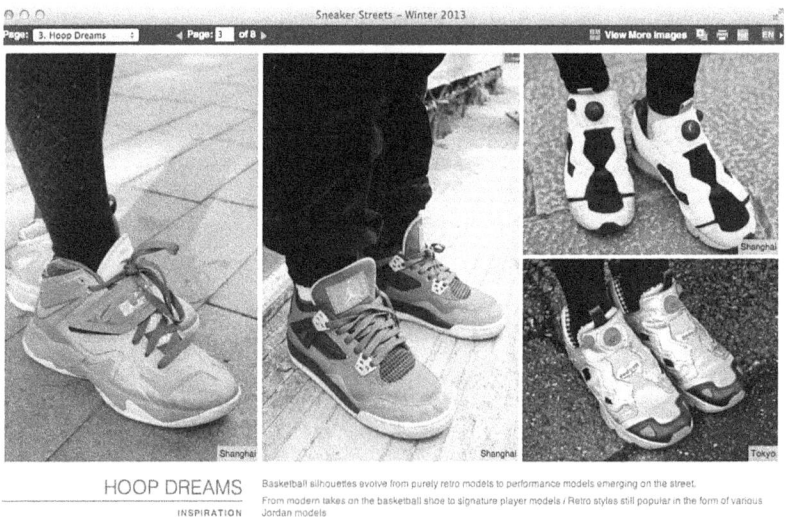

HOOP DREAMS
INSPIRATION

Basketball silhouettes evolve from purely retro models to performance models emerging on the street. From modern takes on the basketball shoe to signature player models / Retro styles still popular in the form of various Jordan models

Figure 2.2. A picture from the trend site, focused on street-sneaker styles—in this case, "Hoop Dreams." Photos were taken on the streets of Shanghai and Tokyo. In the rest of the report, the other cities with images are London, New York, Milan, and Paris.

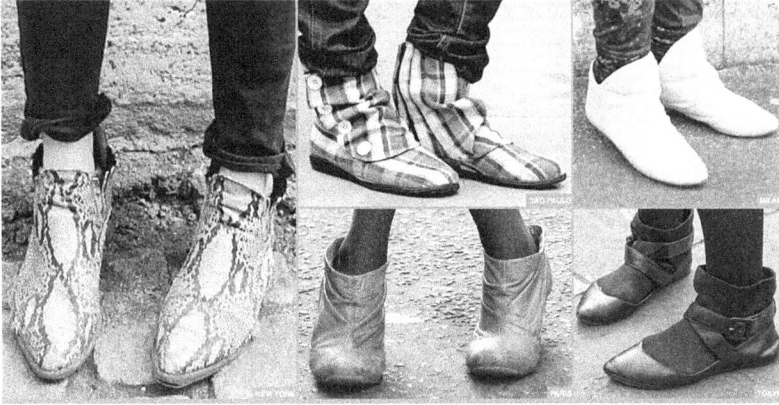

Figure 2.3. An online page under the category "Global Streets: Accessories" from the trend site. Notice the name of the city where the photo was taken at the bottom right corner of each image. In this case (clockwise): New York, São Paulo, Milan, Tokyo, and Paris.

as potential regular providers). To a certain extent, the presence of certain cities as represented by the "cool" people who appear in the picture is explained by the promotional activities that cities and regions participate in to create a brand for themselves (Greenberg 2009; Wynn 2015). Accordingly, that presence can be understood as another way in which the micro and the meso interact to produce a version of the global. Among the trade fairs we can find Berlin's Sneaker Fest, Paris's Sneaker Fest, and the Tokyo and São Paulo fashion weeks. There are other festivals that cater to audiences beyond the fashion industry, combining it with music and cinema: Coachella in Indio, Sonar in Barcelona and São Paulo, South by Southwest in Austin, the Greenroom Festival in Yokohama, Hackney in London, and the photography and fashion festival at Hyeres in Provence, France, as well as the music festivals in Glastonbury, England, and Roskilde, Denmark. Lastly, there is the Rip Curl surf festival in Bells Beach, California. All of them appear in the Global Street section or in some of the other pictures on the site.

The first four cities virtually connected in terms of pictures are almost obvious—and make up close to 50 percent of the pictures presented: people in New York show up in 532 pictures, Paris appears in 511, London makes it into 484, and Milan is in 417. In the next tier we encounter the California trio of Los Angeles, Pasadena, and Indio, which have 273 images; Tokyo

(207), Hong Kong (144), and Seoul (123) follow. Rio de Janeiro (181) and São Paulo (140) are next; and Copenhagen (161) and Gothenburg (132) complete the second group.

In the third tier I've encountered cities like Berlin (88), Barcelona (74), and Shanghai (65)—which are global centers in other circuits, like art, object design, and finance, underscoring how global circuits are not homologous, depending on products and activities—as well as Reykjavik (53) and Amsterdam (47).

The fourth tier is composed of Stockholm (29), Beijing (21), Sydney (17) and Melbourne (7), Honolulu (14), Miami (13), Mexico City (12), and Yokohama (12). Here we can observe head cities of semi-periphery countries like Australia or Mexico, as well as second- and third-tier cities from central economies (Japan and the US), something that continues on the fifth tier (all of them have ten images), with cities such as Sapporo, Kojima, and Osaka (all in Japan) as well as Florence, Italy, where most of the pictures were taken at Pitti Street, home of a famous shirtmaker. The last tier is made of cities with more than one image and includes Buenos Aires (6), New Delhi (5), Fortaleza and Itu (5) in Brazil, Medellin (4), Istanbul (3), Bangkok (3), Madrid (2), and Seattle (2).

Paraphrasing Bestor (2001) discussing the geography of sushi production and distribution, this process creates spatially discontinuous urban hierarchies in which, for the OM designers, New York is a relatively close neighbor

Figure 2.4. Map with the three principal groups of the most important cities for the trend site's "Global Street" page.

Figure 2.5. Map with the three last groups of cities on the trend site's "Global Street" page.

of London, Tokyo, Rio, Copenhagen, and Hong Kong. It is distant—on this scape—from Buenos Aires, Florence, Beijing, and Madrid; and with no relationship whatsoever with other cities that are economically or politically more important—like Chicago, Brussels, Dubai, or Frankfurt—but are absent from the imagined maps of fashion.

Designers also received in real time pictures from the runway. These pics arrive almost immediately as they are taken at fashion-week collection festivals around the world. The resulting Global Streets geography depends on runways enough to be one in which cities more central in the world of fashion are highlighted, so next to Shanghai the pictures come mainly from New York, Paris, Milan, and Tokyo—though fashion week as a format has extended itself around the world. In this case, fashion forecasting works via the observation of what high-end producers in central locations present as trending in the future.

This "city" made out of fashionable people gets more detailed if we look at the neighborhoods that appear in the images on the trend site's shopping service, in which pictures are of actual design products as displayed in luxury boutiques and shops. In addition to the city in which they were taken, those images also display the stores' exact neighborhood locations. In this case, forecasting is about what top competitors in central locations are currently doing.

Though the high-end retail market distribution is different from what is seen in the pictures of the "Global Street," the presence of the top- and second-tier cities reinforces that distribution, as the images displayed come from Paris, New York, Los Angeles, Milan, Tokyo, Hong Kong, Barcelona, and Berlin. The more precisely localized high-end retail city is made up of two kinds of neighborhoods: those traditionally in high-end retail and those perceived as "young," "hip," or "alternative." Even though pictures from Milan are overwhelmingly taken on Corso Buenos Aires, just as pictures from Los Angeles tend to be taken in Beverly Hills—the traditional luxury retail areas for those cities—and in New York they are obtained on the Upper East Side or in Midtown East, along the Madison Avenue corridor, there are also images from stores in SoHo and the Lower East Side. In Barcelona images come from the Eixample neighborhood and in Berlin from the Mitte. In Paris the high-end versus alternative way of framing the ecology of shopping in the city is reproduced in detail, with pictures mostly taken in the central high-end shopping districts (mostly the seventh and eighth arrondissements, but also the first and ninth) as well as a few pictures taken from stores in the Marais (in between the third and fourth districts). The locations of the pictures are neither surprising nor capricious since most of them are of items from luxury brands (Prada, Celine, Ferragamo, Miu Miu, Gucci, etc.) and are usually taken in the areas of the city in which fashion houses or department stores are located. London images come from the Mayfair and Knightsbridge areas of the West End, while Tokyo pictures were taken at Ginza (where department stories are located) and at Aoyama (where fashion houses like Luis Vuitton or Comme des Garçons have their stores). This patterned way of thinking about space will come in handy later to understand how designers organize their actual shopping trips to Europe and to other US cities like Los Angeles. These "cognitive maps" of the world are rarely completely accurate or entirely based on fact, but they can still exert a powerful influence.

WHEN SHOULD IDEAS APPEAR?

While I've discussed the effect space and scale will have on cognitive maps, I have not explicitly highlighted the role of temporality and how the tension between diachronicity and synchronicity is seen in trend-forecasting. In it, designers engage in a peculiar relationship with the immediate past, the present, and the future. Recall that they work though different versions of how the future is forecasted, sometimes from what already exists, sometimes from what others are forecasting, sometimes from what people have done with something already produced. This management of multiple temporalities has a paradoxical result, though: the everyday lives of creative industry workers result in an eternal present, with designers struggling to keep an eye on the strategic and prospective time of the calendar and of what competitors are doing and how to imitate them or go beyond them; the here and now of New York, and the engagement with the actual object; the opening and closing of the workday in China; as well as with the many projects they are working on, and the stages they are at; are they mood trending, shopping, sketching, detailing?

A team like the one I'm describing is usually working on four seasons at the same time; things get even more complicated for trading companies, which usually work doing development for multiple clients. They have to come up with a multitude of styles—without counting the color variations for each, or SKUs as they are known in the industry—they have to work on coming on with trend ideas for prototypes for a season at least a year in advance, sketch and work on the prototypes for shoes hitting the market three seasons away from the present, all while adjusting the work flow according to the orders they anticipate receiving on those. In addition, they oversee final development and production for the shoes that will hit the market in four to six months, working to correct the details, materials, and colors, while also attending to the delivery for a fourth season, the one currently underway.

The latter sometimes alters the temporal sequencing; clients might ask to add an update on a currently successful shoe, which would then be included either for the next season or the one after that, moving objects from the bounded confines of one collection to the next, and causing designers to have to those items navigate across multiple temporal landscapes (Zerubavel 2003; Snyder 2016), with their flow of tasks. I go into more detail on this later, but for now I want to emphasize how design teams operate within the temporal confines of four seasons running simultaneously, having several calendars for each, underscoring how multiple and heterogeneous time regimes coincide in the design process (on time regimes, see Hall 2009).

Designers have to inhabit manifold temporalities, and not just because of the necessary time-zone coordination between New York, Dongguan, and the corporate office on the West Coast (in the case of this company). They inhabit strategic time when projecting a full collection, its success among buyers and consumers, and its outcast against competitors; diachronic time when enduring the calendar and the benchmarks they have to achieve; and the phenomenology of the here and now (albeit extended in space) of being "drawn in" by the immediacy of their craft.

The following section shows how much in planning the future, via the shopping of shoes and accessories, designers become engaged in the "fun" part of their endeavor, while simultaneously starting the process of generating a commodity.

WHERE DO IDEAS COME FROM? PART 2. OR, WHY ARE WE DRILLING THE SOLE OF A SHOE IN LONDON ON A SUNDAY AFTERNOON?

The first trip OM designers take is not far away from their office in downtown New York. They hop on the W train and go uptown on a twenty-minute subway ride, which deposits them half a block away from two of the high-end shopping places in the city (Barney's and Bergdorf Goodman)[2] where shoppers can find shoes from the most recent collections of established brands—mostly from France and Italy—like Chanel, Prada, Celine, Balenciaga, and Sergio Rossi, among others. Salespeople know designers from previous visits, as they show up systematically. The designers look at what has arrived and how shoes are grouped, and they also take pictures of the main floor—though that is usually not done by Nicole, the main designer, but by one of the associates (Pepi) or a junior designer (Ashley) who usually goes every third week. At first, salespeople used to stop designers and shoppers from taking pictures, but new technology (and the fact that consumers also take pictures to send their friends)[3] has made it almost impossible to stop designers from doing so. In fact, floor employees now engage with designers to get better sales commissions. (OM designers buy on average between two and five pairs of shoes, spending close to US $1,000 per visit.) Salespeople also offer information via email on what is about to become available or let designers walk around the floor until they decide to actually shop, all while pointing out the new arrivals.

What happens at large department stores stands in stark contrast to how designers react to both store clerks and other designers at smaller shops. While it's common for designers like Marcia, a Brazilian working at the time for a small brand addressed to the young female market, to point at how everybody in town will run into each other during the "research" period before sketching at Barney's, I had to serve as a shield for a designer who had run into a former colleague, now a competitor, at a smaller shop. Though she was friendly with her only a week before, when they ran into each other in a different context—a leather fair—at the shop we were at she asked to

Figure 2.6. How a purchased item made it into an OM design.

use me as a device to block the view of the shoes she was trying from the competitor. I also noticed that instead of paying with her corporate credit card (as designer teams usually do, since "originals" are usually expensive, ranging from US$300 to US$800), she decided to pay with her own, even though reimbursement takes time. When asked why, she retorted: "If they see the company logo, they'll know we are here trying to pick up some ideas from them. It's not a big deal, but they know a lot of people in the industry and don't want them saying something like 'So-and-so was also here and they loved those shoes.'"

More important than the in-town trips are the four to six yearly shopping *raids* (as they call them, since the design teams visit four to six cities in four or five days) in Europe. They go to established fashion capitals like Paris and London, to smaller towns in the Tuscany area located close to the tanneries and some of the shops where high-end brands create their shoes, to Florence,[4] and to "new" design cities (they've alternated between Barcelona, Berlin, Rotterdam, Antwerp, and Copenhagen for one day or less).[5] There they buy not only shoes but also accessories that will then be used as resources to think particular parts of a shoe. Designers pay with a company card (for the nine trips I covered, expenditures ranged from US$22,000 to US$40,000), and in some of the cities—Paris and Los Angeles, for instance—they have a chauffeur drive them around the city to optimize their shopping time.[6]

Trips always start in Italy, where they stay for a day and a half; the team of four arrives in Florence and promptly goes to a small seaside town[7] to check five particular boutiques. All the shops are near the manufacturing places—a cluster of tanneries and factories—so designers can find items that are made in small quantities, including a one-of-a-kind box of shoes. Many designs for the shoes the OM team goes for happen to be from subcontracted factories for high-tier brands (one design that sells well there will most likely be available from Fendi too, for instance). The boutique owners have access to these lines because of their contacts with the factory where they are produced. Nicole maintains that these boutiques are all well known among "shoe people" or "people in the business"; thus they go there on every trip. The local clerks know them already and they tend to bring out shoes immediately, without much explanation of what the designers are doing or why. Given that salespeople know Nicole and her associates are designers, they bring them small sizes; the industry standard is to produce prototypes and samples in sizes 6 or 7. In their interactions there is little information uttered; we don't know if a shoe is a popular style or whether it is something other designers have bought. The OM designers trust the salespeople enough to let them decide what is interesting. In those shops they look for ideas for upper materials, so they even look at men's shoes. They also look for new shapes, so they may buy a shoe just because they like the heel and want it as a reference for future designs.

They look for what they call "new hardware," focusing on metallic constructions like buckles or studs. They also are very attentive to "new colors" and buy pairs for future reference regardless of the shoe style, heel, upper, or construction. As they walk around, they take pictures, show shoes to each other from afar, and pick up an item to get its "feel." They might try the shoe on or, in the case of boots, flex them, put their hands inside, try to bend them, and touch the materials. They leave the five shops having bought a maximum of twenty items (in most trips the number is closer to fifteen). Of those items, two-thirds are shoes (including men's styles) and one-third are pieces of jewelry or accessories.

After they are done with the seaside area, the designers ask the driver to take them to the second town, which is closer to Florence. In that town there is only one shop they go to, but the store includes a large variety of brands and products (shoes, accessories, jewelry). The OM team goes there because the boutique is really "Italian," which for them means tacky, but the components of the shoes are all of high quality, so much so that even though none of the designs will get replicated as such, the designers buy ten pairs as they envision some of the parts becoming components of future design ideas "good to bring into the US market."

On that same first day, they arrive in Florence and immediately go to what Nicole calls a "very well-known store where other people in the industry shop." It's a very expensive boutique that she also calls "nicely edited," a way to refer to the combination of brands, styles, colors, and materials, and how they are displayed. Afterward they go to four shops on the Via Roma, which don't exclusively sell shoes but carry mixed clothing, accessories, and footwear, too. In the boutiques they also look for "concepts." For example, on the trip I joined, mannequins there were in bondage lingerie. Was that something "in style?"

They also pay attention to the music, asking for instance one of the shop attendants for the name of an Italian pop song playing (it turned out to be a song sung by B-movie comic star Adriano Celentano at the San Remo festival). They use those shops not so much to buy shoes but to get a "feeling" for trends to forecast, something similar to what they might do in smaller venues in New York City. Afterward they go to a European chain store that carries brands like Patrizia Pepe or Estefanel, which are usually not available in the US. They buy three items per store, spending about €200 at each.

The last part of the Florence leg is spent walking through a cluster of high-end shops featuring brands such as Prada, Miu Miu, Sergio Rossi, Celine, and Gucci. These shops carry different items than the ones on Fifth Avenue; in most cases what they have for display is not in the US yet or has not been bought there by the store shoppers—what they see in New York City usually comprises only 20 or 25 percent of what they observe in those *fiorentini shops*. Shoes from Prada or Miu Miu are usually the same but others differ more. New designs come out faster for shoes developed and produced in Italy. Nicole and her team go to these stores more to enter and look around than to shop. They only shop if they run into something they haven't seen on the trend site or in the high-end New York City shops. They buy no more than two products. If they like an item a lot, they know they can find it in London, so there is no need to worry. As soon as they are done shopping, they leave for Paris. If their plane arrived the night before from New York, they might leave and make it to Paris that same night, to be ready to wake up and get started the next morning as early as possible.

Once in Paris they aim to spend just one day there. They go to three distinct areas. First, they go to two big department stores, Galleries Lafayette and Le Bon Marché, which are fifteen minutes apart. There they look for smaller brands, some of them local, like Paris par coupe and Colisée de Sacha, as well as cheaper brands—priced from €55 to €120—like *Mellow Yellow*, and brands like Walter Steiger, who have a presence in the US but a much larger selection in Paris. Afterward the team goes to a mixture of well-known

Le Marais
PARIS APRIL 2013

Figure 2.7. A street picture, a belt, and a men's shoe from an OM designers' trip to Paris in April 2013. The pictures illustrate the variety of matters in which designers are interested: people on the street and what they wear, and actual shoes (even if they are men's). The belt is there to show that accessories can become parts of a shoe.

high-end boutiques (e.g., Sonia Rykiel, Max Mara, Prada) at Saint Germain des Pres, in the sixth arrondissement. With very little time to spend they try to go to Le Marais—again not so much for actual shopping but for the "feel" of the boutiques and the people, before undertaking the last part of that leg of the raid. They then delve into the Rue de Grenelle, an area with brands like Iris, Sergio Rossi, Paraboot (another men's shoemaker), and YSL, which OM designers do not much care for, but the owners ask them to go "because of the exclusive feel of the area." In Paris the designers spend around a third of their budget, buying around ten pairs (though quantities are not set in any way and change seasonally). Prices vary between €200 and €1000 per pair, as they usually buy them on sale at half price. That same night they take the Eurostar to London.

By London the luggage they have brought is completely full, so it's almost mandatory for the team to buy at least one new large suitcase. Once in the UK, they dive in with the reckless abandon that comes when finishing a trip. Though most of the money from the trip is spent there, they often do not even stay the night. London is considered exciting, and it provides a lot of information for the designers in the company. Not only do they buy shoes they were looking for (or that they didn't know they were looking for but managed to "find") but, as on other parts of the trip, they also go for clothes, jewelry, and accessories in their quest to find prints that look interesting. They buy younger styles, including bathing suits. The search for materials continues there too, as some of what gets bought is acquired because it has a valuable leather, a metallic coating, or a splatter-paint effect. The presence of fast-fashion brands like TopShop also means that designers can observe the turnover of trends at a faster speed than in the US.

The first thing they do in London is to go to the main three department stores: Harvey Nichols, Selfridges, and Harrods—each of which has a huge footwear floor. There, they find all major high-end brands, including those I have already mentioned and others like Roger Vivier and Christian Louboutin, for which they have a very extensive selection. Like in Paris, they also look for shoes by domestic brands like Kurt Geiger or Gina, as well as for brands not easily available in New York's department stores, such as C by Chloe, Tom Ford, and Todd's. How the floors are organized makes it easier to spot trends, as they are arranged not by brand but more conceptually, by colors and materials. The shops have a larger selection than the US stores (for a brand like C by Chloe the ratio might be seven styles in London to only two in New York). By the end of the West End raid they have bought close to fifteen pairs of shoes in Harrods, between eight and twelve at Selfridges, and about five at Harvey Nichols (though there they also bought jewelry and bathing suits with particular fabrics or ornaments).

The second part of the London shopping trip happens in the Oxford Street area, where they go to three cheaper stores: TopShop, Accessorize, and River Island. In the last one they just grab a bucket and fill it up with vests, T-shirts, headbands, and cheap jewelry. The rhythm is frenzied, with a lot of young female shoppers (the designers are between twenty-five and thirty-six) running around them. Unlike in the other shops, they receive almost no help from store attendants. In total they buy over twenty items, none of which are shoes. If in other cities the alternatives to the department stores are more-carefully manicured boutique shops, which give away a local feeling,[8] in London variety comes from mass retail shops, which have fast turnarounds and a wide variety of cheap materials to be source later on.[9] If interested in taking a domestic trip beyond New York, designers might go to Los Angeles—for instance a smaller competitor for a similar market does so a couple of times a year—where they visit the vintage shops of Beverly Grove, Silverlake and Santa Monica, aiming to score something that would resonate with the contemporary sensibilities of women in their twenties in large urban markets.

If we were to summarize why designers shop where they do, their practical logic can sometimes feel contradictory: they go to some places because everybody does and to some others because nobody does, and so they feel they gain a comparative advantage. Among the first group of destinations are places like the large department stores of New York, such as Saks or Barney's, where designers systematically run into each other during sketching and development cycles, or the shoe floor of Galleries Lafayette in Paris, where two designers working for different companies reported to me they ran into each other during September 2015, right before they were going to text each other to make a plan and meet to go out for dinner or drinks.[10]

Among the latter destinations we can find, for instance, the Tuscany towns where they buy directly from the shops owned by small factories that are part of the supply chain of large, high-end Italian brands like Prada or Pucci, knowing that some of the designs, materials, ornaments, and details are going to be very similar to what those high-end firms are producing for the coming season—and that because they lack the stamp of the brand, their price will most likely be 40 percent of the full one (e.g., a €700 shoe is available for a range between €200 and €300).

The designers also take between four hundred and six hundred pictures of "cool" people on the street, of shoes people are wearing, of store fronts, and often of the inside of the store too, usually pretending to try the shoes on, but—as I noted when describing what they did at Barney's—sometimes without any excuse or simulation. A European trip is an opportunity for the design team to explore the world of products, but also to have fun with it. While on those trips they share meals and drinks. They also take pictures of passerby and of themselves posing in front of shops and scenic streets, aiming to find "inspiration," while running in exhilaration to make sure they cover all the places they were supposed to. Designers get dinners and drinks paid by the company corporate card—or in some cases through reimbursement— whether it is having sushi at *Uchi* in Austin, after going for a trend presentation at SXSW; going to the then–Milan hot spot *Carlo e Camilla* after sourcing for new materials at the Lineapelle fair and spending the rest of the night walking through the *Naviglie* district talking about their love lives; or having dinner after getting high in Amsterdam, following an afternoon of shopping in Rotterdam—even if the next day they have to be up at 4:45 a.m. to take the train to Paris. They also get to travel to new places, and on top of shopping at the most obvious locales (since I just mentioned Milan, let's say the Duomo area where the high-end brands concentrate) they get to explore small boutiques used by local stylists, like *Nasri e Cavalli*, where—given the relative affordability of what is in stock-, they can also buy something for themselves.

The idea of something being fun spills over from meals, drinks, and sights into language—so much so that during fieldwork I felt it as a term continuously affirmed, invoked, and repeated to the point of linguistic exhaustion. While for an outsider like me the use of the same word in different contexts and to utter different ideas seemed confusing, designers used "fun," "hot," and "cool" constantly to refer to what they thought they should buy on those trips. Though the latter two terms seem obvious for a conversation about fashion, the idea of "fun" to talk about things as variegated as the playfulness of a work of art, the window display of a shop, the renaissance of Stan Smith sneakers, or the particular effect that an ornament might add to a shoe (to mention just a few utterances), sometimes seemed as strange as, later on, how much the different intonations of the phoneme *shi* among Mandarin speakers transformed its meaning.

All this results in what Arjun Appadurai (1986) has called a tournament of value: a ludic way of producing exchange value in the future, value that is not present in the moment as calculation. Designers travel to envision a shoe that eventually will be designed, produced, and sold, but during these trips, objects are insufflated with experience, enchanted for the moment, lived as the markers of exotic locales and occasions. Designers' work also involves gift-giving or a logic of reciprocity, as they usually get to keep some of what they buy after the items have been used for design purposes. This happens also later on in the development cycle, as designers get to keep samples that were developed but eventually dropped by clients or designers themselves, so on top of the shoes being free they might actually be one of a kind. Even if they are within the realm of commodity creation, these moments can be separated analytically from more mundane economic exchanges.[11]

But even when all their shopping is done, the activities necessary for the trip to come to fruition are not over; US customs regulations make it hard to bring such an extensive amount of shoes into the country. The company had to devise three workarounds. One, they have John, the Taiwanese manager of OM's Dongguan office, meet the team on the last leg of the trip to take one of the shoes with him for reference (and to avoid having the OM team bring a full pair back to New York City). Two, and at greater cost, they send one of each of the shoes by FedEx directly to the Dongguan office and travel with the

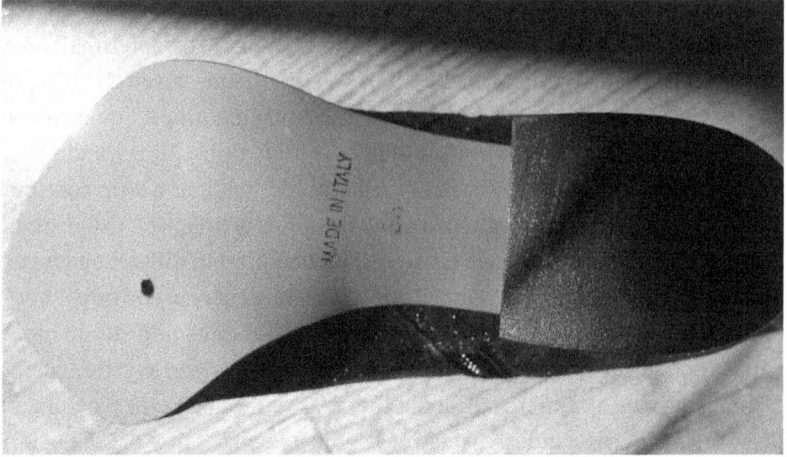

Figure 2.8. A shoe bought in London, drilled in the sole before being brought to the US.

remaining half of the pair. Three, they damage the shoes in such a way that customs agents see them as defective and as such accept them as items unfit for commercialization. In the past, they used to tear them up or make a cut in the construction, but good designs were hard to reconstruct and this damage sometimes ruined them for modeling purposes. Eventually they realized that making a hole in the sole was far less damaging and equally effective. So I wasn't very surprised when by the end of the October 2013 trip, Nicole, Ashley, and John were desperately looking at Google Maps and rushing to find a hardware store that would be open on a Sunday, and then—once they finally found it—they spent three hours before going to Heathrow drilling holes in the over fifty pairs of shoes they had bought. If they were flat, it would be on the sole; if they had heels, they'd do it on the side.[12]

"ORIGINALS" UP CLOSE

In his often-cited short story "Pierre Menard, Author of the *Quixote*," Argentinean writer Jorge Luis Borges tells the story of a critic favorably evaluating a line-by-line retelling of *Don Quixote* by an unknown French contemporary writer. Given that Menard has written the piece in a very different context of production than the early seventeenth century of Cervantes, Borges—instead of denouncing the literal copy of a canonical book—celebrates the work of imagination involved in the fragmentary retelling. The story has been heralded as a unique meditation on the role of context in the interpretation and translation of texts, as well as an important take on what categories of uniqueness like authorship and originality are (and the effects they have).

While not falling into an easy celebration of designers' work, the chapter follows the spirit of Borges and Menard and shows in a few vignettes designers' work across market contexts. The book scrutinizes the work of recombination, as designs are done tweaking what was "originally" produced by other companies, and objects are mimicked as they cross boundaries (as designs are usually used for "inspiration" across temporal, spatial, and price lines). I also show how—in assessing what they decide to move from one context to the next—designers take advantage of what Roland Burt called "structural holes," generating creation and novelty not merely by copying and trickling designs down from one market to the next but actually by acquiring ideas studying existing products, ideas that would then be recombined, converted, and transferred to better fit the imagined needs of a consumer for a different market segment. So, what we've been observing in previous pages and in this section is better understood to be part of a process by which elements become de- and recontextualized, dis- and reembodied in new objects as they are mobilized through different niches. Sometimes it could be an accessory from a mass market on a past season that becomes reappropriated and translated into shoes; sometimes it could be the ornament of a high-end shoe that makes the trip from a pump to a sandal.

I use the words "originals" and "inspiration"—usually in reference to shoes and, sometimes, in referring to accessories such as bags, buckles, or belts as "inspiration items"—not in any substantial or normative way but rather in quotation marks, as that is how designers and other industry types use them. In doing so I hope to go beyond the idea of imitation either automatically sparking innovation (seen in works like Raustiala and Sprigman 2012) or its opposite (Opazo 2016), in which innovation is a term only reserved for change at the level of concepts or techniques. Each short exemplar points to one kind of reappropriation and recombination based on an "original."

Nicole and her team went to Intermix in New York, where she pointed to a shoe that had a similar construction to one they had then sketched; they explained to me how their sketch of that shoe had already been sold to established clients, who had demanded something similar to what they perceived to be a "hot item." The work of transformation was relatively minimal; all the work was achieved by moving the object from one market level to another. Much like in the idea of diffusion, we observe an item reproduced across

different contexts without losing much of its defining character, with designers acting mostly as curators who decide which objects are going to make it
through from one market to another.

Interestingly, while the team had already sketched something similar,
they decided to buy the shoe in question, since it would also perform a second function, serve as "reference" to the team of developers in Dongguan,
as developing constructions from pictures or sketches is harder than doing
so from an actual shoe.

This scene contrasts with the following ones from other outings in New
York, in one those trips at the Dior display at Saks Fifth Avenue, designers
spent time taking pictures of what they called "hideous" sneakers, in the
hope to find inspiration for future shoes in their crystal stubs what they had
actually traveled uptown to see; in another stop on the same "inspiration"
excursion they looked at an Anine Bing shoe last with beads. While they had
a picture of it already at the office, they wanted to check it live, then decide
whether they needed to own it too. Since it had been made in Los Angeles,
with sourcing materials and workmanship very different to what they would
be able to get in Dongguan, the team realized it did not make sense to actually
buy it to "study" it, given how hard it would be to replicate it on the material
OM had at hand—but finding "inspiration" nevertheless in it.

Both of these scenes point to the role that different parts of the object play
in affording for new possibilities; in one case with the designers having already in mind that they would be dismembering (or bracketing in this case)
the "original," and working from one of its details to generate a new design; in
the second one, after the decision that translating the item verbatim would be
impossible—given their knowledge of the materials they work with—resulted
in its role only as a reference for general "inspiration" in terms of the shoe last
as well as more specific ideas to be taken from the beads in it. The last scene
happened at a flea market in Williamsburg, where one of the designers stepped
out to make a quick sketch of the cell-like mesh upper she had observed on a
vintage shoe, dematerializing and reinscribing a finalized product as the opening of a new idea with multiple potential avatars. In that case, the reference
to the original was absolutely erased, beyond any issues of how much their
office can actually replicate the "original." Much like Borges's Menard, designers make something anew while being very close to replicating the original
product by making the final product change in relationship to the context of
circulation (be it through materials, the type of markets shoes will be made
available on, and the seasons under which they will navigate those markets).

IN THE MOOD FOR SHOES

Where does design happen? And when? Does it start when the designers pile up their drawings on the wall of their offices so as to make sense of how they work as a collection? Or rather earlier, when they are traveling to Europe and a few major shopping districts in the US to look for inspiration in shoes, belts, buckles, and accessories? Or even before that, when they scout the very expensive online trend-forecasting service OM pays for, which has the latest pictures of Milan's runway shows, an image taken from the window display of a shop in Le Marais, or a digital picture of a heavily stylized woman and her look in Yokohama, Japan?

The search for colors, concepts, "feel," songs, "hip" people, variety, faster trend turnover, finishes on materials, constructions, uppers, hardware, and accessories becomes crystallized as information on mood boards first; then they become drawings for a full line, which will in turn be made into proto-types, and finally into the samples that will become confirmed, circulated among clients, and then mass-produced. Yet, as I'll show, samples are also put together in a step-by-step process in which the detailing of the different parts of the shoe—in a sometimes-virtual, sometimes-live dialogue with the Dongguan offices—plays a central part.

The previous pages are heavy on details and names, partially so the reader can witness the prodigious amount of information that designers need to qualify and systematize. In doing so, I want to emphasize the practices of assessment they engage to be able to classify and qualify all the information they receive. There is no machine or algorithm to do this even when work-ing through the forecasting sites, just actual information that needs to be filtered, qualified, and classified according to the necessities of the client, the collection, the line, the season, or how the designer aims to establish their identity. The information gathered must also be made to speak to the brand, be relevant, and work with the identity of the products. Designers have to be able to communicate to one another—and to the bosses who approved the bounty—what they like from the shoe. Is it the bottom, the print, the construction, or the details?

Designers work as researchers that investigate and qualify preexisting information. They call looking at magazines (whether they shop on their own dime or their companies shop for them), blogs, Instagram, and shopping sites—and going shopping—"doing research." They dedicate a big part of the day to research when sketching, and often ask other members in their team to come up with things that might fit in their collection—meaning that they would like to be sent images taken from magazines, social media, or virtual shopping, including sometimes less-used sites like Etsy or eBay if they're searching for vintage or vintage-like materials.

So how do designers make sense of this excessive amount of information? They don't use everything they buy to design something new, of course. The amount of items that they have purchased lasts for approximately one line (OM does between six and nine lines a year), and designers also manage to squeeze out information and details from what they've picked up on a trip to last for another half a line. We could say that if each of the lines has about forty-five styles per brand, a shopping raid produces inspiration for about seventy styles. In the images below (figures 2.9 and 2.10; also figure 2.7), I show how bought material becomes a reference for new OM designs: sometimes as an amalgamation of other shoes, in terms of what makes it to the actual detailing of the shoe—how the constructions, materials, and uppers are going to be finalized; other times as direct inspiration to draw new work, vaguely inspired by the architectural lines of a shoe by a major brand; and in yet other instances as the almost direct copy of a very expensive yet obscure item from a small brand from Sweden or a boutique in Berlin. This is so prevalent in the industry that Marcia, a designer from another firm, once said that she would take me to Steve Madden to look at their window and she then would tell me: "This is an Acne boot, this is a Valentino shoe, this is a Chanel shoe. And every other designer can tell you that." This also sparked fear among small-boutique owners in Berlin's Mitte area—so much that one owner, tired of American designers coming to knock their materials off, would ask Pepi (OM's junior designer): "Are you really a designer, or just a line builder?"

Design and production are processes with a vague starting point, happening simultaneously in many far-flung locales. The first decision is made when the CEO and the head designer decide how many collections there will be in a year; this number has lately increased from four to nine, though the timing between collections has become absolutely blurred because of the constant design process required by the fast-fashion market. They also decide how many lines there will be per collection and which consumers the designers imagine the potential shoes to align well with. In doing this, the firm is also choosing which companies will provide the shoe's components (leather, polyurethane [P.U.], insoles, soles, accessories) and which sample rooms and factories will build the prototypes (the first versions of the shoe,

Figure 2.9. Designing with other shoes. A table at the OM office with an OM shoe atop it, surrounded by its inspirations (three shoes from other brands and a belt). Notice how next to them there also are a small trend board from a magazine and a detailed sample-request sheet.

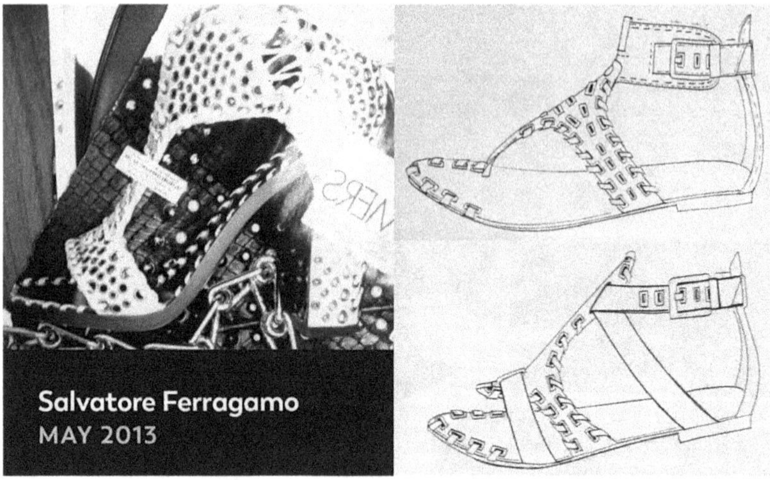

Figure 2.10. A shoe from Salvatore Ferragamo, from a picture sent in an email from one of the associate designers to Nicole, and the two sandal drawings it generated.

Figure 2.11. A mood board at the OM offices, SoHo, New York City, June 2012.

usually done with discarded materials, regardless of how well they match the colors and materials imagined by the designers), the sale samples (which OM will use to gauge interest from potential buyers in seasonal fashion shows), the confirmed samples for quality and design, and the finalized product to be mass-produced (recall that OM produced over 2.5 million pairs in 2013). Factories also compete to participate in this production process. They do so via agents, who coordinate the match between shoe company and factory by offering to produce samples to exemplify their shoes' quality.

Designers synthesize all the "global" information in mood boards to put together a story line about the colors and materials they have chosen for their shoes, and to imagine how they might attract their potential customers. Are the consumers neo-romantics? Tomboy Chic? The mood board starts with designers creating a lifeworld out of how they imagine their consumer to be. (A lot of their information comes from seeing women on the street in New York City wearing their products, or from going into shops to where the shoes are sold to see who is looking at them.) Imagining "the girl" and what she wears is more important as a building block than weaving a coherent narrative. Moreover, it's in the metaphorical work of putting together a one-on-one relationship between the imagined woman and the objects she wears that the narrative slowly emerges. The many pictures taken from magazines of women and their style are seen as a better, more granular and detailed way to connect specific details, ornaments, materials, and colors; they provide designers with a sense of context for those connections. The diegetic work of putting together first a syntax of objects and then a narrative comes out of the work of associating many different details and objects with the imagined consumer. In using preexisting objects, the mood board builds and imagines a future through past and present materials.

To show the extent of the work put into the "Who's that girl?" narrative, I'm moving us to the offices of a smaller-scale, similar price-point company at Sapiranga on the outskirts of Porto Alegre, Brazil, where the concept of creating a mood board and a persona for the girl they imagine their consumer to be gets refined to the point they create a board with a character ("Marina") who wears their shoes. The homunculus (to use a Schutzian reference, in which certain traits and characters deemed ideotypical from a repeated and sedimented situation get stylized) is turned into a full character, including a profession (architect or designer), age (twenty-seven), lifestyle choices (has a boyfriend but lives alone, favors live music with family and friends, always chasing for what is new, considers herself happy, going to the beach—all of which makes sense once one realizes the target woman is an upper-middle-class inhabitant of São Paulo), and consumption patterns (sushi, reads *Vogue* and fashion blogs, tries to find what is unique among mass-market products, practices yoga, has an adopted puppy). The team even created Spotify and Instagram accounts for her, and always ask in development meetings: "Would Marina wear it?" This example is a more explicit and concentrated version of how designers at OM and other similar market-segment brands operate, and it reveals in a nutshell the anticipatory work of consumption that goes into the design.

Designers get the drawing process started by linking how those "moods" and each shoe they are making intersect. A second consideration taken into account is which shoes are going to replace those that occupied the same space in a previous collection. Do they have a sandal for the Coast buyers? Do they have a "crazy" shoe that could replace something they did the previous season that was also considered "out there"? For example, Marcia told me about one of those meetings at her brand, which depends on a large transnational corporation, all designers and some of the sales team were in the room, and everyone was looking at the company's best seller, a boot item, and discussing how hideous it was, that it was boring, bland, they didn't like the construction, and a whole series of *et ceteras*, until the head designer stopped and said that they needed to stop the whining and sketch something "new" on the same construction. They all knew that despite how uninteresting they found the shoe to be, they couldn't leave something resembling it out of the next line.

The process of drawing gets started thanks to the synthesis of the available information, how designers imagine their customers, and how previous collections have been built and constructed. Throughout this process, regardless of whether it is a shopping trip to Berlin, an image from a São Paulo street, or a meeting in an office on the West Coast, the same people meet to discuss information, imagine how the many buckles, shoes, watches, and swatches they bought can become shoes, correct drawings, and discard up to 70 percent of what gets drawn—for a final collection of thirty-five shoe the designers draw up a bit over a hundred. Sometimes they do this face-to-face, although in a lot of those instances what they do is actually show their screens to each other, or email each other and then discuss what they have sent. Other times, thanks to electronic media across locales, the team puts together, in real time, the ideas that are going to organize their drawings.

Mood boards and sketches operate as what STS scholars (Star and Griese-mer 1989; Star 2010; Fujimura 1992) have called *boundary objects*, working to assist communication between multiple constituencies (among the designers, but also when talking to the production team in China or the higher-ups on the West Coast). They serve as points of reference, allowing the translation of the common object into multiple logics. These objects are central in producing what scholars have termed *distributed cognition*, since materials remain flex-ible for group use and capture various forms of nonverbal knowledge, elicited and captured to some degree through the interactions generated by sketches and drawings. Here, the visual representations coordinate the distributed cognition, since they allow for the manipulation of tacit knowledge between individuals. As I hope to show in the next few pages with the work performed by sketches and sample requests, boundary objects are thus plastic enough to adapt to local needs and constraints of the several parties employing them, yet robust enough to maintain a common identity across sites.[13]

The mood board is a particular way to narratively organize materials that are not shoes (there are pictures of dresses, watches, purses, buckles, and wristbands), including inspirations for names and "concepts" taken from lyrics of songs or by the "look" and "feeling" of a particular neighborhood or city. (Notice the name "Valencia" in one of the styles in figure 2.12, fol-lowing the discovery of the city by some trend sites and the style and travel sections of the *New York Times*.)[14] It's not odd, for example, to see the picture of a musician who stands in as representative of a song or style (see Patti Smith in figure 2.11). Next to the board the designers eventually post poten-tial drawings, usually directly next to the images, implicitly comparing what they are aiming to do with what is already circulating in the image market in magazines and sites, and how those objects (their textures, shapes, colors, ornaments, zippers, materials, and finishes) can be "translated" into actual shoes. Though for the barely trained eye this wall is a visual cacophony of papers, where half-sketched drawings, with barely legible instructions detail-ing the materials and colors to be used live side by side with cutouts from magazines, or street pictures from a recent trip,[15] for the designers, it is the taken-for-granted way to communicate to other members of the team: what they are working on, where their ideas are coming from, and why, in the long run, they've chosen one material over another (polyurethane versus leather or a laced eyelet instead of a zipper). In doing this, the mood board also serves a second function: it acts as an "anchor" that fixes meaning for the many sketches that are produced.

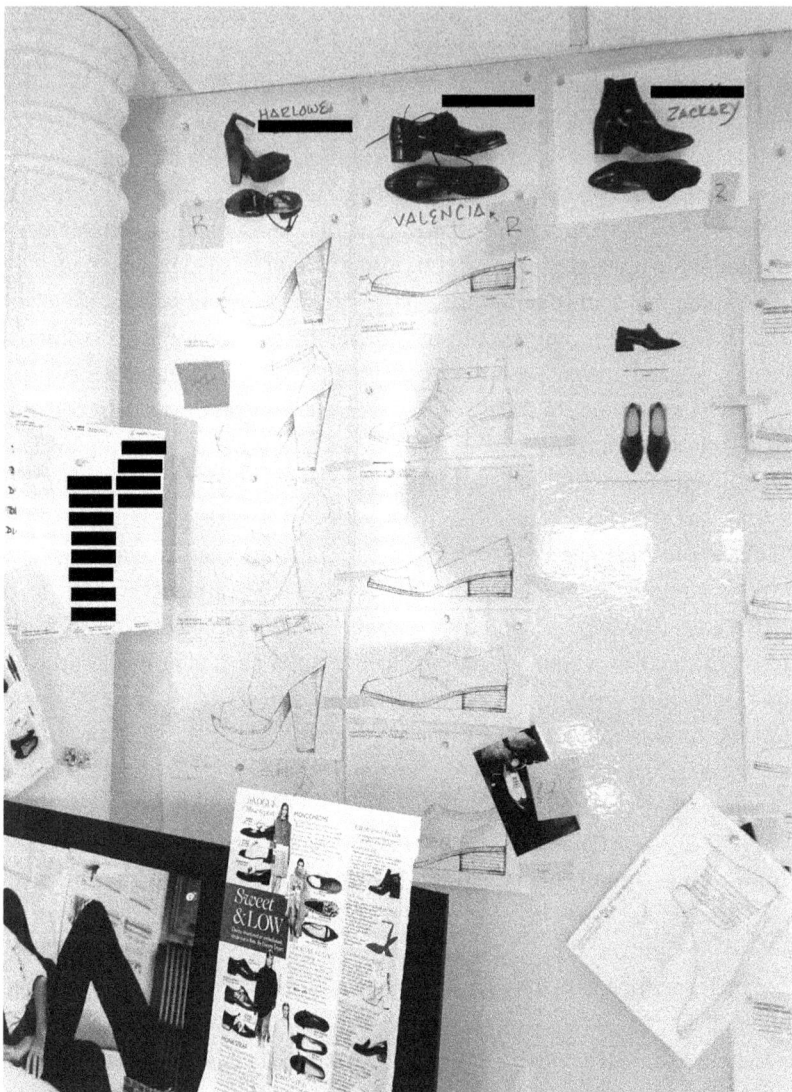

Figure 2.12. A wall at the OM offices, SoHo, New York City, June 2013.

CONCLUSION: NAVIGATING
GLOBALIZATION, REAL AND IMAGINED

Putting together the global as a particular kind of scale has resulted not in the recognition of its heterogeneity but, rather, in the reduction of the world to one vision; not multiplying the viewpoints, practices, and lifeworlds but actually engaging in a myriad of techniques, standards, and protocols to support and sustain that reduction. This chapter showed us how to narrow down a world too vast and sprawling into something manageable to the fingers of a designer or the discerning eye of the consumer who does the shopping. The chapter *also* begins the task of showing *how the global itself is put together*, revealing how large social structures like "the global" are done and sustained through the minutiae of seemingly mundane processes and agents. What I have just shown is how, in the seemingly banal process of choosing certain images, cities, imaginaries, storefronts, what designers are doing is defining the inclusions (e.g., Tokyo, Barcelona) and exclusions (e.g., Maracaibo, Accra) that give form to the particular geography of "the global." In other words, by stitching images, materials, and experiences, designers are not merely giving form to a shoe but to the global itself. Moreover, the chapter underscores that some of the ties that bind globalization—as seen in the shopping trips and the "fun" social activities had in them—are close, intense, and intimate encounters by those in charge of design and development. This section has thus highlighted how much the global is dependent not just on any kind of social relationship by those involved in putting a shoe together but on the "connective tissue" of friendship and kinship.

This chapter ended with sketches next to a mood board, underscoring the heuristic distinction and transition between the predesign and design parts of the process. In this chapter the reader inhabited the real and imagined spaces of globalization designers have to navigate, reenacting the whirlwind of images, materials, and experiences that they have to assess to put together ideas for a shoe line. We've seen them running into cities with cognitive templates about space that they learned while looking at the organization of images on trend-forecasting sites; we've also witnessed their need to be face-to-face with materials, as shoe constructions can barely be reproduced from disembodied images, and designers (and technicians) need to have the actual last in hand as to develop it properly, disaggregating it into technical specifications to work around. We learned about some of the skills they have to develop (taking images without being caught by either storekeepers or fashionistas; assessing the potential value of a cheaper replica of a luxury object if what is necessary is the construction and not the upper or its execution). We also learned how, in the tension between high and low, designers train their eyes both on the street and in front of multiple screens to best characterize the zeitgeist and convert and transfer ideas and objects through different markets, privileging their recontextualization over plain and simple transport, choosing in some cases old things in new combinations, and in other ones new things in old arrangements. But I have not explained *how* this actually happens. In the chapter that follows, I leave behind the messiness of how designers inhabit the process and aim instead for a stylized reconstruction of the process of developing shoes, from sketch to confirmed sample.

Chapter 3

WHEN IS A SHOE A SHOE?

INTRODUCTION: CLUTTERING AS COLLECTION

To make a collection is a way of thinking about the world; the principles and linkages that make a line up imply experiments, possibilities, juxtapositions, and assumptions about what goes with what and why. To cite curator Hans Obrist (2014, 39): "You could say [it] is a method of producing knowledge." Meaning-making processes play a central role in creative decisions about which potential shoes are going to be pursued as projects, developed, and produced. If the mood board showed how metaphor-making slowly made way for a loose narrative and a grammar of objects, what we observe in how designers organize and classify the "bounty" they have accrued in shopping trips, and even the sketch lines they are building, is a different procedure.

Designers operate through a logic I've termed "cluttering." Cluttering comes from the verb to clutter, and I use this term to call attention to the accumulation of objects without an apparent order or syntax. These accumulated objects contextualize or generate a background, which results *then* in the production of difference. Through the grouping and comparison of everything bought in Europe, designers can think of what stands out. If we think of the different grouping of objects as starting from a relatively static state, cluttering allows us to see how the introduction of a new piece brings up properties to forms that were inactive without that particular object in the series, reconfiguring what previously existed. It's also through the myriad sketches that get drawn (and the many avatars they can generate) that designers decide which shoes belong together, form a series, or appear as something that could be narrativized via trends and mood boards.

Cluttering operates, then, closely to what Romantic authors and scholars have called "elective affinities." If the concept has been used in alchemy to explain how certain materials elect to unite with one chemical entity instead of another, and later on in sociology (Weber 1905; Lowy 1992) to name the process through which two cultural forms enter into a form of reciprocal attraction—a process that derives in thinking of them as mutually selecting each other, actively converging, thanks to potential homologies or analogies between the two—what gets underscored by designers is the mutually reinforcing character of the materials that get chosen, as well as the background-forming work performed by the excessive amount of items they need to pare down.

If one is next to the designers as they look at the items they've brought back from Europe, the series that slowly emerges in the pairing of sketches, or the drawing next to and from some "original" items, gives one the idea of impenetrable creative decisions generated next to "piles of stuff" (as Marcia referred to it). There is an integral method to madness. What I am describing and conceptualizing is an integral part of managing excess, working through an apparent disorder as a way to build a working syntax that will slim down the potential ecology of objects for consumers.

While consumers and cultural critics complain about the limited character of what is being offered, the reality of fashion production is this: a key part of the work of designers—as well as of technicians, sales and sourcing people, and quality-control folks—is to allow for small islands of meaning to be put together in what would otherwise be an infinite landscape of objects. The resulting ecology of products comes from designers working through excessive information, slimming down the glut, allowing for consumers to have wide yet relatively limited choices. Andrew Abbott (2014) has called this strategy for managing excess and the overload of alternatives "value contextuality," explaining how items are not considered in terms of their unique and fixed contribution, but rather as part of a holistic combination, paring choices down not by looking at items as things on their own but rather by understanding their context vis-à-vis the other items around them. The process of finding items' value by thinking of them relationally is aligned also to the items' semantic character as standing for something else, which results in two different ways of working on it. One is through metonymy, where things get aligned because of how they can be associated; the second one—as we saw with the mood boards—is associated with how those materials are imagined as aligned (or not) with the consumer the company has in mind and the larger cultural meanings that can be attached to both people and objects.

Cluttering is then at the heart of how both shopping and sketching operate. And it gets combined with a preexisting spread, made out of what has worked in the past and what buyers and salespeople request from the team. For instance, OM designers generally produce 300 percent more sketches than what gets developed as prototypes. If a line is expected to have around thirty-five styles, then there might be 200 sketches in the first run. Most won't even make it to the prototype stage. Of these sketches, 120–140 will become prototypes, and around 90–100 will become samples developed in actual materials to be taken to sellers and clients. As they come back, some prototypes will get discarded. This could happen because designers don't like the way they look as actual shoes, the office in Dongguan lets them know that making them in the materials they thought of would be almost impossible or too expensive, or the designs are not working properly in the materials the designers had imagined.

In figure 3.1, I show how a line begins to take shape, as many parallel sketches are put on the wall (see the numbers above them) and decisions are made about which version of the shoe they are going to privilege and which one(s) they are going to discard. In some cases, variations are kept in to show continuity in the line, so a drawing can become a construction that will be used for a couple of styles, or an upper that will be developed on different constructions.

This changes a bit depending on how important the collection is to the company's bottom line. During intermediate seasons (neither Fall nor Spring but, rather, the smaller fifth and sixth collections of the year, which happen after the larger Fall and Spring ones), designers discard less. They go more for what they describe as "fun" or "fancy," what they imagine to be less necessary shopping for consumers. The emphasis is less on basics like boots or sandals and more on edgier stuff; designers celebrate having more freedom to work on those collections. In the case of associate or junior designers it might be a moment in which the head designer has less control over the totality of what is being selected for development, even if they usually don't get to do so in a new construction, as opening a new last mold and developing an unproven construction is costly.

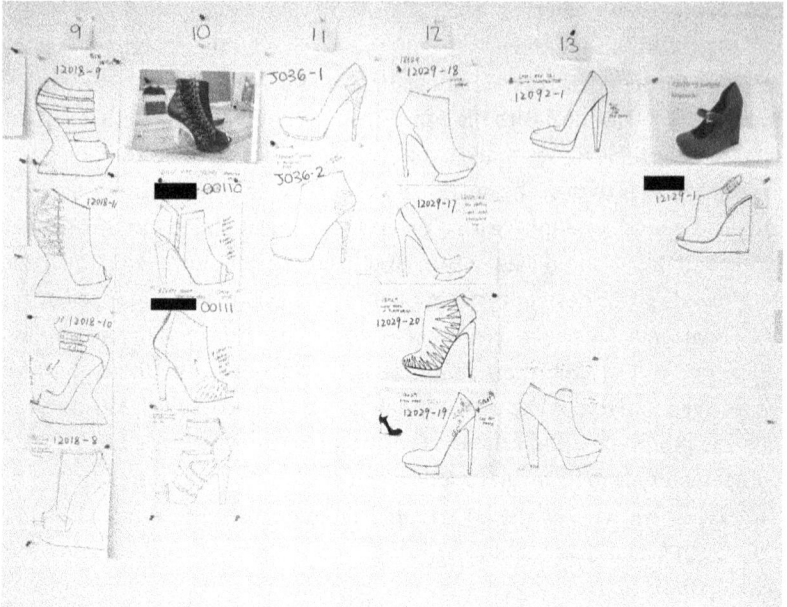

Figure 3.1. OM offices, SoHo, New York City, October 2013.

FLEXIBLE SKETCHES

Kathryn Henderson (1991, 1995, 1999) has shown the role of sketches in organizing production, serving as the "social glue" that helped individuals within teams and different groups in one engineering company. She has also shown how in some cases sketches helped to distribute knowledge and activities by enlisting group participation, and in others allowed for the reading of different meanings by the groups "glued" by them. Building on her insights—and before we progress onto the contingent and variegated forward path of shoes in their careers from sketch to prototype—this section presents an overview of the flexible roles that shoe sketches perform within a design organization like OM.

For designers, sketches perform multiple functions. First, they crystallize and formalize the work of collecting and assessing trends and objects that act as reference for design—we can think of this working at the level of semiotic substitution, as each initial sketch is in conversation with others but also has its own individual history of how it came to be. Secondly, they provide a narrative organization to the collection, so we can think here at the level of semiotic association, as the process of diegesis slowly organizes—via the matching of the drawings to real and imagined characters, moods, colors, and materials—the sketches in a relatively encompassing and coherent way. In both cases, though, individual and sketches in series are the result of cluttering as a strategy for "slimming down the wall," the process through which the collections get edited. This happens both live and in printed matter; one way for head designers to continue the work of slimming down the collection from home is to take out a print out of the wall as it is—usually on multiple printouts reorganized at home as a reproduction of the collection as it stood on that day—and keep working on it.

Thirdly, sketches work as an instructional interface between the designers and the development team in Dongguan. While the wall gets reproduced in the office in China, waiting for designers to come for a detailing session as samples become confirmed, the development team receives sketches individually, but accompanied by all kinds of textual and paratextual devices to maintain meaning stable across both groups. Much like the "standardized packages" that Fujimura (1992) conceptualized to explain how cancer research had consolidated thanks to the combination of flexible boundary-like objects with a standardized set of technologies, sketches are here part of a larger standardized package that gives detailed instructions about the last and all the minutiae that make up the upper part of the shoe. Those instructions are about proportions, as well as about its ornaments and component materials (thereby linking both sketches and instructions to materials sourced outside of the development offices, with agents from local suppliers and in local markets). The Dongguan team also receives instructions on how to best proceed in starting the development process with the making of the upper in discarded materials.

Lastly, sketches link the design team to the sales associates, who are the conduit between the designers and the clients. As reported by designers—this is material not from observation but from interviews and informal conversations—it's common for the sales team to bring demands from department stores, the main client of shoe firms like the one described here. In almost all cases, although designers acknowledge that the sales team and the clients want similar successful items—and we see there a disagreement in the literal character of the homology as seen by the commercialization actors and the design team, which thinks of it in terms of what items from the current collection will be "as successful as" the desired past shoe—there are always last-minute additions, patches, and extras that are the results of consultations between customers, salespeople, designers, and (if the designers are in

Dongguan) the development team, especially technicians. Although the last-minute item repeats at the individual level much of how other shoes came to be—since they are a new iteration or recombination of shoes that already exist, not from the competition but form the firm itself—they usually stand out with respect to the collection's established narrative. In doing so, they go against the fact that most of the collection has been designed through finding what stands out from a sea of repetition, accumulation, and permutations.

HOW ARE DISAGREEMENTS SOLVED?
(ARE THERE ANY DISAGREEMENTS?)

Figure 3.2 is not a board on a wall but a sheet made up of other shoes put together by the designers, which will be used by the head designer to ask the rest of the team to develop a new shoe based on an existing one from the spread. In some cases, the indication is for a whole shoe; in others it could be the detailing, ornament, construction, or just the upper. Designers put together folders for bounded categories (boots, Oxfords, pumps) where they file all of their "research," which results in a sheet like the one copied here

Figure 3.2. OM offices, SoHo, New York City, August 2014.

that gets circulated to the whole team. In there the head designer has added Post-It notes addressing team members' advice ("Pepi loves this one!" next to flat by Zara Basics), sketches of constructions developed after an Oxford, and instructions on how to redevelop one of their own shoes with a different print.

The existence of a sheet like this one underscores the logic behind how shoes are designed within this market bracket. Instead of starting from zero, sketches are always based on preexisting templates, regardless of whether these are shoes the team already has constructions for, shoes from other companies, vintage items, or something used by someone on the street. Designers operate under the logic of permutation, in which the new exists partially as the transformation of the already existing, be it through the replacement of a detail, an ornament, the new combination of preexisting pieces, or the transmutation of an existing material into a new context.

If on the previous section I showed how designers make a big effort to build a line with some narrative coherence, in this section, I'm focusing on the logic behind the operations for putting together a shoe. In doing so, designers for this market differ from their higher-end counterparts—like the designer for OMA!, the brand within the company that does expensive shoes—which start from a more conceptual and narrative organization for the collection, even if still heavily based on "research," and from line builders— the older "shoe dog" men in the industry who work for the cheaper markets— whose idea of design is to "buy everything on a store and copy it" (as a few interviewed designers confided) and who tend to develop their new products slightly altering the constructions they have that have already worked well.

A tradition in the sociology of knowledge has looked not only at collaboration but also at disagreement (Latour 2005; Boltanski and Thevenot 2006) and made it a powerful entry site to understand asymmetries in network circulation and how problems are solved within a community of practice. Following controversies has been presented as the key way to understand where the fault lines in entities such as a teams or groups exist and to actually participate in producing the team as a unit. But to the question of where the controversies in shoe design are, the answer is that they are hard to find among designers within a team. This has to do with the constant flux of activity in which designers find themselves (disagreeing is a luxury they can't afford while pressed for time to finish a product with a fixed deadline, and multiple stakeholders waiting for it), and with the trial-and-error character of how development happens, than with preexisting communality of aesthetic tendencies among team members.

To elaborate on the first factor identified above: The relatively regimented character of time (coordinated by internal benchmarks like sketch review, proto review, trips to fit samples for style, trips to fit samples for comfort, deadlines around big fairs or the timelines of large clients like department stores to deliver finalized samples) and the many other players dependent on them—as I'll show later, technicians, office managers, sourcing people, sample room managers, agents and factories—make futile the "What if we try to do a poodle next to a banana on a heel?" conundrum. While of course associate and junior designers often discuss being creatively stifled, sometimes by insisting on developing shoes the head designer thought as a waste of time (think of the note on Nicole's folder I mentioned before, saying "Pepi really likes this one"), others by discussing it with me later as they found a new job in a company with a smaller line, at the same time the phenomenology of "putting out fires all the time" makes disagreement within the design process a waste of time.[1] Moreover, the chronological time of arguing, consensus building, and teamwork might not be enough to get things done. The finite character of the timeline under which a collection is made—and how much their design work is interlocked with other parts of design, development, and production—opens up the opportunity for decision-making of a less democratic and collective kind. When designers and managers get together for sketch reviews and they collectively look at the sketches for a particular season, there is a strong chance that the designers who proposed the sketch that "deviated" retire it themselves after they see how it plays within the larger seasonal context. In some cases, the head designer might "bump out" some shoes detailed in a way she doesn't care for—not by rejecting them from the get-go, but rather by including more ideas to develop as sketches and prototypes, tilting the balance of the collection in a direction that makes the shoes she did not like superfluous, and as such easy to discard without much debate. In others, an item is tried and developed until it becomes a prototype, only to be dropped as soon as it is made.

Disagreement is also hard to find given the trial-and-error process items are constantly added throughout the sketching, prototype-making, and even sample-developing stages. Head designers affirm that issues can always be solved at the proto and development stages, so there is little need to struggle about particular items. Even when a material comes out not as expected in development—let's say a brown leather has a red finish different than what the designers had imagined—there is always the chance of not discarding it completely but of working around the unexpected. The process of re-detailing a shoe follows in micro a cycle of elective affinities, in which the

WHEN IS A SHOE A SHOE?

transformation of one detail cascades in a new appreciation of the sample and results in designers having to re-detail the upper of the shoe—as the construction does not change—altering its specifications—ornaments, zippers, buttons, etc.—and how they relate to one another.

Designers, recall, tend to produce many more prototypes than the samples that will eventually become developed Moreover, the key before the prototype state is to sketch to the point where the team the constructions they need in the line, some good systems are in place, but still conserve the flexibility to add items later if they feel like something is missing from the collection at large or that an item would make a welcome addition to a weak roster of a particular subcategory of products (e.g., boots).

Ashley told me the story of a meeting in which the head designer of OM pushed back against the idea of having too many preset styles. While some of the production managers and folks from the sales team were in favor of saturating the number of prototypes, the head designer resisted since, according to Ashley, "the reality is that many of the 'last minute' styles we request end up being the best ones. We should always allow ourselves space to add, and with these big lines there are always items that pop up in the last minute that really need to be added. In fact, it is exciting to wait for them." While one would hope that, given the experience's chaotic character and the dependence on other nodes of the infrastructure (sample rooms, development team in China), designers would rather have everything planned from the get-go for the process to be more streamlined and easier to follow. On the contrary, they seem to relish the exhilaration and variability of the iterative nature of what they do.

IT STARTS WITH AN EMAIL

The following email was sent by Pepi (one of the associate designers) to Larry, a US expat who works for one of the agents OM deals with in China (WM):

OM proto request—om-18 constr. November 11, 2013

Hi Larry,

Please have the sample room start working on a proto of the attached sketch on the om-18 construction.

    refer to OG photos for upper pattern.

quilted shaft: refer to OG photo for quilting with random stud detail. The studs should be 4mm and 6mm.

18mm strap width.

Button buckle ornament (BK2) to fit 18mm strap width (the one we opened fits a wider strap width—I will send a revision to the ornament tomorrow—it will be very minor). Please go ahead and start the proto anyway, even though this ornament isn't ready yet.

12mm eyelets, 3mm width (as om-94) -—refer to photo and please try to source these eyelets. I believe a piece of the eyelet has been shipped to you already.

Round cotton laces.

Size 5 zipper detail.

Zipper puller detail as om-63 OG—but smaller. Please just source similar D ring (about 10mm long as noted on my sketch) and make leather puller w/ stud 30mm long.

4mm binding on strap detail and counter detail.

Shaft height = 153mm.

Back trim with loop/tab on top. Top belt strap passes through back tab (belt strap passes through and is not stitched down).

Refer to sketch for additional measurements/details.

This boot has an inside zipper.

** *please do not wait for ornaments to start the proto.*

Please let me know if you have any questions.

Many thanks,
Pepi

This email (and sketches like the one I'm copying below) marks the beginning of the movement from sketch to confirmed sample. In it the designers let the people in the sample room know the details of the sketch and on which construction it's going to be built (developing new constructions is expensive,

TALL JOIE WEDGE
(IF CONSTRUCTION IS
NOT READY - MAKE PROTO)
ON LOW WEDGE

Figure 3.3. A sketch sent to WM, the agent's sample room OM works with in Dongguan.

so the uppers are put on top of previous models' constructions). This shoe is from a series that has a relatively complex ornament (not ready yet), but Nicole and Pepi are counting on it being able to be add it to the shoe once the rest of it has been developed as a prototype. Early prototypes are mostly done on discarded materials (a lot of suede, from what we can see in the pictures), which pushes designers to look attentively to imagine what the shoe is going to look like in the final materials and colors, once it is detailed in full. This is an acquired kind of knowledge, which is developed through the many boring hours spent working on sample requests, looking at the pictures included in the reply emails and the follow-up exchanges.

A second file ensues, soon after the initial email that contained instructions and a sketch. This second file includes a sample request in an Excel sheet with precise descriptions of the upper, including categories like pattern, binding, laces, studs, eyelets, zipper pull, button buckle, zipper, and upper stitching; and of the lining (the upper, the insole binding, the sock, sock stamp, heel, welt, outsole, etc.) that gets sent to one of the factories in Dongguan. The sample request spreadsheet is there to control and fix the image and make sure it does not proliferate. As many scholars from different

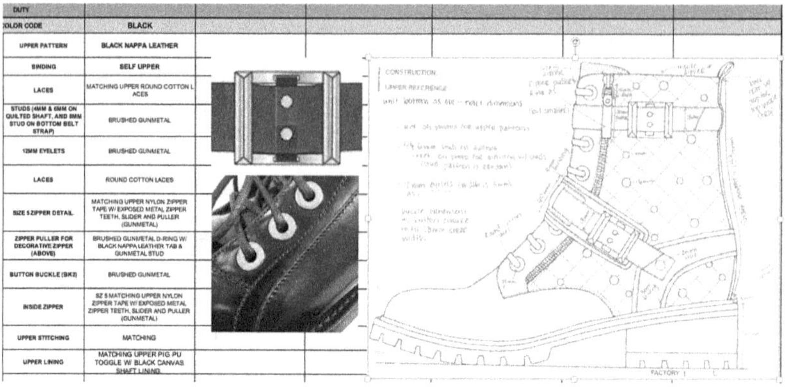

Figure 3.4. A detail of the Excel attachment included in a sample request to WM.

traditions (Mukerji 2014; Gruzinski 2001; Wagner-Pacifici 2011; Huberman 2003; Galison 2004; Burucúa 2016) have signaled, far from the univocal character that people sometimes attribute to them, images are hard to control, and multiple paratextual supports are necessary to make sure the many groups that are bounded by the sketch "read" in them the same. This further contributes to illustrate the tension between standardization and flexibility at play in processes of distributed cognition, especially when the different constituencies are located in various global sites.

With these specifications the office in China will produce a paper shoe pattern. They first have to wrap the last in tape, then flatten it on the table and draw on top of it a pattern with the details sent from the New York office. Technicians have to understand whether the desired materials can be used to produce a shoe with such a pattern, the standard measurements, and the allowance. Then they develop the pattern in discarded materials to put on top of the desired construction and produce a prototype. The construction of a paper shoe pattern is a privileged location to observe tacit knowledge in depth, as the materials have to be developed following a set of measures specified in an email, but there are no formalized set of rules on how to proceed. The amount of extra space that has to be left for seams (what in the shoe business is called the allowance) can only be learned through repetition in practice, not in school but in the making. It implies the capacity for technicians to mentally map materials and standards and to physically know how the pattern should be constructed around the last. To make sure the work is done by properly trained craftsmen and not by a machine—as paper patterns are sometimes developed by sample rooms in China by reproducing the drawing in a machine divided by two, having the profile sketch of the shoe be the base that will be doubled and then finally flattened and developed—some designer teams actually send the sketch not as a profile but at a three-quarter angle, impossible to duplicate and transform into a paper pattern.[2]

The following communication is what a "detail" email looks like. In it, the team not only changes the materials but also, in aiming to correct for the materials that they are using, uncovering how things that we usually try to explain to each other in a tacit or embodied way—the feel of a material, how to weave together a welt, how the welt and the upper are supposed to fit—are so codified that instructions can be given electronically to a distant location. While in one of its most important formulations (Polanyi, 1962: 55) connoisseurship appears in tension with measurements and grading, in this case we see the complementarity of tacit and codified knowledge, as messages are transmitted in such a way that not only prescriptions, formulas, or instructions are sent but also how things are to be done is communicated by a pictorial example of how to work the material.

Ommw-01610—Change Rope Welt to Woven Leather/Pu for Fall

Hey Larry

For Fall we want to use a leather/PU woven welt instead of rope for OMMW-01610 construction. Please prepare a prototype with the woven welt as the attached photos:
   4 pieces of leather/PU are woven together as attached photos
   edges are folded
   Woven piece is a tubular shape with roughly the same
dimensions as the OG's rope
   Insert into welt using the same method
   Let us know if you have any questions!

Thanks,
Pepi

Once that first shoe gets developed into a prototype, Nicole and her team receive an email with a picture and detailed information. There is also a second picture that comes in the email: the same shoe as tried on by the foot model in the sample room. To guarantee that the designers know how the materials and the design react as shoes are worn, the sample rooms—and the OM office too—all have a "fit girl" who tries on the shoe. The standardization is such that when Anna, WM's fit girl, is busy with some other brand, Larry—the office manager—lets the designers know they were looking at in the pictures is the foot of another model. In this way Anna's absence functions as what Bruno Latour has called a "tiny barrier." This is a less obvious technical device through which distance is black-boxed—a phenomenon to which I dedicate chapter 4.

> Subject: 正在寄送電子郵件: P1070802.JPG, P1070800.JPG, P1070801. JPG
> sending photos with WM another fit gal Anna is busy.
>
> Larry

After close scrutiny of that file, someone in the team redraws on top of one of the images the sample room sent, making some of the indications clearer.[3] The prototypes are done with discarded materials, which can be seen in the preceding emails, pushing designers to imagine what the shoe will look like once colors and materials are finally detailed. Designers project their shoes without certainty about how the colors, grains, and finishes of the leather will come up until they have the developed swatches. Part of their work once they do get the materials to develop the samples is to see if they have come out as imagined—more often than not they are developed by the sample room in China—and, if not, either to discard them, to avoid wasting time developing a shoe that won't result in something saleable, or to correct the sample request sheet, indicating that the color is slightly different than imagined, or maybe altering a complementary detail, which the designer envisions as coming out better given the change in color or finish. That sheet will be sent to the rest of the design team, and to the development office and sample room. All involved will get an individual item account of how to work on the sample, as well as a second sheet listing all the styles that were first developed as prototypes and the information on which ones were dropped after the designers contrast what they imagined with the reality of the materials they received.

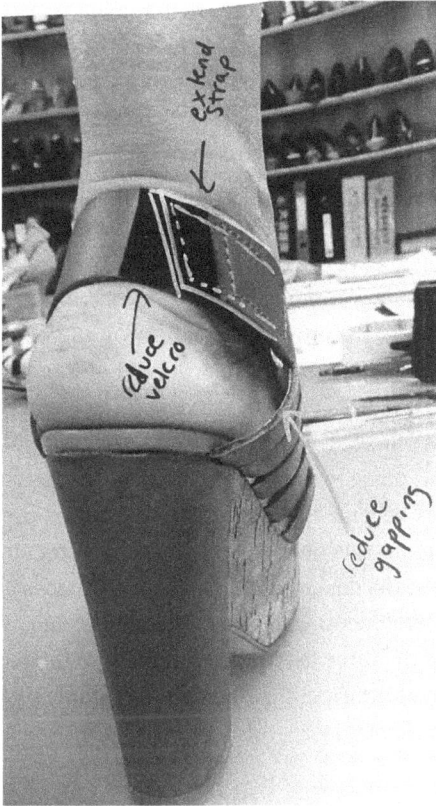

Figure 3.5. A picture of an actual sample,
drawn over with corrections.

Once again, on both sides of the design cycle and of the globe, participants have to communicate each other their feeling for materials, the standard measurements, and the patterns that are produced. In all this work, the attached pictures work as conscription devices, enlisting group participation. They are also receptacles of knowledge created and adjusted through group interaction aimed toward a common goal. The pictures convey to us the sense of collaboration at a distance: that problem-solving happens in multiple sites and among agents helping to distribute knowledge.

That this stage of the design work happens in two faraway time zones has particular consequences in terms of how the head designer's work is temporally organized. If the workday starts when Nicole wakes up in New

York and, before going to the office, checks the emails that arrived from Dongguan during the early morning hours on the East Coast, it has actually never ended, as Nicole's first morning email answers the queries and concerns of scheduling and capabilities in China. Later, when she arrives at her office, she works with her team in assessing the constraints and developments signaled by the China office; past noon, they contact the West Coast to let the team there know where they see the designs going. Communication ensues the whole day until they leave the office. As South China goes to work, so does Nicole, for a brief hour of furious emailing—concerning both how detailing is coming out and how the prototypes look, to OK them or to start planning the changes to be requested the next morning—before going to sleep around 9:00 p.m. or 10:00 p.m. ET. As this stage comes to an end, she'll fly to China to work at the OM offices, going to the sample rooms and revising how the corrections she has made to the prototypes and samples come back.

As some things become untranslatable without co-presence, some key actors travel (more on this on chapter 4). As shoes get closer to becoming confirmed samples, the design team travels to Guangdong Province for the final phase of development. Once there, they meet daily with the sample-room managers of the three factories, sometimes in the factory's office (the factories are always out of sight!), others in the sample room, some more in OM's China office.

IN DONGGUAN (FOR NOW)

It's 5:45 a.m. in Hong Kong, or so it says on the flight display Cathay Pacific Airlines has on the remote control for its multimedia devices. We are on a flight that left New York City some seven hours ago, on our way to the former British colony. Most lights are out in the business cabin, but Nicole has been working for the last couple of hours. She is flying business thanks to an upgrade afforded her by the thousands of miles she has accrued while traveling from New York to China to oversee production for OM. On her screen she is detailing one particular shoe that has not come out as she expected, asking production to widen the strap on the back. She was in the Guangdong Province city we are traveling to just ten days ago, but she is coming back right after the Western New Year to make sure production is completed before a different landmark arrives, the Chinese Lunar New Year. The season she is working for won't be in stores for a couple of months, but things have to be kept on schedule, since the production is organized around six lines plus up to three smaller clusters of groupings added in by sales request. She's completing the detailed production sheet now since she has to hit the ground running. She will be picked up by a local driver, who will take her from the Hong Kong airport—after almost sixteen hours of flight—straight into the design office OM maintains in China to hash out the details with the design managers in one of the factories her company does production with. By the time she gets to the factory's design office to work, it will be around 3:30 a.m. eastern time.

She will be staying in Dongguan for five days and will fly back to New York City once she feels the design for the season has been finalized. After four years of working for the company, she has realized that it is better to break what used to be long trips—lasting between two and three weeks—into two smaller units: one lasting ten days and a second one, usually a couple of weeks later, to correct the prototypes she worked on with her team during the first trip, and to make sure that they have come out as she had expected before the shoes finally become samples and physically travel to the US to be shown to sellers and, later, produced and distributed. She has to constantly communicate with two of the factories in China; with a third, which has its main design office in Miami; as well as consult with the owners and president of the company on the US West Coast.

As Nicole wakes up the next morning, she takes advantage of the time difference to check on the project she left for her two associate designers to complete back in New York City. It's Thursday at 6:00 p.m. ET and her team has not yet left the office.

The preceding fieldnote, from January 2014, works almost as an upside-down counterpoint to the timeline under which the OM team works when in the US. It also underscores the odd temporality and territoriality under which shoes are designed. The office OM has in China feels like a doppelgänger of the one in New York, aiming to black-box distance via the reproduction of the design floor verbatim in Dongguan.

There are walls with drawings the designers left the last time they were there, including the same numbering, variation, and serialization seen on the walls in the US. There also are numerous older mood boards, shoes produced in past seasons, designs bought on European trips, and copious sample requests with detailed instructions. The office has two permanent employees: John, the Taiwanese manager we last saw in London helping Nicole and her team buy a drill, who studied shoe production in London; and Sherry, his second in command, who is from Guangdong Province; and who before working

Figure 3.6. A wall at OM's office in Dongguan, January 2014

in the shoe industry studied English at her local university, a very common path among "office girls" in the Chinese export industry.

The twin character of the South China operation does not end there. We can better understand how complex the relationship is between modularity, replication, and codified and informal knowledge by observing how similar the process of detailing shoes face-to-face is to the process of doing it via electronic communication.

Maybe because I started this ethnography by observing the process in New York (which is how designers start learning about the process too), but I got the eerie feeling that the online process worked almost as a template for how shoes are detailed in person. I was surprised to notice in Dongguan how similar the live routine was to its online version. Once in Dongguan the team meets daily with the sample-room managers of the three factories, sometimes in the factory's office (the factories are always out of sight),[4] other times in the sample room or in OM's office in China. This routine happens Monday to Saturday, from 9:00 a.m. to 10:00 p.m. Nicole supervises how the shoes are coming along and repeats the process she did over email, but this time she does it live. She sees how the shoe fits the foot model, and also tries it on herself, as to see the fit on a "US" leg like hers. She also grabs the boot and tugs it, aiming to see the quality and resistance of the leather, how much the shoe bends if pulled. The photo in figure 3.7 was taken at OM's office, with Sherry trying out some of the boots produced by WM, the agent they work with the most. The day after we would also go to WM's offices, and have their fit girl try other shoes as Nicole went over the details of the sample request to make sure that things were coming out as she wanted, aiming to get an idea of the fit of the shoe—noticing whether the heel is comfortable, whether there is too much space between the back of the boot and Anna's actual heel. Part of what explains this new trial of strength (Latour 1984) of the shoe prototype is the movement from the standardized foot of the model to the designers' "American" leg and foot. Designers point at the anatomical differences between US and Chinese calves, feet, leg length, and knee-to-foot distance as something that has also to be accounted and adjusted for. We get to witness

Figure 3.7. Nicole inspecting and drawing on a boot worn by Sherry atop a table in the OM office in Dongguan.

once again—and at a different site and moment of the process—the tension between standardization and tacit knowledge.

Once she gets a "feel" for how well the parts fit, Nicole redraws, this time not on top of a drawing but on an actual shoe developed with the sample materials. The shoe will get resampled in the next forty-eight hours. As soon as it is, either we go to the agent's office to see how they have been reworked or the agents visit OM's office. Two of them bring their own fit girl, while Sherry still tries on WM's shoes. Corrections are drawn with a silver pen to make the notes for the people at the agent's office as clear as possible, so they can properly transmit the information to the technicians on the sample floor (they are translated from English to Mandarin, and sometimes Cantonese). Nicole also draws on top of tape to show where straps and buckles should be if the measurements are not correct (figure 3.8). She then writes the corrections down on a sheet of paper. Sometimes, if things have been developed as she wanted but not coming out as expected, she develops a new sample request, changing the measurements, the detailing, and sometimes even the material to take the shoe in a direction closer to what she had expected (figure 3.9).

These processes get reproduced at the agents' offices. In fact, in my visit to Dongguan, it got reproduced almost as a standardized procedure at both FC and WM offices (the third agent OM deals with is a smaller operation and usually brings the shoes to OM's office). Both agencies had a room exclusively filled with OM products; both had a set fit girl to try the shoes on; and both had a team of contact people who spoke English with relative fluency. The processes of inspecting, correcting, detailing, and resampling are also very similar. The fit girl jumps on the table; Nicole revises the shoe, draws on it, and compares the actual measurements to what it said on the sample request—she usually compares them out loud with John, who goes with her to all of the fittings. If satisfactory, the shoes get an OK; if not, a new sample request is made with all the corrections detailed, and we'll probably see them again later, this time at OM's office. Even when knowledge gets transmitted face to face, designers and technicians resort to sample requests as the key device to control the inarticulate power of sketches—and of the eye (Mukerji 2014).

This is true even when, instead of being at the agents' offices, we actually make it into a sample room to inspect how the parts of the shoe are coming along. Being at the sample room allows Nicole and John to inspect if studs are being stitched properly, that the insole is being stitched with the proper materials from the sample request, whether the leathers have been finalized the right way and, if not, what alternative ways of treating them might give

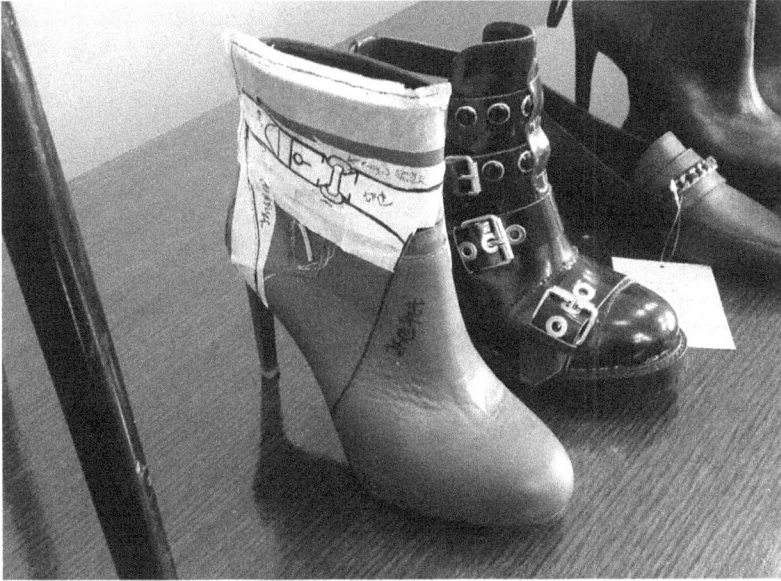

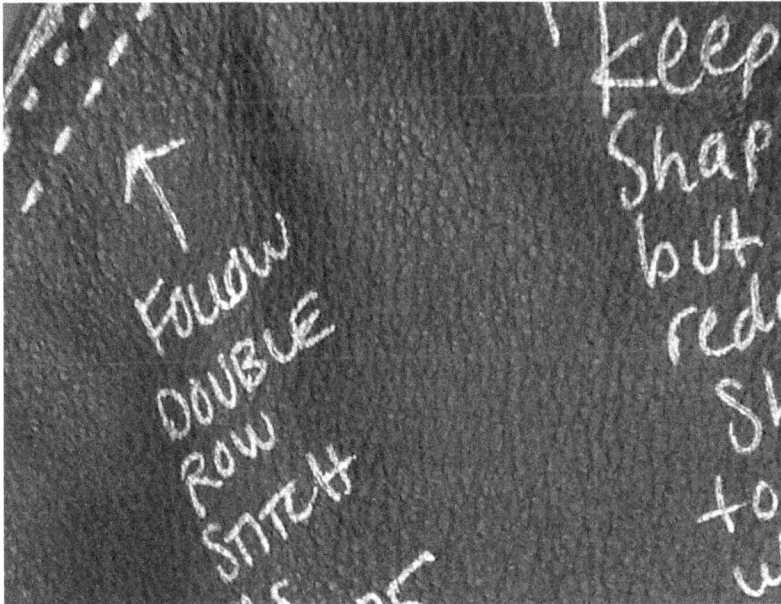

Figure 3.8. Corrections and instructions drawn over a pair of shoes.

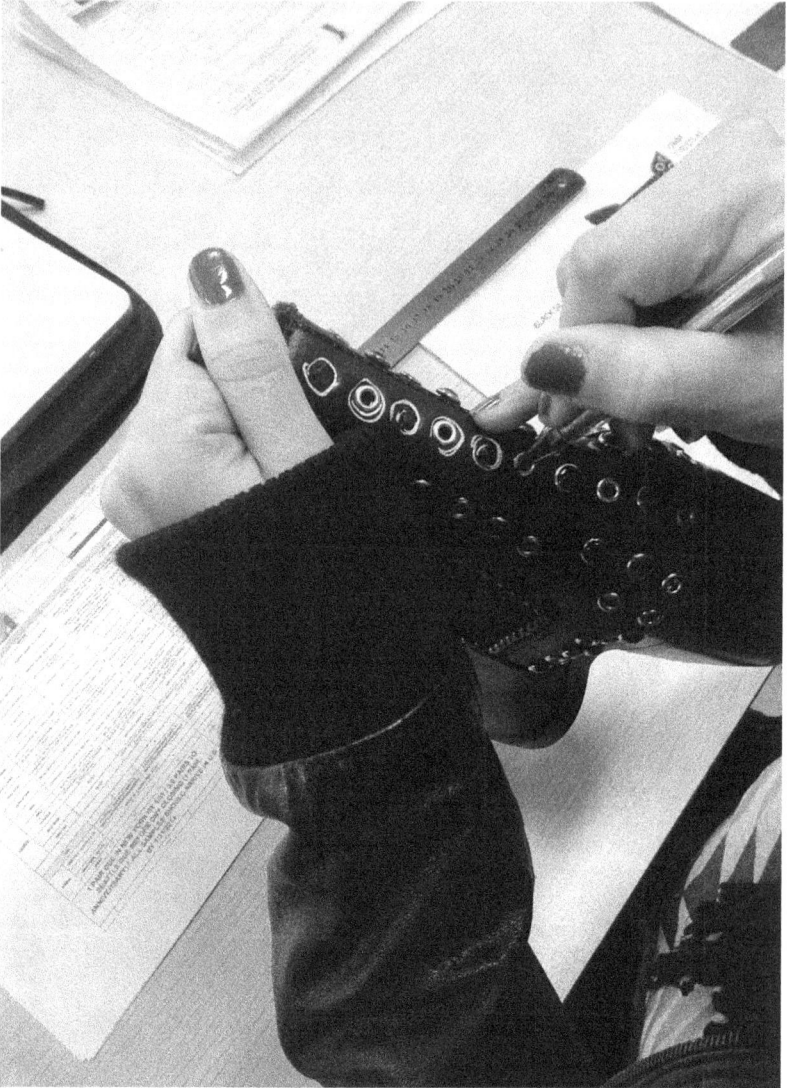

Figure 3.9. Nicole drawing on a shoe, comparing it to the sample-request sheet below.

them the right shine, etc. This mostly happens when designers are checking the status of a sale sample; they only make it into the actual sample room to inspect whether samples are being finished, if the sample-room technicians have incorporated the corrections properly, to check with them if there is a mistake, and to give any last-minute instructions on how to correct any issues. Even though this building is different than the others we've been to, with actual machinery on display—a ground floor where shoes get glued, hammered, and sealed, and a second floor where most of the stitching is done[5]—once Nicole, John, and Jeff (the US expat who works for WM) wanted to check how a sample was actually coming out, they repeated the procedure. Anna, the fit girl from WM who came with us to the sample room, entered a room with a large meeting table and finalized shoes on the shelves, and stepped up on the table so Nicole could see the fit and decide whether more work was needed.

THE MULTIPLE LIVES OF AN AVATAR

The literatures on commodity chains and on networks have both contributed to a "black box" (Latour 1987) understanding of how a firm operates within a global organizational ecology, hiding the many procedures by the myriad intermediaries that help it work like we see from the outside. The commodity-chain scholarship does so by understanding the firm as central to the relationship between input (raw materials) and output (finalized product), without much interrogation of the multiple variabilities of how that process can happen. I want to show, on the other hand, how the emphasis on production instead of design has contributed to an understanding of the firm as a homogeneous entity, hiding from us how a chain—its links, phases, stages, and the hands through which the commodity circulates—is a highly fragmented and idiosyncratic social formation, itself the result of many smaller but precisely calibrated networks, made up of provisional relationships each step along the way.

Focusing on empirical micro situations has three consequences, and I'm here returning to the three main arguments I said I was going to advance at the beginning of this part. The first one is that it helps us to restore the multifaceted and sensory texture of objects before they become quantifiable or homogeneous abstractions to be sold and bought. While the final object produced is indeed a commodity with exchange value, looking at the process through which it happens allows us to unlock the history stored in the product, as well as the multiplicity contained within the homogeneity we call a shoe. I've shown the heterogeneity of the process by pointing at the sourcing of "the global" in the shoe, seen in the different ways in which—with different levels of co-presence—other places figure in the design; relatedly,

I've shown how these processes of assessment become a "tournament" of value, in which shopping, looking at images, and putting together mood boards operate as a ludic way in the present that hides the production of exchange value in the future. Temporality once again plays a role, as it conceals the tension between exchange value and the other valuation regimes (play, gift-giving, and collecting) that take place in the shoe-development process.

Moreover, I've shown the different phases of commoditization, dequalification, and singularization through which a shoe passes within production itself. I've shown the multiple forms and guises under which shoes appear: they are used as reference—figure 3.10 shows discarded shoes that were used as references for coloring leathers—dematerialized, rematerialized, classified, and dequalified until they become goods.

I want to stay on this point for a minute and discuss how we can see the many social lives of a good within the realm of production alone. While the literature on the economies of qualities (Callon et al. 2002; Karpik 2010; Hansen 2000) has explored what happens when goods go to waste, become singularized by use or by devices like branding, or enter into the secondhand market, little has been said of how a good has many potential lives in its production cycle. Shoes are prototypes—made out of discarded materials—; samples—a shoe with the same materials than the final one but without the approval. But they are also icons with effectualities but no materials (as in the trend), as well as finalized goods that are bought to either become supply for new products or parts to be decomposed and recomposed into a new object. Furthermore, as we've seen, some of these shoes become singularized within a background landscape of other shoes as to be made a reference for what constitutes originality and innovation.

Immediately related to this, there is a second consequence: the paradoxical production of innovation. I've shown this through the quasi-palimpsest-like process of design, in which designers work through copies of copies to produce difference. They organize this through cluttering, a way of accumulating objects, ideas, and sketches in which the large quantity produces a background or context for what then appear in contrast as distinctive or unique (the preferred categories are "hip," "hot," and "cool"). As much of the tacit-knowledge literature has already explained (see Polanyi 1962; O'Connor 2005; Harper 1992; Wacquant 2004; Sudnow 1978) designers learn how to find difference in the practices of repetition. In this embodied repetition, creative workers learn to answer the question "What comes next?" not as something

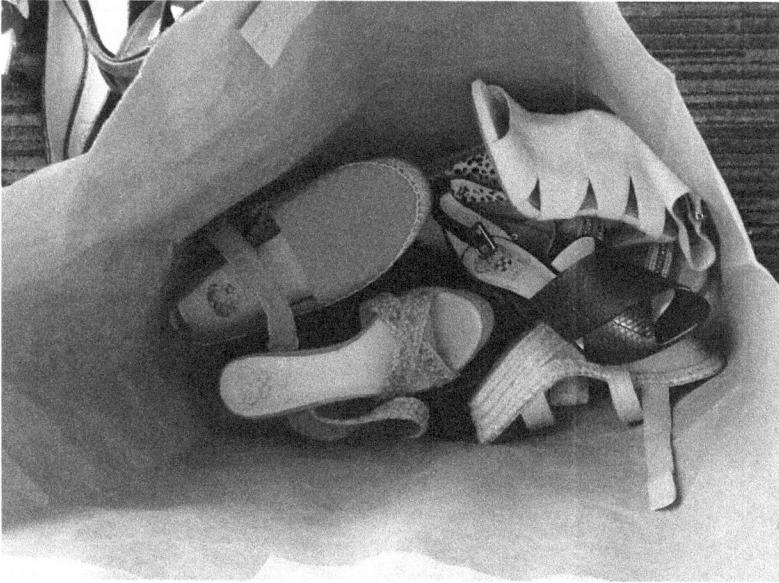

Figure 3.10. Commodities serve as supply to other, similar commodities: Shoes by competitors on the floor of the OM design room in New York City (top). The life of a commodity in this cycle can also end up in declassification, with shoes going back to being undifferentiated rubble (bottom).

that is preformulated, or following logical or formal rules, but rather as procedures that aim to produce a knowledge from the senses (in this case visual and tactile) that helps to guide the designer as she goes uncovering the next step in the design and production process, as well as what is enticing for others about the final product.

The design cycle illustrates the tension between reproduction and innovation in a second way, as novelties emerge as displacements resulting from each line being both a repetition and a new event at the same time. What gets repeated are the procedures, the information-collecting practices, the searches for difference with competitors and with previous collections, the searches for "hot" items awaited by both the firm's salespeople and buyers from shops like Nordstrom. What emerges as new is a result of the search for homologies with previous successful seasons (Which were the signature and the hot items? What was the spread between flats and heels? How many ornaments did they use?) and equivalent seasons in past years (How many sandals to produce if the collection is for Spring or Summer, for instance) while being precluded from repeating those outstanding items, given the constant search for novelties that characterizes the industry.

We could say, following the work of Becker and Faulkner (2009; Becker, Faulkner, and Kinrshenblatt-Gimblett 2006), that making shoes is a unique opportunity to see how culture operates via "shedding," helping us to see the "variance increasing activities" at work in helping users to select, from a varied landscape, what is going to be considered an "original" production. Much like jazz, shoemaking involves a paradoxical relationship between routine practices and originality, in which actual choices are better explained by the context and background-producing procedures, and in which the creation of value is best understood not as a deviation from established routines (Stark 2009) but rather as an exercise built on routine practices and well-known conventions that signals—through constant repetition and accumulation— that which might emerge as distinguishable.

Since some of the changes in design throughout its inception are explained by the exchange between the design and support teams, it's only logical that the chapter dedicated to opening up the black box of the input part of the commodity chain should show the interaction between the design and production phases. In doing this, I advance the third consequence of this first part, showing how some of the comparative advantages of agglomeration economies—which are not supposed to travel—are indeed reproduced. While colocation offers unique advantages, collaborative knowledge production is not contingent on permanent physical co-presence; it's also produced under conditions of temporary physical or virtual co-presence.

This itself has a couple of important implications, which makes them even more salient given the paradox of this being a chapter focused on design that has as much as possible sought to background the support work (Becker 1982) that happens in China: to change the picture of the lower-value node in the chain as unskilled or with little participation in the production of knowledge. Though there are numerous studies of knowledge, they tend to focus on the global production of software, economic expertise, technology, and engineering; there are seldom studies of globally distributed cognition, collaboration, and knowledge production in low-end manufacturing. Thanks to understanding the formation of clusters in South China, we can see the power of the little routines, standards, technologies, devices, and infrastructure that take time to set up and that explain also why capital cannot move somewhere with cheaper labor immediately. Gary Gereffi (Hamilton and Gereffi 2009) has recently made this point by using Becker's (1995) Latour-inspired take on the power of inertia to discuss the levels of interdependence and integration that make it difficult for capital to leave and for industrial upgrade to happen immediately. The combination of the specialized cluster around Dongguan, communicational advances, and the constant travel by people and things allows for the kind of knowledge that is costly to acquire, transfer, and use in a new location to become less "sticky" (Von Hippel 1994) and as such transferable from one locale to another.

The second implication is that, as I've hinted in many sections of the chapter, we need a better account of how electronic communication helps sustain embodied and tacit knowledge and, at the same time, how embodied, kinesthetic knowledge can become codified and transmissible.[6] While designers touch materials, bend shapes, get the "feel" of a color, and discuss whether things are starting to look "cool" in such a way that one would imagine their work should always happen with them in the actual room next to the materials being turned into a shoe, firms have managed to do design work in such a way that sometimes it's hard to understand if there is any meaningful difference between work done in New York City via email communication, at OM's office in Dongguan, at an agent's office, or even in the sample room itself.

While I've emphasized how this chapter aimed to open the black box of global design and development, we can also observe the work that modularity (the inscription in documents; the repetition of meeting rooms with a central table; the fit girls; the codified sample requests; the redrawings on top of sketches, photographs, and actual shoes) does in terms of aiming to settle and simplify the heterogeneity of putting a shoe together, replacing it with a codified set of procedures by which a shoe is produced and perceived as a homogeneity.

The discussion of cluttering can be thought of as yet another practice through which scale-making is achieved. One of the key points to this chapter is that it provided a novel anatomy of the elements that make the global possible. On top of collaboration, networks, or standards, I focused here on how looking at design, cluttering, the tension between innovation and repetition reveals how much these elements are not born out of top-down and homogenizing processes but out of messy, locally negotiated contingent practices—underscoring again how much the development of a shoe is at the same time the assembling of a scale.

THE END?

This first part of this book has ended with a set of relatively finalized samples. Shoes will arrive to the US in two waves. The sale samples will travel first—sometimes by FedEx, other times by a courier hired to hand-carry them—to be shown to the company's own salespeople and to be displayed in OM's New York City showroom and in the specialized trade fairs that happen at least eight times a year in New York, Los Angeles, and Las Vegas. Clients can thus decide whether they are interested in ordering them and, if so, how many pairs they would like to request. Once OM receives the finalized information on the potential demand, orders will be confirmed and the samples will turn into actual shoes to be sold in stores, moving from the sample room into mass production at the factory. Final orders will then be shipped, enter the US legally through customs, and be distributed at department stores like Nordstrom. But is that really the end of the process for a shoe design? Or is it a new beginning?

If I were to widen the frame on the picture that initiated this part of the book—an event to celebrate OM as a brand and supposedly give consumers a "feel" for the backstage of how shoes are designed—we would have seen, close by, a table with very similar designs by a competitor.[7] This points immediately to the possibility that our work aiming to understand in full how a cultural product is globally assembled might not be over, as we need to study the next phase of the commodity chain: how do objects circulate once they leave the firm? How do other companies decide to copy the designs by OM? When do they imitate them verbatim? When do they alter their features?

The second part of *The Perfect Fit* deals with how things are seen on the floor in South China by those actors who have been all but black-boxed here: technicians and fit models. How does this complicate the picture of distributed cognition that we've established in this first part? How does it move the designer off the center of the story? What do we learn about the kinds of knowledge that can be disembodied and formalized? And what does all this say about the competing ideas about what a shoe is and how taste is achieved?

PART 2

Feet and Fit

Chapter 4

THE WORLD
AT HER FIT

Scale-Making, Uniqueness, and Standardization

INTRODUCTION: BRIBERY AT THE FACTORY?

If you are a foreigner and spend a few days in Dongguan, there is a strong chance local folks and expats will take you out for dinner on Bar Street, an area where you can find all kinds of food, from stylized versions of Cantonese dishes to the regular menus of cosmopolitan kitchens (Indian, sushi, Italian, Contemporary American, French) that can be found in most international centers. Located in Dongcheng District, the area runs for some six large blocks on Dongcheng South Road, and spills over onto the first block of the adjacent streets. It is close to the offices of well-established developers and to some of the trendy hotels where designers stay.

OM's team regularly stays at the Pullman Hotel, which caters to local customers, offering large shrimp or crabs grilled on the street on large, improvised charcoal containers. If you pass by in the afternoon, you can see the crabs still alive, slowly being sorted and prepared on the sidewalk. As you walk further north along Bar Street, the wording on the signs and awnings progressively change from Mandarin to English—albeit with a few typos or plain linguistic mistakes. The restaurants become more secluded, divided more starkly from a sidewalk that is now noticeably cleaner than it was on the first couple of blocks. Some newer locales have opened at the end of Bar Street, near its intersection with Dongcheng East Road. If you make it all the way to where Bar Street takes an inverted, L-shaped turn, you'll find an Italian restaurant, Maccheroni by Salvatore, which has been a staple of the area for the last ten years. It's not uncommon to see multiple tables with foreigners (Italians, Spaniards, Germans, Americans) who are either eating on their own as part of their weekly rotation of dinner options while they work in Dongguan or as the guests of locals. In those cases, reunions are frequently to do business, where groups made up of both foreigners, expats, and locals discuss potential work collaborations or blow off steam after a long workday. The restaurant has recently expanded, taking over two adjacent shops, and customers flock to it not only because it is a well-known and reliable purveyor of good-quality Italian meals (and wine) but also because of its outdoor seating.

On a night in December 2015, I dined at Maccheroni by Salvatore with a couple of American designers and the managers (a married couple in their thirties) of a Taiwanese trading company, which produces shoes for the European and US markets. A small trading company, it had recently scaled down its family-owned factory into a smaller operation. Instead of running two full assembly lines, the company was now composed mostly of a fully operating sample room, and a relatively large quality-control division with a dozen employees. For production, they used the factory floor of a business partner: the son of a good friend of the woman's father. But sometimes, if they were expecting larger orders, they used production space in the behemoth factories run by agents in charge of the final production of shoes developed by other trading companies and smaller factories. As the couple explained how happy they were that they had been able to secure a large order from a West Coast US company, they tried to explain to me the difficulties they encountered when trying to place some of their orders with this kind of massive factory. Some of the issues would be obvious to scholars studying the coordination of complex systems, such as social networks determining access to production space: orders are prioritized (i.e., in hierarchies dominated by foreign brands), production quality varying by type of machine available, and quality control varies depending on the extent of access provided by the plant. But there was one issue that was certainly unexpected: in order for the samples to get approval—a necessary step for the factory to produce your shoes—she contented you have to bribe the fit model.

When she saw the surprise on my face, Grace—the Taiwanese woman who had inherited the role of manager of the trading-company from her father,

Simon—unpacked how this happened. She explained: "Think of it as if you were thinking of something like Steve Madden—but without the designers." The image captured not only the scale, scope, and importance of the operation (Steve Madden is one of the largest brands in the US) but also its transnational ownership: originally from Seattle, the factory had recently moved its headquarters from Taiwan to Dongguan, where it operates in Houjie, the shoe district in the "world's factory." Grace's analogy also made explicit the fact that, without designers, those in charge of authorizing that the shoes meet the standards of quality for mass production are not the technicians, the sample room managers, or the inspectors but, rather, the female fit models. *They* get to say whether shoes are comfortable and good enough to meet the technical specifications for large orders.

In her dealings with large factories, Grace explained the problems she had encountered in getting her shoes approved. After a series of rejections, Grace noticed that other similar companies made it through, and that sometimes she would see how representatives from the factory engage in long conversations with the models before they did the fitting. In all of those cases, the fit models would approve the samples, which would move forward for development and production. Given her knowledge of the players in the shoe market and the quality of what they produced, she was surprised to see these approvals when her own shoes were being rejected. Though her company decided in the end not to place orders with that large factory, she came out convinced that the decision to approve shoes as fit for large production had to do with the fit models' inordinate amount of power.

Although I do not have any way to know if Grace's story is true, I had heard similar rumors from other managers and fit models. These rumors were supported by the prevalence of the *guanxi* economy, which certainly infuses all orders of Chinese social life (see Guthrie 1999; Wang 2009; and Yang 2011, among many others). Yet there was something in Grace's account that captured my imagination beyond the anecdote itself: the power of a female foot to dictate how shoes are to be produced.

In other chapters, I emphasize how the process is seen differently according to what is being prioritized: for example, whether shoe making starts with a design idea (for designers), with a line (for agents and traders), or with a last (for technicians). In this chapter, I show what happens if we take Grace's story seriously and center the production process on the shoe fitting. By examining what appears and what does not appear when we think of a finalized object like a shoe, the fitting process offers a fantastic entry point for tracing not only issues of visibility and recognition but also the invisible careers (Shapin 1989) that support designers' work.

MODELING THE SHOE

Among the manifold definitions of modeling, there are four that help us to understand the conceptual and semantic network around the activity of fitting: (1) fashioning or shaping a three-dimensional figure or object in a malleable material; (2) displaying clothes by wearing them; (3) use (especially as a system of procedure) as an example to follow or imitate; and (4) a person or thing regarded as an excellent example of a specified quality.

The meaning of the first two are obvious: fit models in both China and the US are used to helping in the development and design of shoes, as well as displaying them to clients during the commercialization period. The third definition best encompasses fit models' central role in the making of standards, signaling where their power lies. To preview the main argument of this chapter, the "foot stabilization" that results in brands always working with the same model—whether face-to-face or online—allows for designers, technicians, and production managers to understand what they are looking at, whether it be a sheet of measurements, an image with a prototype, or a sample to try on. This a less-obvious technical device through which procedures are simplified and settled from a distance. It is also the kind of work that STS scholars have conceptualized as *invisible work* (Shapin 1989; Star and Strauss 1999).

As I will show in the next two chapters, fit models allow for the production of standardized shoes. They are an obligatory point of passage for design ideas, materials, and sketches, as well as central players in a larger infrastructure of scale-making. In previous chapters, I have shown how a world was made to travel toward designers via images of other designs, products, shops, and customers. In this chapter, we'll see another procedure of miniaturization in a double sense—of the comparative scope of a foot, usually the smallest female shoe size, versus the whole range of size variation in multiple locales—for making the world flat. This results in a foot that becomes an immutable mobile (Latour 1986; Law 1986), moving from China to the US, or from the US to China, without distortion. Moreover, through the fit model's foot, we see all the translation between multiple cultural standards—sometimes across size conventions in different regions, other times according to gendered expectations—and how both sets of standards are intertwined with imputed racial and national bodily characteristics. I focus the final part of this chapter on the many consequences of this translation.

WHAT'S IN A FOOT?
(AND HOW TO WORK WITH IT)

Arlene puts her right foot on the table.

We are on the penthouse of a building in New York's Midtown, where a small shoe brand has its showroom. Both Marcia, the former designer, and Pepi, the current designer, define the brand as marketed to "Brooklyn-like" women in their mid- and late 20s. Arlene has been standing for a couple of hours, working closely to correct the lasts—a mechanical form with a shape similar to that of a human foot, used by shoemakers in manufacturing—for the shoes of the fall collection. The designers have been preparing for a trip to MAGIC, a trade show in Vegas, so this is a good time for the fit model and the technician to work intensely on fixing some of the lasting and fit issues on samples they recently received from China. Clint, a veteran technician in his 70s who has been working in the industry for over fifty years, sits next to Arlene. My presence gives them an excuse to take a break, and for Clint to explain why a foot matters in shoemaking. He focuses on the particularities of Arlene's right foot (see figure 4.1) to explain why technicians use a live foot, as well as how they work around the tension between one foot's peculiarities and its role as a standard. And I say one foot because they mostly go by her right foot; as Arlene explained, her "left foot is a bit fuller."

For outsiders like me, it is unclear why the industry does not utilize wooden or rubber mannequins or the last itself to measure how the shoe is coming out. For "shoe people," the answer is obvious: while the last manages to give you volume, Clint said, it's a rigid object. Yet, as he noted, "the foot is malleable," which presents all kinds of challenges. How do you account for the quirks of a foot that is supposed to be standard? And how do you use the information a malleable foot gives back to you?

The malleability of the foot, along with the fact that it is a part of a person treated (and produced) as an object, point us toward the idea of *affordance*. This concept was first coined to study perceptual relationships between animals and their environments, focusing on how the properties of a landscape impact animal behavior (Gibson 1979. The concept arrived to the study of cultural production via scholars of cognition and became an important part of the cultural-sociology toolkit after Tia DeNora (2000) employed it to study how people use music. The term points toward the possibilities of an object at hand and how these depend not only on the morphology of the object but also on previous meaning-making and uses, as well as on other qualities and contexts associated with it (Keane 2003).

What's more, it makes sure that we understand social semiosis (Peirce 1894; Veron 1998) not as a process where the meaning attributed to objects is open ended but in which "thinking with things" (Daston 2004; Henare, Holbraad, and Wastell 2007) results in an understanding of objects as constraining the possibilities of both meaning and use. Using the foot of an actual woman as the modeling object to render volume instructions to make a shoe allows information that would be otherwise rendered mute (or only revealed by the technician) to be voiced out loud by an authorized agent. Yet this process constrains other ways of measuring fit. For example, to measure across the volume of the last, the feet would have to be cut. This results in the need to develop ways of bracketing what is subjective about each foot from "spilling" over the objectivity of the standards (Galison 2004), as well in ways of training the modeling woman to become the standardized foot. They also open up, as I'll develop later in the chapter, a field of struggle, as it is unclear who gets to talk about the fitting foot qua object and who has the ultimate authority over fit: is it the technician, the fit model, or the designer?

While the model foot is supposed to be a stand-in for every foot, and for a base and last to generate a design, it is actually an object of its own that renders through its imperfections more useful information than a solid and perfect three-dimensional representation of what designers imagined. Unlike the metal bars under which most measurement devices have managed to disembody and leave the flesh behind (Crease 2011; Alder 2002)—as when a foot is measured at 30.48 centimeters and not an actual foot—what we encounter here is the establishment of standards working from one body to another. In the fit process, a whole metrological system plays around the knowledge of how one trained person's actual foot responds to the varying states of the object: What are the necessary changes to the last depth to adjust the shank curve when changing the height of a heel? As the curve augments, it changes the weight distribution and the length that the base of the shoe needs. How does the technician account for those differences if—when measured on a table—the flat and the high-heel base are the same? When working on a pump versus a sandal, how does he (all technicians I met during fieldwork were men) account for the fact that an actual foot spreads out in a sandal? Does the base need extra width, even if the difference is one or two millimeters? And relatedly, how much lighter should he advise the insole be made to account for this extra width?

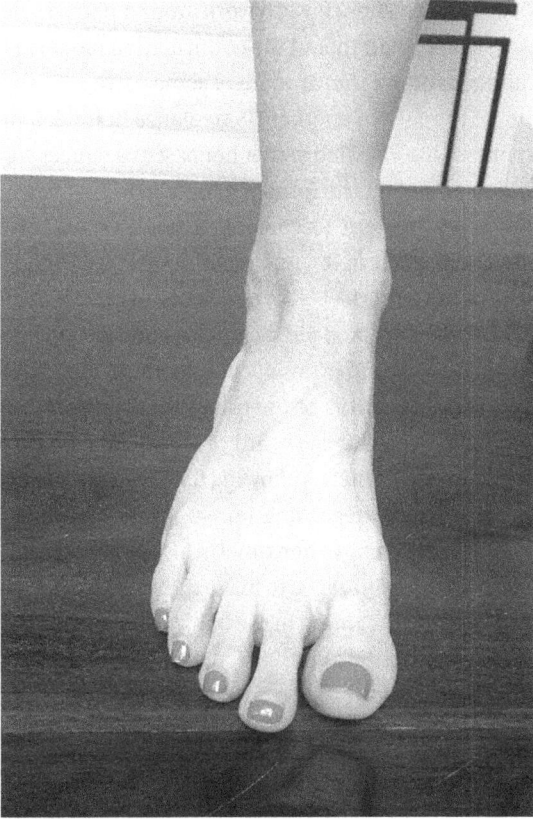

Figure 4.1. Arlene's right foot on the table.

When working with Arlene's foot, Clint is constantly on the lookout for two different things: first, that her foot overpronates, so the weight of her foot rolls inward and she tends to push off almost completely from her first two toes; second, that her second toe is actually longer than her big toe. This throw off the toe sweep—how toes are expected to align—as molds are made with a particular sweep in mind. This is a particular problem when the they have to model pumps on her, much as having a small fifth toe is a nuisance when fitting a sandal. Of course, these are just two peculiarities of one fit model. In some of the other fitting sessions I witnessed, OM designers worked around Anna's low instep, so if something fit well but was gaping over her feet then designers usually ignored it, as they knew how to account for her right foot. Connie—a model for a large factory—self-reported that her technician always had to know how to work around her very delicate calf—which was less "strong" than that of the confirmation model in the US—and skinny foot, understanding that if there is some extra side space it should not be an issue. In the case of another US freelance fit model, Brace, she has already incorporated the knowledge that her past as a dancer comes to haunt designers working on her, in the form of a high arch.

In all of these cases, "perfect" feet are called "golden standards" within their own companies and are selected with careful scrutiny. Fit models embody a contradiction: each has a "perfect" foot that follows or is close to twelve different standard measurements, and yet technicians and designers have to learn how to work around the peculiarities of each "perfect" foot. Technicians and designers have a series of "tricks of the trade" for fitting and adjusting what does not seem aligned with the standard that they imagine for the product and market. Sometimes this means allowing for more space between foot and shoe or leaving a gap or disregarding how tight the upper feels on the fit model if she has a high arch. Other times, this entails cutting around the insole at the ball area circumference to make the shoes more flexible, stretching the leather or cutting the lining in the ball and ankle area to make sure to account for the wrinkles in the material that would unnecessarily harden the shoe and make it uncomfortable or too tight, even for a skinny foot.

Arlene is one of a kind, Clint explains. She was selected in a casting call over twenty years ago because of her foot measurements (even though, as we've already seen, her feet are far from perfect or standard). But over time she has developed a full vocabulary to describe the things about shoes that don't work properly. Technicians and fit models develop a work dynamic that turns them into a unit: as much as the model knows the peculiarities of her feet (or foot), the technicians know to make calculations based on how feet conform *and* depart from the standard measurements. Experimental information that would be considered "noise" in other metrological contexts—for instance, the various imperfections of the model in replicating the standard—is in this case incorporated as vital data. The more that technicians and models work together, the more designers get used to a particular foot, and the more they transform that noise into how they manage the standard. While the technician-designer pair works in tandem, over time they develop into a metrological unit. The more they get used to the peculiar and subjective character of the working object, the better they can actually render it as a standard and contain the particularities from corroding the generalizable.

This chapter underscores the importance of the foot through a study of cultural production, and by using conceptual tools developed to understand the construction of scientific knowledge, much like the role of "nature" in STS-inspired literatures. This is not a capricious choice. The foot of the model, as I will show in the following pages, is hard to domesticate, and as such, to quote Latour (1988, 158) again, it is what stands for reality, since "reality is that which resists." It works as the referent toward which the whole infrastructure is oriented. It is the anchor that allows for and yet limits the work of actors. A key to this—and to all labors of adaptation—has to do with the fact that in the case of the foot, actors *cannot* move beyond it, it actually can't be taken out of the body! The foot works as an a priori presence around which a whole system of reference is built.

The following two short exchanges allow us to see how the organizing presence of the foot operates even in absentia (either when one of the actors—in this case the usual fit model—is not physically present, or when one the people involved is not part of the designer-technician-model triad). Nicole, the OM designer, had to explain to one of the US-based managers overseeing production in Dongguan that if there was a gap between the shoe and Anna's foot, it was OK. The manager was concerned: "How come there is a gap!? How can you send us a boot that was done in a proto having a gap?"

Nicole responded, "Don't worry! We all know about it and have learned how to fix it and calculate around it."

In the second exchange, Ashley, an associate designer at OM in New York, explained to me how she could still work around and account for the differences. After receiving an email from the sample room featuring a different fit model than the usual one, she explained, "I look at the kind of measurements and key places—the instep, the ball, the calf . . . because in this case this is a boot—[to] see if it pinches her, where it looks like it might be too tight or too loose, and compare it mentally to what I know from Anna's foot. I sort of calculate mentally the difference between the two and go from there." Once again, while both fit models are supposed to be "standards," there is an interplay between the internalized standard, which Ashley articulates as developed and learned through both physical and visual interaction with the fit model, and its relationship to the putative industry standard, which serves as the base by which technician and designers adjust their measurements.

When examined from the outside, a fit model's work seems tedious. Not much happens daily. Sometimes she stands so the technician can see the difference between static and weight-bearing fit; on other occasions, she sits (and when she does she might be checking her cell phone).[1] Regardless of her position, the technician works like a detective, trying to read, in the traces of how the shoe reacts to being worn, a more "real" reality about how well fit works and what problems are in need of correction.[2] In this dynamic, the relationship between causes and effects is inverted, since the technician can never definitively pinpoint the source of what looks (or feels) "wrong." What the technicians conjecture about is a set of outward signs that need to be assigned causes, and, as I make evident in the rest of this chapter, how to bracket issues related to the peculiarities of the actual foot.

For long periods of time, the fit model can look absent-minded, even passive; at others, she engages with the technician or designer and offers feedback: "I'd move the strap a bit, or it hits the anklebone." With more experience, models gain confidence and knowledge, and can point out what does not work (sometimes even aesthetically, as they have a different viewpoint of the shoe). But I was struck by two characteristics of the encounter: first, the seemingly unfocused character of what goes on; and second, how the more time the technician and model spend together, the less they talk about what they are doing, instead engaging in seemingly random conversation about daily life, peppered with comments about the shoe. This dynamic is even more apparent in larger companies, where technicians and models interact face-to-face for longer periods, and in China, where most of the initial fitting and sampling work is done. For a company that works with six to eight fashion seasons a year, with a few lines per season and two rounds of fitting and confirmation, one can imagine that fit models and technicians effectively meet face-to-face year round.

A similar effect takes place in the US: although designers and technicians only meet in person every other month when there is a new line, they do so for two full and furious days, fitting nearly sixty shoes per day. The fitting session is as much an occasion to provide feedback and correct the shoes as to catch up with each other's lives. Either because of the long-term temporal arc of production or because of its concentrated character, in both cases, work is conducted at a tacit level, allowing the interaction between fit and standard to be worked out in minute detail amid discussion of the many other things happening in actors' personal lives.

OF MEASURABLE, IMMUTABLE, TRANSLATABLE, AND MOBILE FEET

The transmutation of all the little changes into standards is another avenue to observe one of the main themes of this book: how a projected object slowly becomes one, so that designers, technicians, and production managers across the globe can interpret a sheet with measurements or an image of a prototype or a sample being tried on (as we described in chapter 3). But what are those elusive standards? And more importantly, how do feet get matched to sizes?

Most producers for the US market fit shoes with either a 6B or 7B female size as their reference (the letter refers to the width).[3] It is unclear why these sizes are the norm, but is likely related to a long history of this infrastructure. For instance, it may reflect the most common women's shoe sizes in the 1970s, which were 7 and 7.5 for everyday shoes and 7 for "fashion" shoes. The growth of Americans over a generation has also resulted in changes to average fit for female shoes, which is now something closer to 8.5 or 9.

When asked about the convention, designers and technicians seemed unsure of its origin and rather referred to the functional possibilities of starting at 6 for fashion and 7 for comfort shoes. In the words of Josemir, the Brazilian sample-room technician who produces Arlene and Clint's shoes in Dongguan:

> It makes it easier to grade. Once you establish everything on 6, the only calculation you have to do is how to grow things proportionally for the other sizes. Besides that, most things are now calibrated as we start working either with 6 or 7—in their [Arlene and Clint's] case, 6. When you have to work on "mama" brands [comfort brands], things are harder to calibrate because you don't have fit models for every potential size. It's a lot of work to calculate the new width and weight, but that's why I am here, to calculate those things.

Josemir has a fit model in his office, though like many other "fit girls" in China who are not employed by a large company or factory, she also does office work, be it following up on samples or entering inventory numbers for invoices to suppliers. He uses his fit model–cum–administrative assistant for many of the non-designer brands that his trading company produces. Josemir's company produces shoes for the US, but also for the northern European, South African, and Australian markets, which creates added headaches in terms of conforming to different national standards. He can't use his fit model for the brand Clint is a technician for. The way their system works calls for all of the fitting and measuring decisions to be made in New York.

Recently, Josemir's office tried to do a casting to reproduce Arlene's feet in China. As told by Pepi—the brand's US designer, who had worked previously for OM—the office received measurements from at least forty potential models in Dongguan, but none matched Arlene's exact measurements. These casting procedures are common in larger factories in need of a single fit girl

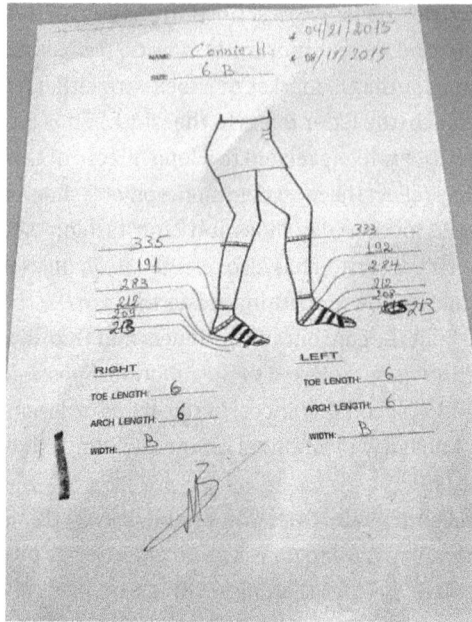

Figure 4.2. Measurements for Connie H., a fit
model at a large shoe factory in Dongguan.

to try out most of the products for a given market. But this is sometimes supplemented by attempts to render a model's foot. Women are asked to powder
their feet and then stand on a sheet to imprint the exact way their body
weight impacts their step. This is also a way to "read" the foot's arch, ball,
and waist to help technicians not only to understand the foot in nonstatic
situations but also to predict how the quirks they need to correct relate to
their current fit models.[4]

Pictures depicting the measurements of a fit model to be are a regular and
repeated procedure (figure 4.2). To understand how volume relates to form,
candidates put their feet into a machine that measures the girth (in millimeters) of six different areas: the top, the ball, the waist, the instep between
dorsal and plantar joints, the heel instep, and the ankle—plus the calf, which
is of central importance for boots, the most important item in the US winter
market. In some specialized places, for instance, the SENAI center in Novo
Hamburgo, Brazil, experts help local businesses develop measurements. I
was able to witness not only the first machine I described but also a second

device that models would stand on to record the weight distribution of their feet, in a more precise and updated version of the "powder on the foot" trick.

While in Novo Hamburgo I also collected more varied information about the operation of fitting standards for the US market; which markets higher-end shoes than those made for the American market in Dongguan. Figure 4.3 illustrates the multiple logics that are inscribed in the foot-measurement chart. As on every other form, the ability to inscribe measurements to make them become disembodied, reproducible, and translatable in other locales is essential. The form depicted is identical to Connie, the Chinese fit model, showing the standardization of forms and techniques across the industry. But we can witness one difference in its use: the separation between fit models

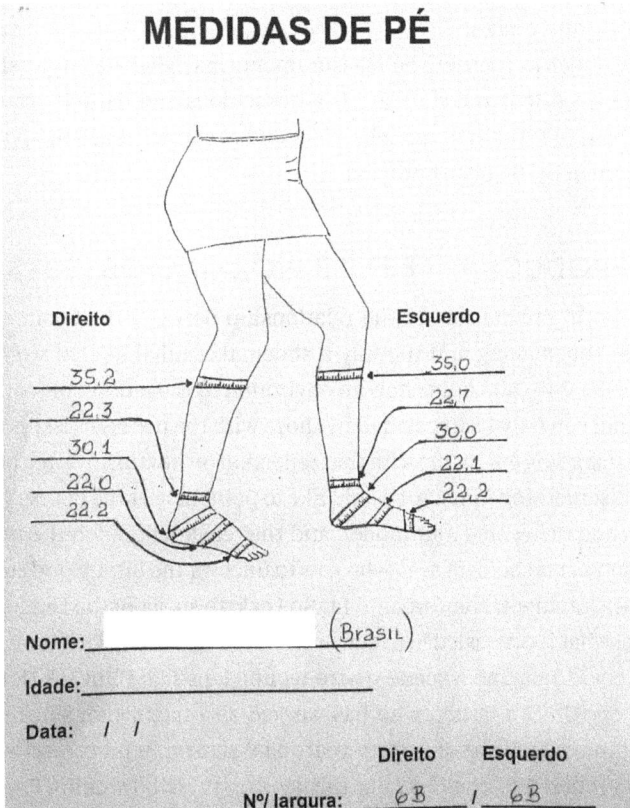

Figure 4.3. Measurements for Carmen, a fit model for the domestic market at a shoe-trading company in Novo Hamburgo.

for the local and export markets; for example, development companies have to recruit different fit models for different markets, as evidenced by the name section that explicitly references a Brazilian company. Notice that while the second form (figure 4.3) is also from a model who stands at a size 6B, the measurements are very different. The "Brazilian" 6B is larger in every measurement by between one and two centimeters. This is a meaningful difference that results in technicians having to navigate multiple embodied standards within the same company; it also sorts models from the beginning as serving one market or the other. Yet another form of control segregates models by market: the ability to replicate standards and avoid translation issues by making explicit *what* belongs *where*. As I will show later on, one of the key issues brought up in the attempt to replicate a set of measurements on actual human bodies is the problem of coordinating and translating across millimetric differences.

But as much as focusing on measurements may give the impression that the fit between feet and standard is a miraculous and natural occurrence, models have to train their modeling feet and eventually become spokespersons for them in the fitting process.

PRODUCING FEET AS WORKING OBJECTS

In a beautiful meditation on the relationship between the techniques involved in shoemaking and the way a shoemaker inhabits that world, Heidegger (1982, 240) highlights how an environment is made out of tools: shoes and leather can only be uncovered by those with the necessary skills to decipher what is going on. In line with that reflection on how uncovering an entity demands something from us, I would like to point here at the necessary skills for someone to become a fit model, and the tension between the fit model herself and her technician as to who gets to uncover the intra-world subtleties about measurement, comfort, and fit. So I ask, to speak in the Heideggerian parlance: what is concealed in a foot, and how do we best make it transparent?

One could imagine a scene where technicians like Clint (in New York) and Simon (Grace's father, who has worked as a technician since starting his business in Taiwan some forty years ago) scream in unison across eight thousand miles: "If I could try out the shoe on myself, I wouldn't need a fit model." Clint said this verbatim, while Simon demonstrated the sentiment by describing how he would sometimes try on a larger women's size (usually a 9 or bigger) and work on it if the fit model was gone. A key part of what a fit model learns is knowledge well within the technician's lore: describing what she feels when trying on a shoe, identifying issues and considering how to correct the issues that might arise, and properly delivering these comments. It is kinesthetic: part of it is about the relationship between the singular and the general and another part is about how to develop a proper vocabulary to articulate this.

Technicians (and, to a lesser extent, fit models) call this "developing a feeling" and see this as the threshold that indicates when a model goes beyond being "just a foot" and becomes a full professional. Josemir explained this to me as the moment in which models move beyond feedback that could easily fit within binary distinctions of loose/tight or ugly/beautiful and can articulate a more complete understanding of the relationship between problems and potential solutions. Part of this requires technical knowledge. For instance, understanding why a shoe might be tight around the toe might require knowledge not only about the proximate cause (the front) but also about the heel construction causing the tension. As Josemir explained, having a knowledgeable fit model meant that a shoe that had been rejected six times could finally be approved. In addition to this technical know-how, "developing a feeling" also requires a particular kind of subjectivity, one that can not only comprehend the reaction of its own foot to a particular material but that is also cognizant of creating the standard and being attentive to a consumer who may have very different tastes and biographical contexts.

Annette works as a manager for a trading company. She started in Brazil but has worked in Dongguan for the past five years. She emphasizes that the process of moving past being "just a foot" takes at least a couple of seasons. To become acquainted with a particular brand, fit models have work for at least two seasons to experience the whole range of products, from sandals to boots. Connie diligently makes this evident when saying, "After working for three months at the factory [even after having had a previous job fitting], I was not good yet, I needed to relearn how to work for a different brand, to give different comments, to feel a different fit according to the market." This process becomes even more complicated when models work with multiple brands in a sample room, at a trading company, or even at a factory, where they have to be able to understand a range of brands and, in consequence, consumers and markets.

There is something like a global agreement about how long it takes to learn how to feel and talk about the necessary corrections both *in foro interno* and *in foro externo*. Connie in Dongguan agreed with Brace in New

York and Lorena, Carmen, and Jackie in Novo Hamburgo: it takes up to a year to develop the necessary skills and vocabulary to give useful comments to the technicians and designers. Learning what kinds of details are worthy of feedback is mostly a matter of "forces and intensities," as Lorena, one of the Brazilian fit models, explained. How much does the material press on the foot? Does it impinge in every position? And what *is* the material, and how much can it mold itself to the foot without hurting it? Moreover, sources of discomfort often come from body parts that depart from the standard for a particular market. Brace referred before to how her history as a dancer made her self-conscious of her instep and arch as compared to those of the "regular" consumer; on a different occasion, she noticed that she has to take into account that if something barely fits her calf, "it won't be of use to a customer in Indiana."

Fit models are asked to learn how to explain sources of discomfort on their own feet, as well as to bracket those issues that make their feet singular or that depart from the expected measurements. Though there is variance among the parts of the foot that need to be accounted for, there are two areas that are consistently signaled as significant by technicians and models: the instep and the ball. The latter is of particular importance for models working with heels, as it is where most of the weight resides. Learning how to distribute the weight properly—especially during marathon-like sessions of fitting fifty to sixty pairs of shoes in one working day—and how to account for (or discount) the pain that develops in the area is one of the most important demands on a fit model.

Trust is a critical element in the relationships between fit models, designers, and technicians. When designers and technicians trust the comments provided by models, they implement those corrections and then ask models whether they can feel the changes made. In other words, technicians use fit models as both their source of information and as credible experts with an experiential knowledge they cannot access. This distributed model of knowledge involves a "trial of worth" (Boltanski and Thevenot 2006) in which the fit model's knowledge is validated with each incremental step, and in which her worth becomes solidified as well.

We can see this as we revisit Clint's testimony about how Arlene was, in retrospect, one of a kind, not only because her foot had the desired measurements but also because of her ability and vocabulary to talk about her feet and shoes. We can also see this in Grace's testimony about her own fit: "My foot is not perfect. I can fit maybe for some wider stuff, but I know the technical

Figure 4.4. Technicians working with a model at a trading company.

stuff and how to talk about it. Some models have the perfect feet but they don't know how to communicate; they are bad at it." Despite expectations for models to be equivalent to the other models within the infrastructure, and for them and their feet to be transmuted into tools, fit models are also expected to be sources of knowledge. This is so important that many fit models who work for large companies develop consulting careers over time, giving independent specifications to factories, meeting face-to-face with factory technicians and production managers, without the intermediation of sample-room or development-office technicians.

Figure 4.4 shows a preamble to one of these occasions. The image depicts a model pointing at the strap and describing its problem to ensure that the technician's assistant takes a proper picture of the fit. Later on, she takes notes on what she verbally communicated to the technician and elaborates a small report with specifications of the things that did not work for the shoe. If she decides that the shoe does not work properly, the sample will be sent to the factory to be reworked. If she approves it, the pictures, her report (seen in figure 4.5), comments from the technicians, and the sample itself will all be sent to the offices in the US. From that point, the company begins its own fit and approval procedures, relying on its own fit models to produce a similar document, which is usually attached to comments by the production manager, with issues beyond standards and fit, focused on patterns.

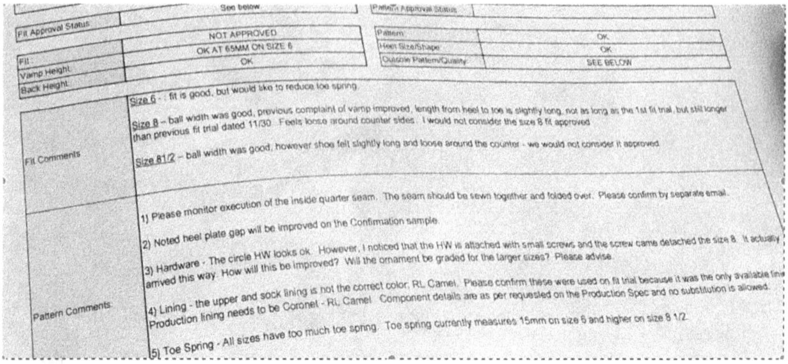

Figure 4.5. The report written by the fit model after the session shown in figure 4.4.

HOW TO SUSTAIN REPLICATION?

Given that fit models are counted on as one of the few expected constant factors in what is an otherwise precarious stability-seeking process, the production of feet as standardized working objects, docile items that lend themselves to comparison and generalization (Daston and Galison 1992; Epstein 2007, 31), involves also taking the necessary steps to maintain the feet as identical to themselves for as long as possible. In the words of Jackie, a Brazilian model who usually works for high-end US brands:

> You have to be careful not to gain weight, since in gaining weight, the shape of your foot might get altered too; but I've never had any issues with that. The thing I'm on the lookout for is wearing too much low-heel or no-heel shoes. It's not forbidden, but your foot gets wider and your ball adapts differently if you do that too much; it sort of 'rests' too much. It can affect the fit. . . . You actually have to be careful about working out too much, you have to be careful not to be too muscular, have to do it moderately because you do not want to do anything that will alter your arch or your calves!

As Jackie explains, fit models observe how their weight, shape, and exercise impact variation over time, and they generate strategies for controlling it. Echo, a Chinese sourcing agent who moved out of the factory into the office through her work as a fit model, adds another factor: motherhood. Pregnancy and childbirth often transform a woman's distribution of body weight by altering hips, and her feet react accordingly. In her case, motherhood transformed her foot from the 6B size of most of the models for the US market to a 6W, a wider standard used mostly for cheaper shoes and comfort brands.

To ensure that standards remain stable, models in large companies are measured every six months. This is partially to make sure that the measurements being mobilized while fitting the shoe are the same as before. But there is a second (and perhaps more important) reason related to the coordination of fit across multiple sites: to verify periodically that the primary standards do not drift. This is done by comparing the relative values of the standards maintained in separate locations. For companies that work with many feet in several locales instead of relying on just one model, the problem is how to make all these feet comparable. Companies use each minimal transformation that results in an adjustment to provide instructions about how to compare fit across the now-differing units and adapt to the new measurements. Or, if the changes are dramatic, they provide a catalyst to hold a new casting call to hire someone who better replicates the preexisting size.

This points to an issue that is central to all standardization-making projects but may be unique to this one: how to coordinate replication and transposability in nonexperimentally-controlled settings when all of the standard-holders are bodies instead of materials, forms, or measuring devices. I found the image in figure 5 tacked to the cardboard wall of a trading company, which distributes shoes to the US, the UK, and Australia. The figure simplifies, disembodies, and inscribes reference information about the fit models

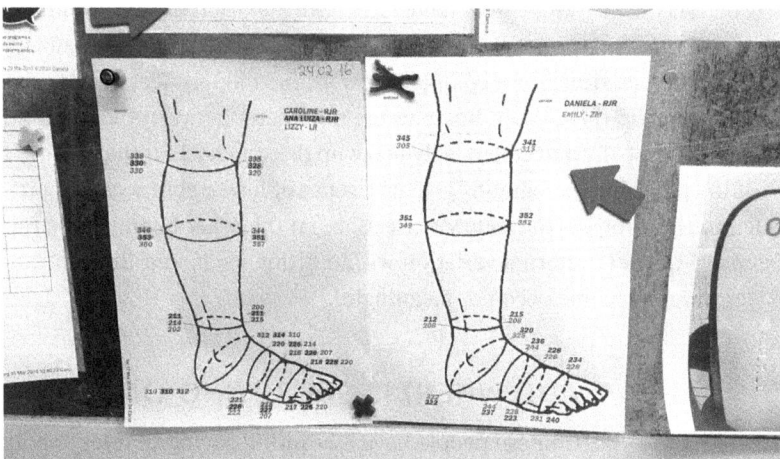

Figure 4.6. Comparative drawings of fit models from multiple companies.

the company has working for each brand. It also provides an immediate comparison between the models for the trading company and those who work for the brands themselves. The image shows reference information for a US and a UK brand. The information gives us the seven measurements used to classify fit models (including the extra one higher on the calves, for boots) but fails to provide information about particular quirks in important areas like the arch, ankle, and toe sweep, or about how the foot pronates. Because these data are harder to disembody graphically, technicians need to know how to work with and around coordinating feet.

When simplification is not enough to produce replication, companies dispose of bodies that are "matter out of place" (Douglas 1966) in facilitating standardization. During my fieldwork for this project, I saw multiple instances of shoes being readjusted by replacing not just the samples but the actual fit model in China. When a US technician complains that shoes are either too big or too clunky, the company often hires a new fit model with measurements that almost match those of the US fit model. I also observed a US-based model (where approval happens) complain that the shoes from China were too wide—because the reference model from the sample room had recently changed.

Christine's reflects this pattern in the industry. Christine is a freelance fit model in Dongguan who has vast experience in the industry. Her measurements are exactly identical to those of a US-based freelancer the company employs, which allows Marius, the Brazilian technician, to have final approval of samples in Dongguan without circling back with the New York office. When all of that does not work, I observed the technical office in China take advantage of a visit from European fit models, to have them and the local counterpart go to the office of NOVI, a German company in Dongguan specializing in secondary services, for a complete scan of the models' feet, ankle, and calves. They did this to coordinate to the millimeter between the multiple bodies that globally and collectively make up the standard for the brand.

If the preceding paragraphs give us a sense of how stability can be provided to this process, the following section, on the other hand, shows the extensive range of internal variation within fitting itself, and the contexts under which each one becomes meaningful.

WHAT (AND WHEN) IS SHE TRYING ON?

According to Echo, Chinese people have a beautiful saying to refer to a fit model's body: her left foot is called the father's foot, while the right one is the mother's. The difference in measurements between the two has resulted in the international (and unspoken) convention of using the right foot for measurements and fit. This poetic way to refer to a more permanent variation encapsulates the micro level of difference I will underscore in the next few pages. Since the devil is in the details, it is not my intention to take the reader into an inferno of minutiae, but to show the disparate kinds of information that get translated and simplified over time to make standard sizes. In the previous section, I wrote in passing that most of the fit models I interviewed claimed to have needed one year to learn the technical vocabulary, knowledge that goes together with the embodied sensations provoked by the shoes. The temporality of this somatic relationship, which ties bodily sensations to a particular vocabulary to express them, is best explained by the fact that models have to learn how to evaluate different kinds of shoes in terms of fit (flats, sandals, pumps, boots); materials (leather, polyurethane, cow suede); the combination of materials used for the internal lining (how much they "sweat"); and with reference to the market for the shoe (style, comfort, etc.).

Divergences in how leather reacts offer a strategic entry point to illustrate the variability of the fit process, and open a window to the manifold roles that time plays in said mutation. The first divergence comes from whether fitting takes place in the morning or in the afternoon. If the latter, suede may have expanded and thus be too loose. The second divergence relates to a different temporal arch, one having to do with the reaction of the leather as the sample is inserted on the last. The leather expands immediately but will return to its original form once the last is removed. This time sensitivity is countered by machinery that cools the leather, allowing them to see how it will look on its final form. The third divergence has to do with when shoes were brought into the fitting room by the trading company to have their models and technicians work on them. When leather shoes have just arrived from production, they are stiff and have not had time to accommodate. According to Clint, "shoes have memory" and so "it's a matter of time, if you let them rest a bit, to become looser on their own, go back to their regular form." Leather seems to be perceived as a capricious material with an exact turning point. If technicians work on it too early in the day, the material might be too hard to manipulate. But if they wait too long, the material might become too loose. Technicians keep this in mind. So, in addition to the fitting tests I described, they also add a "thermal" test to see how the materials react to particular temperature and humidity conditions.

This attention to one particular material—albeit central for the market segment I've studied—and the demands it imposes on the temporality of work routines is complicated by the fact that feet are also materials that change over time. All fittings for production are done in the morning, when feet are considered to be at their best. While less-precise fitting for prototypes and early samples can be done at any point of the day, fitting for production is done only in the morning. (This was true of all sites I observed in both Dongguan and Novo Hamburgo.) Indeed, a factory fit model like Connie, who works only for production, never works in the afternoon.

Models are also asked to walk to see how the shoe reacts to different movements. In some cases, models are even asked to take shoes home and wear them over a weekend (or sometimes longer) to see how they react to usage; doing so also better enables the models to give instructions about what is working and what isn't from the sample. Marius, one of the Brazilian technicians whose work I observed, confided that he found the restricted timing of fittings a bit absurd. Despite being a perfectionist about shoes, Marius acknowledged that the "real" women who will wear the shoe actually have to walk in it the whole day, and by the end of it will have the foot at its widest.

The differences between fitting for samples, corrections, and confirmation are not only about the time of the day but also in the level of rigor that is exercised while evaluating correspondence in each case. For the latter the correspondence has to be absolutely perfect, so much that shoes are not approved for production if there is a millimetric difference with what was expected and how the fit model feels but will be sent back to the factory—even multiple times. The fit for samples and corrections involves guesswork that serves to steer those involved in moving the sample into production closer to what the measurements of the confirmed sample should be.[5]

Fit models also learn how to account for size differently depending whether shoes are for the domestic or international market. For domestic products, they learn to make the fit looser (*fofinho*, in Brazilian Portuguese). They also learn to account for materials differently if they are for lower-tier brands, which generally use cheaper materials that are less receptive to the contours of the foot (for instance, polyurethane in comparison to leather). As a result, the instructions that models learn to give are different from comments they would make for shoes made with higher-end components.

LASTING FEET

In the preceding pages, I have discussed how feet become the objects and subjects of measurement, and how they are trained to become an immutable entity, as models learn to transform their feet into the standard for a shoe size. In the next section, I explain how feet are produced as translatable and mobile objects. This boldly happens, in two different yet intertwined ways: (a) as world-making around the foot, via the generation of an infrastructure; and (b) by bringing the world to the feet, adjusting said infrastructure to take the geographic location of the fitting foot as a key node for shoe development and approval.

What is the infrastructure that develops around a foot? As we have established, feet are not alone when working during a fitting. The immediate ecology of tools and the tensions between the fit model and the technician (and even the designer) offer interesting lessons to those who study how knowledge is distributed, and the tension between embodied and disembodied forms of knowledge (see Fourcade 2010). The fitting is a scenario in which there is a struggle over which kind of knowledge is privileged. The knowledge of the fit model draws authority from disciplining the body and from working the body from within to establish the object of knowledge. On the other hand, the work of technicians reveals a kind of knowledge that is actually based on the constant effort to distance it from the body and to move away from the corporeal the object of knowledge. This is a discipline that works from the outside in, attempting to extract and circulate what has been known while leaving the body (or, more precisely, the body part) behind. To quote Steven Shapin: "The historical trajectory of standards . . . is often described as disembodiment, as in the detachment of the body from A BODY. But under another description that process is a different kind of embodiment, the transference of standards from flesh to metal." What are the metal-like tools that allow this codification to happen?

A fit model always works on top of a table. This is something that can be improvised almost anywhere, as evidenced in the multiple pictures in chapter 3 that depict tables in showrooms or at OM's offices in Dongguan. The fitting table is not an ad hoc arrangement between tables and chairs but a device of its own, made up of flat surface; a stepladder; a small, built-in padded wooden bench for the model to sit on; shelves for the technician to store his tools; and a hollow foundation to accommodate multiple chairs (figure 4.7). When confirming a shoe for production, there are usually three or four people working around the table: designers and technicians sit literally at the feet of the model to look at the shoes she tries on. Most development offices I visited in both Dongguan and Novo Hamburgo had very similar fitting tables.

Technicians carry a series of tools with them. These include rulers and tape measures (with inches and centimeters, something less usual in non-US

Figure 4.7. A fitting table at a large development
office in Dongguan.

contexts but of central importance within offices that produce for the American markets), templates or calipers for measurement, scissors and a blade
(used to make small incisions around the ankle or ball of boots), and a base to
make sense of how the shoe and the last react to different constructions and
heights. In all cases, a fixed wrench next to the table allows them to mount
and dismount the shoe from the last, as well as helps them in opening a last
to better work on the shoe. In some cases, depending on whether they work
in adjusting the surface and volume of the last, technicians will have rasps

and standard and circular surform tools on hand in case the wood on the last needs to be corrected.

Designers and technicians use silver markers to make corrections on most shoes, although they sometimes use a white pen for black and gray leathers.[6] While this may seem insignificant, I have yet to see technicians use different markers in a fitting session (and I have observed them at seven different sites).

Details like these offer insights into how ingrained the conventions of an infrastructure can become. Designers, technicians, and fit models expect corrections to be made with those markers regardless of the company they work for, and even if the context does not collaborate with it. In some cases, they do not write directly on the material, but rather on paper to indicate changes that are then superimposed and glued on the shoe. In one case—according to Connie, who works for a large factory similar to the one described by Grace in the first pages of the chapter—the fitting team even used the silver marker to document the changes to be made directly on her foot. Technicians work on the last and the fit, while designers correct the upper. This division of labor reflects the interest of one group on fit and functionality and the other on aesthetics.

Even more important than the immediate ecology of fit and correction is how this early fitting information becomes objectified as a last and how it returns to the model's feet. Two things that happen with the proportions that the designer imagines for a particular shoe point to different articulations of infrastructure. First, as I've shown in chapter 3, the numbers on the upper start as a paper pattern, and then are developed into an upper for a prototype with a material that vaguely resembles what the final shoe will be made of. Second, the numbers for volume are worked on a fit model, adjusted, then sent as precise specifications to a last-making facility, which produces a wooden last with a machine—though lasts are made of wood by a machine, there are more artisanal procedures to shed off details later on. The last is then sent to the technician for corrections and approval. It is only after the two rounds of fitting and correction that the last will be mass-produced, as it is a key component of how shoes are put together on the assembly line, where it is used to give volume to the shoe by gluing it on the upper. By that point, the transformation of what was at first a foot with its own quirks into a size 6 (238 mm or 240 mm in length) or 7 (248 mm) is official. This is a highly contingent process, full of small procedures, adjustments, and working through the knowledge of the deviation from the standard to establish a number.

In adopting a numeric form, a last becomes an immutable object produced by inscription. As such, it can be easily transported back to the center,

Figure 4.8. At a last-making facility in Houjie, December 2015.

where it will then be combined with other similar objects. Much as Latour (1999, 32) reminds us in *Pandora's Hope*, to create and inscribe a reference is—following its Latin root—to bring it back with us. Fit models, technicians, and designers work around variations that would compromise the object as a heterogeneity and turn it, instead, into an objective standard to be followed by large swaths of the female population. To paraphrase the classic work of Theodore Porter (1995): the use of numbers, perhaps the most rule-bound of abstractions, results in the appearance of the exclusion of personal judgment.

In figure 8, we can see both the machine by which all the specifications finally become a last, as well as a coded last in the hands of Josemir, who will
take it back to his office to compare it to the foot of the fit model and to the
measurements he sent.

BRINGING THE WORLD TO THE FEET

Josemir's trip from the last-making shop to the trading company where he
works is a short, five-minute drive through the Houjie area. Most of the buildings house small factories that provide services to shoemaking enterprises:
from full sample rooms to smaller operations that only glue or stitch; from
technologically-driven shops like the last-making factory to labor-intensive
tanneries for polyurethane instead of leather. Compared to Josemir's sojourn,
other shoe companies have longer distances to travel, depending on where
their correcting and approval feet are located. For instance, in the case of
Clint and Arlene, the approved samples have to be air-shipped twice: the
first time for the fitting, and the second when products are confirmed. On the
first trip, after having worked with the designer's specifications on correcting the shoe, Clint sends one shoe to China, so the last-maker can compare
what he is working on with what Clint approved for fitting (not for styling
yet). "After China works on it," as he explains, a pair of corrected samples will
be returned with the previous fit shoe he had sent. If that works after trying
it on Arlene—and most likely after a few more corrections—he'll send them
back to Dongguan as the fit- and design-approved samples, to be then sent
to the factory for production.

If everything goes perfectly, Clint finally destroys the first half-pair. He
used to sign the shoes and mark them with a red dot to monitor the measurements in the global back-and-forth (figure 4.9). In email messages, he used
to call it the "go-by shoe," meaning what they are using in the meanwhile.
He tells with comic gusto an anecdote where the China office was asking
him constantly for the *Gobi* (spelled like the desert) shoe. He asked around if
anyone knew a shoe with that name—as shoes are internally given monikers
like *Stephanie* or *Verona*—until they realized what the sample-room people
in Dongguan wanted was the signed and approved sample.

Perhaps the clearest exemplar of the centrality of the approval process is
the routine of a Brazilian-Chinese company that coordinates design by having the line-builders who work daily in Dongguan and Campo Bom meet in
the company's New York office four times a year. In those meetings, held in

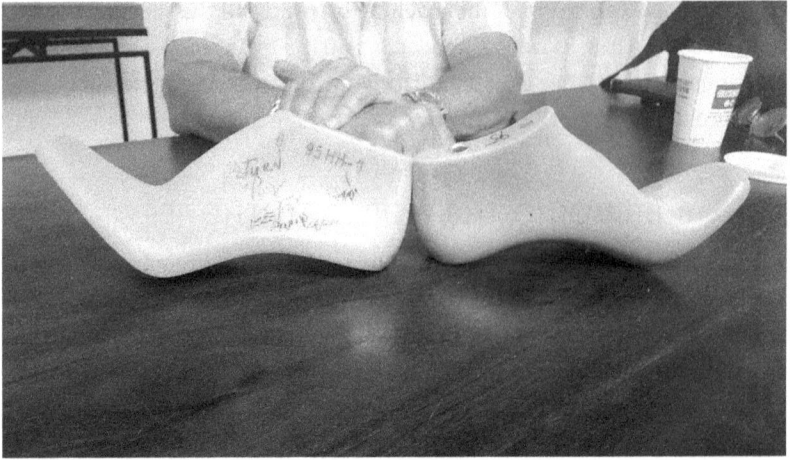

Figure 4.9. Clint and his lasts for pumps and sandals; observe the signature on the right one.

the office of what used to be a shoe factory, they fit every shoe on the feet of the owner's wife. And I say "feet" because they take advantage of the size difference between her left and right feet (almost half a size). Thus, she is used as the final reference for both markets the company works with: Europe (her left foot), and the US (her right). In their approval routine, two technicians—one for each market—work the shoes first with fit models in China. If they approve fit, the confirmation samples are sent weekly to Brazil, where they are worked on a conference call via Skype with the owner's wife. She then enters the technical specifications and approves whether the samples should go into production (or not). This example highlights fit models' central role in the correcting process, the importance of having fit models with the technical capabilities to understand the issues and how to correct them, and the ability to identify whether problems indicated on a first round have been adjusted. When one foot has approval power, fitting is a hydra-like endeavor, with multiple nodes around the world.

Larger companies have fit models in both New York and Dongguan, which adds a layer of complexity in terms of producing standards. While they use Chinese fit models for brands targeting younger and more fashionable consumers (who are usually expected to have narrower feet), they rely on US models to do fitting at the development offices and factories for more "casual" brands. These are brands that need to take into account wider widths, the needs of older women's feet, and a fuller foot volume overall. As much as they need that second, fuller foot to travel, they also have technicians (usually Brazilian, Taiwanese, and sometimes Italian men) who travel from Dongguan to New York at least four times a year to assist in the development and correction of prototypes. If designers stay put, technicians also physically bring the prototypes with them.

Travel takes place when delegation at a distance becomes impossible and some things become untranslatable without co-presence. During key confirmation moments (i.e., finalizing the prototypes, producing and confirming samples), technicians, models, and designers all have to meet face-to-face. Prototypes, samples, and lasts all have to be tried on, and that process is dictated by where fit models are (especially during sample making and confirming). Traveling fit models report that they prefer moving and working in China directly. As Melissa, a model for an American comfort brand, put it: "It's easier to work with the brand technician in China, but especially with the factory one, I feel like things do not get *lost in translation*" (my emphasis).

The traffic in designers, technicians, prototypes, and samples is dictated by where the fit models are located, as well as by whether the "feet" can be matched and coordinated across multiple locations. In the case of the OM, it means that the US-based designers not only travel five to eight times a year (once for every collection) to work with Anna, their fit model in Dongguan, but they also develop a cutout of her right foot to work with as a reference in the New York office.

The most extreme example of this was narrated to me by a former production manager for Clarks, who had to coordinate the five feet the company had in the world, across sites in London and New York—where the designers worked—as well as in northeast Brazil, Nicaragua, and Dongguan—where the company had its development and production facilities. His work involved measuring the different feet every six months and casting when one of the women resigned or needed to be replaced. In fact, one of the major nuisances I observed in fieldwork for those involved in producing reliable standards was the agony of replacing a foot that was already fully accounted for within the development infrastructure. This was such an issue that most of the models I spoke with are often called by companies they used to work for to see if they would be interested in returning to work full-time; and, if not, whether they would be willing to work as freelancers during confirmation and production, given that they already knew the brand and its quirks were fully integrated into their work routines.

CONCLUSION: FEET AS OBLIGATORY PASSAGE POINTS

This travel through a few cases gives us a comprehensive list of the requisite humans, tools, and tacit kinds of knowledge that help us elucidate the range of activities needed to make standardization techniques work in different, highly localized settings. What all cases share (captured in the dictum "Never approve a shoe fit on a picture," to quote Venus, a designer and former technician who was developing her own shoe line) is the centrality and indispensability of the fitting feet within this particular part of the shoe-producing infrastructure.

In other cases (Sterne 2003), the search for something that can reproduce an embodied function outside the body—as in the early technology of sound reproduction—resulted in one element taken out of the body (e.g., the eardrum dissected from a dead person) as an attempt to produce through it a replica of how the human ear transduces sound. Though there are numerous parallels between early sound reproduction and the attempts to disembody standards from the body of the fit model—including the idea that there are isolated mechanisms that can be separated, reproduced, and operationalized; and even if they are part and parcel of the same history of the senses, in which the ear stood in for a particular part of the body as much as the foot stands for the female body both real and symbolic—the builders of early sound-reproduction technology were more interested in reproducing the effects than in searching for the causes of what was being heard. On the other hand, although it shares the abstracted character of the enterprise, in which abstracting the foot from the body is a prelude to abstracting inscribable measurements of the former into paper, the production of standard shoes focuses instead on an element impossible to disembody. Thus, the technician (and sometime the fit model) plays the role of investigator while working to find out what causes a particular effect on a shoe.

That feet act as an obligatory "passage point" (Callon 1986) underscores the paradoxical centrality of a minor and invisible kind of labor, as well as a particular dance of expertise between technicians and fit models. We have seen this in some cases by understanding how and where prototypes and samples are mobilized; in others, by looking at how the models are actually mobilized as to have development pass through them; and still in others by looking at the veto power models like Connie have at large factories. This point serves to support once again one of the key story lines of *The Perfect*

Fit, to see the paradoxical constitution of the global, as a scale that can only be rendered globalized through localized practices and objects; in this case, feet. To be blunt about it, the biggest possible thing—the global—ultimately depends here on the smallest of things: a human foot.

This chapter—and to a certain extent, the one that follows—wages a bet in the form of a question: what would happen if we were to do an infrastructural inversion and foreground what usually appears in the background? Or, to put it more bluntly, what would happen if we put women's feet at the center of a fashion-making infrastructure made up of heterogeneous and disparate elements (Thevenot 1984, 9) such as tacit knowledge, shipment forms, confirmation samples, lasts, measurements, technicians and designers, and sketches? Putting the foot at the center of this infrastructure ends up being not just an analytical exercise, but also a better way to understand some of the processes I witnessed that were unclear if looking at it only from the point of view of the designer, the heroic figure of creation and imagination. Moreover, throughout the chapter, I have borrowed from the constructionist toolkit of social studies of science and technology to explain the development of a cultural commodity. In this regard, thinking through how something is put together and works like an assemblage is not a capricious choice where anything goes, but rather an entry point to see where construction stops and where it can't go beyond: in this case, the presence of a foot that anchors and organizes the circulation of prototypes and samples until approved for production.

To put it simply, feet work as an essential circulation node, underscoring fit models' unexpected centrality and power from that fundamental circulation point. But we know very little about what things *look* like from that vantage point. Who gets to talk *about* and *for* those feet? In the chapter that follows I explore what are, for a fit model, the consequences of having "the world at her fit."

Chapter 5

CINDERELLA ON THE PEARL RIVER DELTA

Who Has the Power to Translate?

INTRODUCTION: FROM GLASS TO GOLDEN SLIPPER

Thanks to the monumental collecting and editorial work of Charles Perrault (and to a lesser degree of Walt Disney) we have received a particular version of the many existing tales within the oral tradition about a young woman with a little glass slipper.[1] According to US historian Robert Darnton (1984), no less than 105 versions have been recorded, and books cataloguing all the variations number them in the thousands. Though what we've received is a fairly stable narrative object, fairy tales were told and retold in many cultures before they were written down. That they have subsequently been written and rewritten, and folklorists' work has been central in organizing our knowledge of what existed before as well as of which versions of the story we get to know, is significant.

It's not strange then, that though written almost a thousand years before the European versions, we know little about a traditional Chinese story, the

Tale of Ye Xian. In it, the protagonist is also a young woman with a step-mother who aims to favor her stepsister, and whose beauty gets discovered in a public celebration, after which she loses her golden slipper. The slipper eventually finds its way to the King, who engages in a town-wide search for the shoe's owner. There are some noticeable differences with the story we know: Ye Xian gets her slippers from a magic fish instead of a fairy god-mother; the King only learns about her beauty via the indexical character of a shoe sold to him by a merchant; and she loses one of them at a village fete instead of a royal ball. But a lot of the story holds, including the relationship between beauty and virtue, the passive character of the heroine, waiting to be discovered and rescued by a man, as well as—more importantly for us—the semantic character of the relationship between fit and uniqueness. The heroine is, after all, the only person who can actually fit the shoe!

But there is of course much more that we can learn from this tale about shoe fitting, beyond its gendered character. The story is one in which the heroine leaves her home behind—as most fit models did when moving to Guangdong, mostly from provinces like Sichuan, Hunan, Hubei, Henan, Hebei, and sometimes as far as Heilongjiang in the northeasternmost part of the country. In our story, thanks to the power of a foot, she gets rescued from poverty as well as from the ignominy of factory work, moving from being an interchangeable and nondescript piece into a unique and recognizable node in the production of beauty. Much as happened to Ye Xian, she gets "discovered" because of her foot's delicate and small measurements, which serve as synecdoche for her unique character as a person—though being "beautiful" is less of the job description, most fit models are expected to be more stylized than other "office girls" working at development rooms and trading companies; and it's also one in which the woman in question is young, under thirty years old, and usually single and without kids.

In the pages that follow, I focus on scrutinizing in depth three dimensions of the relationship between fit modeling and power: (1) the relationship between ordinal and nominal measurements (Fourcade 2016), following up close the dance between uniqueness, average, and standard as a way of conceptualizing fitting feet; (2) the asymmetrical relationship between models, technicians, and designers, and under which configurations each one is authorized to talk *for* and *about* the feet; and (3) all the translation work necessary to make shoes move from one market context to another.

BEING STANDARD AS BEING UNIQUE

Career fit models talk about the measurement moment and how it called attention to the "perfection" of their feet whenever you ask them how they ended up doing this for a living. They always narrate it as part of a story of discovery—in the US and Brazil in a formal casting situation, in China most likely while working either in a shoe factory or already as an "office girl"—in which being measured on those six key spots was the starting point of a career.[2]

The power of discovery—be it by a coworker, a friend who said "I think you are a 6, you should come to our company," or even in a casting setting—and its charismatic inscription on the measurement sheet is such that it allows the woman, who was until then "just" an "office girl," a factory worker, or simply someone eager to work, to transform her self-identification in an instant. The moment in which the measurements determine the standard character of the foot (a standard that as we've seen is also unique, given how few women actually have all the proper measurements even if their size is 6 or 7), transmutes the person who owns the foot into someone imbued with special character and, as such, able to cross certain professional and gender boundaries that had been sealed before. Though, as I explained, there is a temporal arc to how these women become fit models, the patina of the first moment continues with them over time and lights up the faces of those recounting that occasion to me.

Regardless of the location of the interview, reactions were always similar. For instance, in Dongguan, Connie, who had proudly shown me on her phone her measurement sheet we saw in chapter 4, recounted how "a friend at a mall introduced me to her friend who saw my feet and immediately said I should work for their company. I did not believe him at first, but then he called and said 'I remember your feet since I knew they were like a standard across 6B.' So I finally went to the company and measured it and they said: wow, it's a standard size 6B! Please work for us." Similarly, on our way from New York to China, Brenda—the standard model for a large US company—explained to me how she had been working for two and a half years and a friend from college told her about the ad for the company in her town in Connecticut, and she was worried because she did not know much about shoes and did not want to expose herself in an interview. Nothing like this happened. In her recollection, she went to her casting meeting "and they measured my feet and they were just like, 'You are hired,' they did not want to talk to me or anything. It's all about measurements; you know, you either have it or you don't!" Finally, in Novo Hamburgo, Jackie explained to me her joy as, after high school, she was hired on arrival and told immediately how she "would have a great career ahead of her, since she had great feet." She explained later on how this was repeated to her time after time, especially after she threatened to leave and was told: "You have great feet, we want you to stay, please!" These testimonies are representative of the many conversations about discovery I had with fit models and technicians.

One could argue that the process of inscribing that uniqueness on the page—not only do fit models recall that initial moment but they also usually have their first sheet saved on their phone and can show it immediately if asked for it—accelerates the process of self-recognition that social psychology has—since the pioneering work of Charles H. Cooley—conceptualized as the result of multitiered social interactions with other people. Particularly interesting is how much the measurement sheet works in this case as an agent in generating "the looking-glass feet" allowing for fit models to embody their new relationship to part of their own body and the self. Cooley argued that there were three steps to the dialectic between self and recognition: (1) the imagination of our appearance to other people and the corresponding associated feelings; (2) imagining that others are evaluating our behavior; (3) developing feelings and reacting to the imaginary evaluation of ourselves as objects. What we see here, then, is how the inscription of the disembodied image of the self onto paper fixes and accelerates the process of developing an imaginary evaluation of who they are, as well as their capacity to imagine themselves not just as subjects but as objects, able to understand themselves from the outside as a unique foot and to act accordingly.

Some of the consequences of this can be seen at the interactional level; others have to do with the evaluations that designers and technicians make when talking about the performance and behavior of some of the fit models within their work environment. In any case these all go beyond the career advantages of being a model in comparison to an office or factory worker: being paid a better salary; knowing that they're doing work with a specialized character of what they do and how hard it is to replace as a contribution; being paid also in kind with shoes by the company or factory; having the opportunity to generate a career in development or materials after having learned all the technical intricacies of shoes from the inside; or working only part of the day if their work is mainly in production and confirmation.

What one gets to see because of fit models' special character attribute is their ability to avoid the gendered segregation that is central to how the industry is organized. As I explained already, technicians are men, designers are women, and "office girls" is proper semantics for the coordinating work at the office. In general, there is little continuous interaction between the lower female category of workers and the others. Moreover, fit models cross over both at work and outside work, socializing with technicians in a way that is impossible for the rest of the local female workers.

At work, any fitting scene becomes a relatively intimate affair, with the technician working at the fit model's feet. The extension of that scene over time forces the pair into engaging with each other in banter and conversation. Brazilian technicians and Chinese models speak in "work" English but still manage to communicate with one another. Take the following exchange between Marius and Christine, who have been working together intermittently for over five years, since they were both part of the same development office for a large European conglomerate, and keep doing so now. (Marius is in charge of development and approval for a smaller US firm that orients production to the UK and Italy, and Christine works as a freelance for the size 7 shoes they produce for those European markets.) Theirs is a good entry point into the technician-model dynamic.

Christine is taller than most other Chinese fit models and has long hair. She was elegantly dressed for the occasion, coming to the fitting session with skinny jeans that left her heel and ankle exposed once she removed her high boots, knowing she was coming to wear mostly summer flats and sandals (this was during a December field visit). Like many other fit models, she started working for Paramount, the very large Brazilian-backed factory that developed and produced shoes for the US market and brands like Nine West. Her measurements are similar to those of the brand's US model, which is a significant starting point; more important—according to Marius—is that they have worked together before, and that he trusts her expertise. He trusts her so much that he can have final approval on fit that shoes do not have to go back to New York. And, as he makes explicit, "her comments are very important, almost central, in being able to develop new constructions and lasts."

During this makeup fitting session Marius focused on one shoe, an espadrille flat that was a left over from a previous session where they had worked on twelve pairs. On the designer's previous trip, she had to go three times to the factory, even if—as in this case—it was only to fit one pair; that is how much he values her fitting opinion. The shoe had a gaping issue and Marius had cut the vamp to adjust it. She stood as he worked on it, and said, "This is much better, no gap at all." Almost immediately after; and, to be sure, he compared it with the first sample he had sent to the US, and explained to me how her fitting was now much more comfortable, that while before she was able to enter the shoe it was a lot of work, and there was a gap on the front, Christine nodded, posed for the few pictures he was taking with his phone to send to New York, and said, "This is perfect, you should approve—not only the gap is gone but the shoe is better; before, the outsole was too stiff." To which he replied: "Thank you, my dear, I really owe you dinner after that."

As I asked her some questions about her life in the industry, he joked that I was in front of a very strong personality and that sometimes because of that they butted heads. She laughed it off while saying, "Thank you." The end of the fitting scene was punctuated by Marius telling Christine that he had shown me a few days earlier—when I met him for dinner and to talk about his life within the profession—an image of them together, within a larger group of friends, taken for the Halloween night celebration in Dongguan. Christine acted surprised and asked which picture. I told her that it was one where she had a fake blood stain , the result of a wound caused by being stabbed with a plastic knife, in classic spooky fashion. He said that "she was too fashionable, and even then her costume was too clean"—he "had to work to put more blood in it." She smiled; the whole fitting scene—a bit staged for me on this occasion, of course—gave the feeling of two longtime friends working together.

The level of intimacy between Christine and Marius is prevalent in the industry, with technicians usually becoming attached to the fit model in different ways, sometimes recommending them for work (so much that it was fairly common for me to interview fit models and technicians together); in other cases even refusing to work if it wasn't with the same fit model over and over, especially for approval. So, while Clint seemed pretty much a tandem with Arlene, until a few years ago, when his first fit model passed, he only worked if he could have her do the fitting and comment on the corrections. Sometimes those attachments become romantic, so for instance Arlene is married to her former technician, who is now the president of another shoe company in the US, and I encountered three more couples that met interacting like that. During my fieldwork I captured a lot of anecdotal stories about the technicians and the fit models becoming sexually entangled (the US designers that would tell me those stories would say "they fooled around"), and in the few times I went out with people in the industry (a constant activity, especially for the expats and the visiting foreigners) it was only the fit models who would dare to dance with the Brazilian technicians—even coming to look for them at parties—crossing over the imaginary boundary, which segregated them by gender and that was so effective otherwise.

On the other hand, technicians and designers often comment on fit models' moodiness (their wording), as a consequence of their role's special character. This is particularly true if the model works for the sample room of a development company they depend on, so they work with them certain regularity but are not exactly colleagues, and they don't share the intimacy described above.

After one fitting for OM, John—the Taiwanese technician who ran the Dongguan office—started imitating one of the shoe models, making fun of her face of disgust when something did not fit, her brusque manners, and her overall performance of disgust when it came to how OM shoes fit her. How much that "attitude" was unexpected from a relatively subservient and docile office workforce can be better seen when compared to a second model OM sometimes worked with at that company when the first one was busy with a different brand. On a couple of occasions, both John and Pepi mentioned how the second model—who was only called in from time to time—adopted a more subservient persona when working replacing the first one. They mentioned how "nice" she was and how happy she looked was when called "up" from the stitching room.[3] While descriptions like this end up with someone blurting out that the fit model thinks she's the queen of the place—as Pepi did when recounting to me her work interaction with Anna at OM—they pale in comparison to the story of Linda, a Brazilian fit model who worked in Dongguan for ten years before deciding to change her role within the industry to become a scheduler for a Singaporean company that had previously hired her to do fit. Her story highlights—almost *in extremis*—the empowering relationship between fit women's feet and their self-identification.

LINDA, THE QUEEN OF THE FITTING ROOM

I met with Linda thanks to Marius, who recommended her highly, given her ample experience in the industry. A few times in our online communication she mentioned in passing that her boyfriend was also in the industry; he was yet another Brazilian technician. When we finally met, imagine my surprise when the person who showed up with her was none other than Josemir! I had suspected so from looking at their respective *WhatsApp* avatar pictures, and because of a story he had told me the previous year about his divorce and how he was now partnered with a Brazilian fit model, but was still very excited to meet an amorous couple from the two parts of that unique metronomical tandem. We sat on a lounge in the Bar Street area for a couple of hours and talked mostly about her work. While most of my questions were addressed to her—I had seen him at work a few times and had already conversed with him one-on-one—Josemir intervened to emphasize or highlight some of the things she had to say. Though they did meet at work as I'd suspected, he had known of her for a long time, since college, he said. When I asked them about whether they had sympathy for each other then, he confessed that he had actually only known about her feet, since a mold of one of them had been used at SENAI—the technical school in Novo Hamburgo where he first trained and then taught—to teach future technicians how to fit and correct.

I have to confess I found the whole story a bit implausible, but eventually got sent an image of the *pé de silicone* (as they call it in SENAI) from one of the professors who taught development at the university, and it matched hers exactly (or at least it matched the image of her measurements on a Brannock machine she had procured for me). Moreover, her right foot has been copied to train technicians at Formas Kunz, the artisanal last-making facility used by most shoe export companies in the Vale dos Sinos area, inspired by the Bauhaus-styled Fagus factory in Alfeld, Germany. And according to Linda herself, one of the last places she worked for—a Brazilian agent who did shoes for different levels of qualities within the US (and sometimes Europe)—had also copied it and worked with it for a while, after she left, though as Josemir interjected "they couldn't replace her expertise."

Much like other Brazilian models, Linda started fairly young, at nineteen, after answering an ad from a local newspaper. She soon discovered that she had two advantages compared to other models: she seemed to be a perfect size 35—the size 6 of the local market—and both of her feet were identical. The latter feature means that she can try on and give advice on full pairs, instead of always having to do all of her work mostly on her right foot, as is customary. When I asked about getting her measurement sheet,[4] Josemir exclaimed: "You can go into the streets here and ask for her measurements; she's a rock star, everybody has them." She started working for Topazio, a large Brazilian trade company that operated later on in Brazil Paramount, before it moved all production to China; many of the Brazilians I met in Dongguan and the Vale do Sinos area had at some point worked for them. Unlike her work in China, she emphasized, with the few companies she did fit for in Novo Hamburgo, that in the afternoon she always worked on something other than fitting: sometimes in cost, sometimes in materials, others

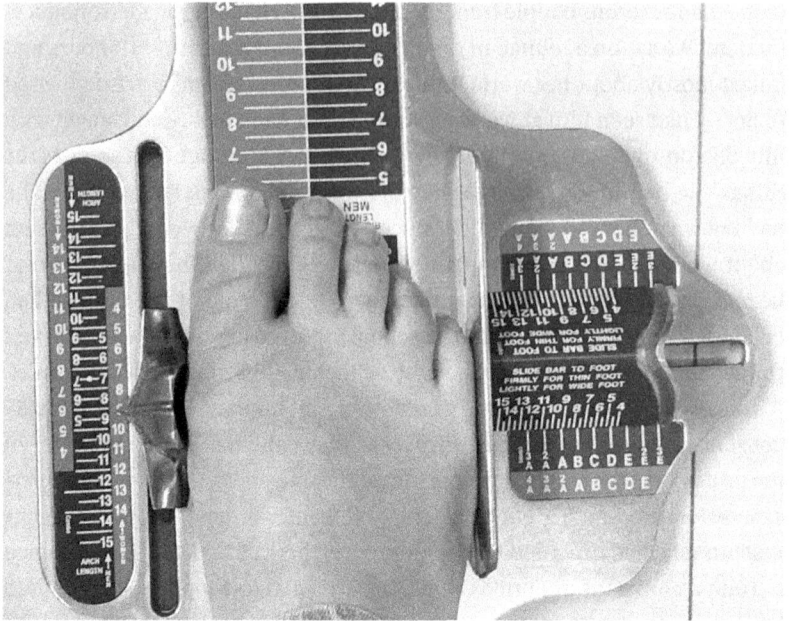

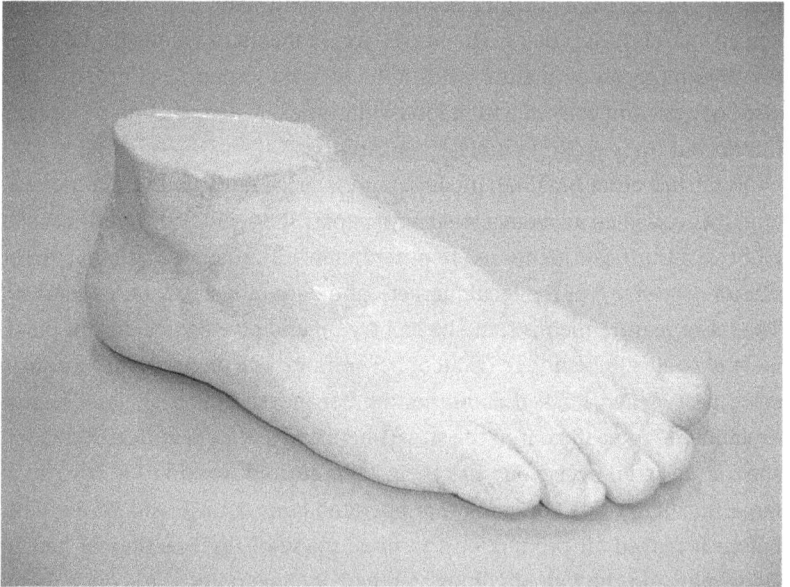

Figure 5.1. Top, Linda's left foot, measured by a Brannock machine. Bottom, her right foot, molded in silicone.

in development. That plus, "always watching what technicians were doing" gave her the chance to learn her trade in a technically competent way, even though she had not attended a school for it.

Josemir's assertion that Linda is the ultimate pro, *a numero zero* instead of a number one, was backed by the outside people who had put me in touch with her, as well as by one of his own stories, in which he narrates the anticipation of finally working with her and how much doing that had only confirmed her reputation, given that she had both helped to easily correct a shoe that had been rejected multiple times by the customer—she'd realized the issue was solvable by opening the last more on the back, though the problem was at the toe—as well as had approved ten shoes, which were all confirmed for production by the office in the US. In reminiscing *à deux*, they still raved about how that first shoe style is still a best-selling construction for the company he works for. Though he couldn't say enough good words about her, and she had nice words to reciprocate about his work as a technician, she chose to establish a comparison with someone else as her equal: Manuel, an Argentinean technician trained in Brazil who had been Josemir's boss when they all worked together.

> My foot is very famous, it's not something I liked to do, and all the technicians I worked with know it, but they all know my foot and say it's the best. When I met him [Manuel] he said, "for once we finally worked together, not in Brazil but in China," he said to me "I finally met the best." And I always heard about him, he's the best. Now I could say we were the best team.

Thanks to her reputation among fellow Brazilians in China, she has been able to profit more than other fit models, as she's complemented her income working for one company with multiple freelance gigs for approval and confirmation, for smaller outfits that did not have a model of their own or that were interested in having her as a way to solve approval within South China without having to spend another round of samples moving from one continent to another. She charged eighty dollars per hour, regardless of whether a company needed her for only ten or fifteen minutes—as sometimes smaller companies are only producing six to eight new shoes and even fewer new constructions as to need specialized commentary and work. Even if she would often get bored, left alone on the table by technicians and designers, working like that—sometimes for six hours in one afternoon—would net her a much more robust income than the two thousand dollars someone like her usually gets paid (in some cases, on top of salary, Brazilians get paid housing and travel allowances). Although for her making five hundred dollars in one afternoon was a nice bounty—on top of the free samples she took with her, as one time she took all hundred of them from a collection—the amount of money companies save by eliminating one extra back-and-forth is relatively incalculable if one takes into account the coordination issues involved in the travel by people and shipping materials, the comparisons and adjustments between multiple *medidas do pé*, and—more importantly for trading agents working under the temporal constraints of fast fashion—the time that was saved by her just being there.

She recalled for me her experience during one of the last times she did freelance approval work, a time when she literally had people at her feet. She said she is a very bad morning person, even though most production confirmation work is done in the morning, and because of that she does not like to stand on the table, or sometimes even to walk with the shoes. So on that occasion she sat, instead, on a chair in the middle of the room and asked the Chinese production guys to bring pairs for consultation one at a time, she then would ask them to try them on her, and ultimately decide whether to approve or not. She said, for her, "It's 'come to me'" (while gesturing with the index to an imaginary someone). "Normally the fit models need to walk," she continued. "I only put the shoes on, not even stand up." As Josemir said to punctuate the anecdote at the end (while the three of us laughed): "She's a real queen."

CAN A STANDARD-BEARER BE CHARISMATIC?

To return to the four definitions of modeling, fit models also conform to the fourth dictionary definition as, paradoxically, their unique qualities for standardization transmute them into people with special powers. As such this case goes—to a certain extent—against the grain to how recent conceptualizations have imagined the relationship between standardization projects, subjugation, and morality. Whether analyzing the role that standards have played in life insurance and defining what counts as "subhuman" (Lengwiler 2009), the role of conformance to standards in engendering oppression and subservience (Thevenot 2009), the way borrowers under a certain score are classified as "subprime" and as such pushed into a market with more uncertain and adverse conditions (Fourcade and Healey 2013), or the role that rankings play in transforming the educational experience of most US law students (Espeland and Sauder 2016), most analysts have taken a page from the critical theory manual and observed how people have almost inescapably become prisoners of the instruments for rationalization they engender. The role of fit models like Linda opens—on the other hand—an interesting avenue for inquiry, pushing us to query what happens when the production of standards results in a subordinated position and role whose occupant is nevertheless celebrated as the possessor of special gifts (and sometimes abilities).

The emphasis on the preternatural worth of models' feet pushes away the idea of the charisma of the object and persona as purely relational, and with it also the arbitrary character of the attribution. What is celebrated is the ability of one person to conform to one measurement as much as they can, so much that those who are deemed "perfect" feet are in a league of their own, even if a tiny difference separates them from other 6B or 7B models. In that respect this ability is closely related to the revelatory role of oracles—or the Arthurian idea of removing the sword from the stone. All they need is for the Brannock, the centimeter, and the scan to say so.

But though there is of course an oracular character to the attribution of worth to a fit model, there is a second part to it: expertise. After all, charisma is performed and confirmed when the special gift is mobilized to produce miracles every time it is called upon. And this second part—seen in the story of Linda, in Marius' ability to approve shoes in China (without having to check with the designers in the US) being contingent on the expertise of Christine, and in general in the binary distinction between being "just a foot" and a professional model—is where the claims of special magic in a rationalized position born out of the instrumental need for global coordination can be better found. Though there is a cultural work at play in producing the charisma of the fit model's role beyond the woman who occupies it (what Weber called "charisma of the office")—seen in their displays of self-importance and "moodiness"—expertise is more significant, as those who know can "put their feet to better use" (as Clint put it) and go beyond the sympathetic magic of the role into becoming someone who is fully able to speak for their feet and to solve the many pressing issues that shoe fitting conjures—especially given the fast-fashion context that has transformed the pace of the industry.

That this charisma is mobilized from a subservient position opens up a field of contestation: can models always speak for their feet? The history of metrological conflicts suggests that they are intimately linked to conflicts in authority (Mallard 1998). If technicians impose themselves to designers on the strength of their mastery of numbers and of how to work them, the fact that this authority is actually embodied on the peculiarities of an existing human agent opens up a space for conflict within their lore. The power of the quirks of a model's foot is such that technicians like Marius lament "working so much to conform a hundred percent to a standard that actually fits one person, the model herself!"[5]

WHO SPEAKS FOR THE FEET?
FROM MANNEQUIN TO WOMAN

This distributed version of cognition—residing in feet, tools, sheets, and technicians' skills—is one in which the technicians' general stock of knowledge (Schutz 1964; Berger and Luckmann 1966; Vera 2015) serves them well enough to bring steadiness to the process by having an abstract idea of how to best organize procedures of measurement, correction, and fit. That said, this knowledge needs to be developed, molded, and refined at a firm-specific level, with actual concrete details, specifications, and calculations hinging malleably upon fit models' actual body parts. It is precisely the tension between the routines technicians bring with them and the fit models' individual characters that we can use as an entry point to study how power is configured among the different actors involved. In the pages that follow I explain the continuum that goes from mannequin to woman, from dependence to autonomy, and what this says about gender and expertise.

I came to this categorical distinction after conversing with Tatiana, a former freelance fit model who had worked with multiple technicians. When asked about the differences that she found she responded: "Some technicians treat you as if you were a mannequin, forgetting you are a human being, more than a foot. And there are some who are very polite, who treat you respectfully, like a pro. And there are some who think you're going to . . . like, that you're fit, that you're also doing everything, that you're his employee, his assistant."

Fit models are reduced to a functional part of their body (the foot) when they are mostly unfit to give good comments on fit—much less provide a solution to the fit issues awoken by the problem they've identified. Technicians reduce them by means of synecdoche, by calling them "just a foot." Most of the times that I saw that reduction at play, it had to do with fit models who spoke little English (Josemir's ex-wife's career floundered in the transition between Novo Hamburgo and Dongguan because of her lack of language skills and her inability to acquire them over time); who lacked an expert vo-cabulary and were unable to go beyond the loose/ tight, good/bad, pretty/ ugly binaries when discussing the shoes; or who were office workers who happened to have a standard size but were called upon to try shoes on spo-radically and otherwise mostly did office work. In those cases, technicians did all the expert work and models were reduced to being just mannequins, their feet absolutely spoken for. If one could say that models fit within this collaborative organization of knowledge because of their ability to provide embodied standards and knowledge about it, in this case all they seem able to provide is the first part of the equation.

The foot's synecdoche-like character appears under a second guise in the industry, as that which becomes anthropomorphized, resulting in de-scriptions of people in which the shape, length, and volume of their feet are conflated with their actual physical characteristics. I witnessed an example of this when one of the US models for the comfort market came to Dongguan to do approval and work on the specs directly with technicians at the factory. When the local model asked why she was being brought in—in fear of being replaced, despite being one of the full-time models for the company—the Brazilian technician laughed it off by inflating his cheeks in a Dizzy Gillespie–like gesture that was supposed to indicate the other model's supposed fatness.

The topic of the second model's visit continued while going out at night, this time involving the designer for the team that included the local fit model and an expat leather technician, who—after seeing the American model—asked why she was in town. "Is she a star? Does she have perfect feet?" The designer replied: "Well, perfect, you know, fleshy, US-style. It's a size 7, with meat but short. You can't get it here, it's a fuller foot." They also laughed. I was surprised later when seeing the object of these two scenes was a slender blond woman who was even more petite than the Chinese model she was being compared to. This was quite common throughout fieldwork; I often found little correlation between feet and bodily shape and listened to the subsumption of body type into conversations that were actually about the foot's shape.

If mannequins are reduced to just being a foot, and have their feet spoken for, more knowledgeable models are expected to be megaphones for their feet, instead of having the technicians operating as ventriloquists. When technicians trust the models and what they have to say about fit, both parties can work together with designers in other key parts of the sample-producing process: looking at how the design holds, whether the construction and upper fit well, and the look of the materials while on the foot. Most fit models reported that in higher-end lines the technicians tend to treat the models like equals (as we saw with Marius and Christine), taking their comments and corrections almost as if they were their own.

Technicians celebrate when models develop a "feeling"—as I explained in chapter 4—and are happy when fit girls participate within the coordinates of the knowledge provided by technicians. I was surprised when, after interviewing Josemir and Linda, I went the day after to see a fitting session with him and met his new local fit model. When I asked her about what makes a good fit model, she reproduced some of the key categories advanced by the couple the night before: "developing a feeling," "being more than just a foot," "knowing how to give indications," "saying more than loose/tight." We could even put these categories in correspondence with a lot of what I saw during fitting sessions, and furthermore when talking to both members of the metrological tandem together at interviews, with technicians both qualifying and organizing the models' comments, taking advantage of their understanding of the whole process, interpreting the experience of the fit model within it. In that case technicians consider the fit model a central yet subservient part of the process; in Tatiana's parlance, an assistant. Much like a modern Pygmalion, the technician in this case makes the model anew, training her, treating her like a repository of valuable information, but without developing a full autonomy.

But sometimes this does not happen, and knowledgeable fit models push against some of the technicians' diagnoses. What is at stake there is who has jurisdiction (Abbott 1998) over the correction and approval of shoes. Technicians usually appeal to the abstract character of their own expertise, given that they know how to translate the comments into measurements and grade into mathematical formulas—and try to make the fit model into someone to whom they have delegated some of the technical issues, but without challenging the centrality of what they know.

The question about who has the power not only to identify what is wrong with a shoe—or to give a diagnosis—but also to correct it, offering a solution, is of major importance, as the struggle over who gets to make inferences and provide an approved treatment for a problem constitutes what scholars of expert knowledge have identified as the major tenet of the lore: who gets to control, who gets to supervise, who is qualified to give treatment. If technicians could battle designers because of the abstract and imaginative character of designers' knowledge about shoes, confronting it with their own technical experience and their concrete, everyday internal knowledge of what a shoe is and how it works—they use here *their* own abstract and formal expertise to disqualify the experiential knowledge of fit models.

Nevertheless, the relationship between designer and technician, and between technician and fit model, changes when the two dyads become a triad. "Do you like it? What do you make of it? What do you see from there?" Those three simple sentences from a designer are powerful enough to transform someone who has until then been either a puppet made to speak by the technician as if he were a ventriloquist, or a megaphone for one part of her body, into a subject—knowledgeable about aesthetics, capable of autonomous decision-making and of self-fashioning through her taste judgments (on this see Mukerji 2016; Simmel 1957; Craveri 2005; Crowston 2013). Even when fit models recognize that technicians might know more about shoes than designers, they bonded better with the latter, who—according again to Tatiana—"act more humble, are easier to get along with, [they are] someone who respects you and your opinion, and asks from you other things than just if it's tight or not." On a few occasions I saw models giving their honest opinions to designers about not liking a particular shoe much, or saying they would not buy it.

If until then models had learned how to render part of themselves into an object able to be a spokesperson and give instructions—to become the standard representative of every US woman out there wearing a size 6 or 7—to develop enough empathy for the body and taste of some unknown woman as imagined by a brand—then after those questions are uttered, models slowly recover their own voices as people who not only know about measurements, pinches, and materials but who also have opinions as dedicated consumers of fashion.

And consumers of fashion they are!

Much like the designers described on chapter 2, who come from Europe with a bounty full of potentially free "original" shoes, fit models can keep confirmed samples and, sometimes, unique shoes that never made it beyond development into production. Linda's answer to how many shoes she had was that the first time she did a job for a good company, she took all of the shoes they offered her because "she just liked them all too much." Over time she became more discerning, though she had a hard time making up how many shoes she had, other than telling me she had a room full of them and that they were organized by color. Connie mentioned how she had also kept many shoes, enough to call them her "collection," and explained to me that she has kept even some items that are uncomfortable to wear but are absolutely stunning to look at. Those have a favorite spot—visible from the outside—in her shoe closet; she even showed me a picture of one of those pairs, a stiletto boot, the heel too steep to make it comfortable to wear. While these are of course rewards of symbolic and monetary value, exceeding and complementing the salary models make, they're also a way for the brand to slowly construct the fit model's sense of fashion. Some companies include in their contract that fit models have to constantly wear the shoes the brand they work for produces; sometimes designers have to abide by this too, though it's usually informally enforced in that case.

When meaningful interactions with technicians and designer do not happen, though, and models complain about the underside of their trade, they report "being left alone the whole day on a table," "feeling bored" or "useless," "doing something that does not add up to your life." This is true for most of the "pros" I talked to, who often have to accept that technicians are men who are not interested in listening to them, even if they know what they are talking about.

When I asked Linda what the hardest thing was to learn about fitting—expecting a response about materials or "feeling"—she bluntly answered that it was people, especially the technicians, because they do not listen. She even said: "They don't want to lose with a fit model, it's their ego. I had a lot of technicians, they would say to me, you only fit, you don't say what I have to do." It's because of that exhaustion that she left her fit career behind a few months before I met her and was working instead as a scheduler, in charge of the rhythm and the pace of development and production. She said she loves shoes and "was probably the best at fitting," but her level of frustration was such that she just "couldn't do it anymore."

TRADUTTORE TRADITTORE?

If the sense of the expression "at her feet" was self-evident in the previous section, I want to emphasize here a second way standardization work is dependent on the translation of a model's fit into larger categories of users. In this case the meaning is less about the tricks of the trade adjusting for a standard, and more about the cultural imagination that is behind sizing the foot of a Brazilian woman in China while thinking of the Midwestern female consumer market in the United States. The power to make the standard work—as adapting it to the foot of the model is made worthwhile by what we get out of the idea of using it as a reference—highlights that a standard is something through which agents can bring things back to the center. The standard-bearer's charismatic power gets betrayed—to play again with the Latin root of *tradire*. As we eventually learn in the multiple work of translation what we find is indeed a betrayal of the resemblance to an "original" point in the series, as well as of every one of the involved stakeholders.

This is a different kind of "adjusting for" work during and after standardization, predicated on the ideas that designers, technicians, and line builders have about their customers, and in consequence about how to transpose and modelize a model's measurements into a body different than her own. After all, the development of shoes is based on a foot that—as I showed in the previous chapter—exists as an outside referent and is yet in tension with the consumer's imagined (and actual) foot. This translation work operates in the tension between the role of mimesis and the power to replicate a distant other, in some cases known somewhat directly—as in the case of US designers, who are nevertheless from New York—and in others imagined (by fit models and technicians). Anthropologist Michael Taussig (1993) has called this "sympathetic magic," calling attention to the power of replicas to explore difference and eventually *become* the Other. For him this mimetic faculty—the ability to make models and to imitate—has been unleashed by the modern technologies of reproduction and accelerated the chance for the replica to take the power from what is purported to represent.

On my first trip to Dongguan during January of 2014, I witnessed a scene that would repeat itself all throughout the four years of fieldwork, at the end of many detailing and fitting sessions: once the fit model tried on a shoe, the US designer tried it on herself too.[6] The scene points to what happens when the standard foot is not enough. One part of the answer to that question is easily understood via participant observation, as what designers do is to bodily restore tactile knowledge: some of the key things they check for are the leather's quality and resistance, how much it will "age" and creak with use, and whether it bends if pulled. The fit model narrates these issues, but they are hard to transfer from one body to the next. The second part of the answer is more surprising, as designers explained what they are doing is to try it out on an "American" leg.

The designer will not just see how the shoe fits the foot model but will also try it on herself, to see the fit on a "US" leg like hers. Part of what explains this new trial of strength of the shoe prototype is the movement from the model's standardized foot to the designer's "American" leg and foot. Designers—as

I'll show in more detail in the next section—point at the anatomical differences between US and Chinese calves, feet, leg length, and distance between knees and feet as things that need to be accounted and adjusted for. Though in most cases—when working on pumps, flats, or sandals, for instance—designers let the model be the key site for validation to happen, the belief in differences not at the foot but at the leg level inspire them to act differently when working on boots. In this trial we get to witness once again—and at a different site and moment of the process—the tension between standardization and tacit knowledge.

All the developments described are based on being able to transfer findings, techniques, and infrastructures from one kind of body to another. There is a tension in the process of standardization between the need for generalizability and the local test scenario, framed by tacit and local knowledge. So, one of the key issues as the production of a shoe progresses is to how to loosen the boundary between the sample room as a laboratory and the "outside" world. The section that follows interrogates in full what happens when trying to replicate awhile having an Other—in this case, usually a US customer—in mind. In the next few pages, I describe four different kinds of translation issues (though they are of course interrelated *in situ*).

BETWEEN MARKET, CULTURE, AND BIOLOGY

Carrying out something similar to what in scientific contexts has been called a bridge study (Epstein 2007, 2009), US designers engage in translation work to imagine how a future shoe will look on an "American" foot. This kind of ethnonational conversion involves a comparison—especially at the level of the calves for boots, the main item in Fall collections—between the model's leg and foot and what they consider a typical US foot. The alleged differences intertwine cultural and biological attributes. Sometimes the differences are explained as "cultural"—in the US the prevalence of sports, and wearing fashion early on in life leads to more muscular feet; in China women have flatter feet because they don't grow up wearing heels. And sometimes differences are presented as biological, so "Chinese" models have narrower feet, wider calves, and shorter toes in the designers' descriptions.

The first time I heard of the difference between US and Chinese feet wasn't from an American designer, though; it was when, after figuring out the existence of fit models, I was interviewing Grace's then–business partner, Marshall. at her family trading company. Marshall is a Taiwanese man in his mid-thirties who had studied in the US. Moreover, his explanation of the distinction between US and Chinese feet was not a direct answer to a query about national variations but rather one about how they cast women for fit modeling. He asserted that what matters the most is that customers get the foot they want—and in a company like theirs, which produces shoes for many different markets, that means having multiple fit models to suit a range of clients' needs. When asked to clarify a bit about those needs, Marshall went beyond the "wide versus skinny" foot dichotomy I was expecting:

> You know the feet of different ethnicities is very different, the Chinese foot is very different from European, American or Russians. For instance, the Russians—at that time I learned later they were producing shoes for a Russian brand—they have very special foot, so if they found someone like that, they always want to see the same one, you know the bone is more protruding here, something like that. And lots from Europe and the US, because they do a lot of sports when they are young, so more muscle on the foot, not as boney you know. A lot of Chinese, they don't do a lot of sports or activities, so the foot is very thin, and also very wide. Yeah, every country is very different. . . . It's not only the perfect foot, sometimes the foot is big, in China you see the girls are short so they have small feet, it's sometimes you can hire someone with big foot, you want to do that because you don't have 7.5 or 8 or 9.

Although the strategy described in chapter 4 worked following an idealized standard that was actually performed and produced while concurrently working on and with the peculiarities of an actual foot, this procedure works by anticipating a different idealized future (Beckert 2013; Schutz 1959): that of the peculiarities of a niche market, with companies orienting themselves accordingly, by having a clear understanding of what the fit model's actual foot can perform in relationship to the feet of most of the customers in the markets they are producing for. In doing so, designers, technicians, production managers, and even fit models work with an implicit stereotypical theory of cultural difference. In this local theory culture, biology and markets become intimately intertwined, explaining why a particular kind of model is better for a particular region of the world (or the opposite).

Looking into how markets are matched with models, and especially at what explains the difference among feet, is yet another important window for observing how the global is both imagined and produced concurrently, as much at the infrastructural level as it is when designers scout for ideas and trends to translate into designs. For instance, Chinese feet are described as flat—in comparison to the US—and thinner, and the explanations given for these sometimes have to do with biology, as when accounting for shorter toes and rounder calves, and sometimes with culture, as when explaining how some of these characteristics are a consequence of not growing up wearing heels, or of weighing less because of diet and having not engaged in competitive sports at an early age. The peculiarities of US women who play soccer—something much less prevalent in the rest of the world—are usually highlighted when explaining this phenomenon.

The variability in ethnonationality when aiming to replicate through sympathetic magic a distant other's feet is presented as an advantage of South Brazilian trading companies vis-à-vis their Chinese counterparts. Brazilian feet in Novo Hamburgo are portrayed as less limited than Chinese feet, since—to quote Christian, a developer for the higher-end US market—"South Brazil has all kind of girls; we have Brazilians, Germans, and Italians"—he refers here to the large Italian, Portuguese, and German migrations to the area, something I'll develop in detail in chapter 6—"so we can serve better multiple markets."

There is a tension between homogeneity and heterogeneity in all of these accounts, with internal homogeneity complicating the possibilities for replication, and with a variability in which market is presented as more or less homogeneous depending much less on the country's actual ethnic composition than on the volume of product they produce for that region. In that respect, Brazil appeared in most of my interviews as divided between north and south—not at the level of consumers, but of models—as women in the north have to walk more, and because of the temperature usually wear sandals and open-toe shoes, which results in them having both stronger calves and flatter, wider feet. Europe, on the other hand, when named appeared not as divided into multiple national markets but rather as a unit when referring to replicating feet in Dongguan.[7] Regardless of whether a fit model works for a Spanish company, for the Dutch market, or for a British department store, the name under which standards are subsumed when she is asked who she works for is always the same: "Europe."

In this intimate relationship between bodies as they are imagined and invoked, and bodies as they are part of an actual infrastructure, we manage to see the cultural work of producing classifications that are presented as abstract and universal. This nevertheless generates certain features that are incorporated into artifacts that will then be circulated back to consumers. In trying to understand where they come from, I want to point to one ethnographic scene I have already presented, one testimony obtained in an interview, and the step-by-step process of assembling the infrastructure of production for a new market in Mexico for a trade company that had worked until then just with the US.

Sometimes the relationship between ethnonational variation and replication has been learned the hard way, as for instance, when the fit models from the market the shoe is being developed for are unable to try on the finalized samples successfully. This happened on several occasions during my fieldwork and, as I've explained, resulted on at least two different occasions in having the US reference fit model travel to China to try some of the comfort shoes being developed on a wider foot. This kind of taken-for-granted routine at the epistemic level collided also with the realities of how the infrastructure was setup when Marcio, one of the Brazilian technicians I interviewed extensively, described to me how complicated it was for him to work for the Russian market, given that the standards put in place for that market were different enough to alter, for instance, the proportions of boots. Both Brazilian and Chinese traders follow the proportions set historically by German and Italian makers. This requires not only the hiring of a model just for that market—one with a protruding metatarsal, as signaled by Marshall, the Taiwanese production manager—but also the development of different lasts than those used for the US or Europe at large. This leads to Marshall compromising his own technical expertise in trying to generate the proper replica, and forcing him to learn some procedures anew.

Translation issues are relatively common knowledge, and technical workers have learned to work around them or to replace the nonworking parts (usually the fit models) when necessary. Stereotypes about what the feet of a consumer for a certain market are like are accepted as received lore and presented to outsiders like me as facts to deal with. That is why I found the "putting a foot for a market anew" experience of Venus working for Mexico very much revelatory of how those stereotypes are produced. She described the experience to me as one in which she sat in multiple trips, for days at a time, at different locations of the department store she was producing shoes for in Mexico City, observing the feet of the female customers who were going to the floor where shoes were sold. While she also paid attention to what they said about the shoes on display, she was far more interested in listening to their complaints as they tried shoes on—paying attention to where the shoes pinched them, the areas where the foot hurt against the leather, or where they looked too loose—and, more importantly, in taking notes, pictures, and sketches of feet and legs. This happened so frequently that sometimes clients felt uncomfortable around her and wondered "Y esta qué mira?" as she would scan them from the floor up. When pointing at a picture of one of the samples developed in Dongguan, she explained to me that the lady in the image "tiene un pie más mexicano." By that she meant with a much higher instep than in the US (but relatively similar to China) and with a smaller ball. In her narrative, biological and cultural explanations were intertwined once again in producing the alignment:

> A lot of women in China have a very high instep. And Mexican women have a foot that is flatter, like in China too, but the difference is that they have a very pronounced heel, because girls start wearing heels when going out much younger than in China or even the US. For the US market the foot is wider, in Mexico women are more delicate than in the US, the ankle is thinner.

The explanation she gave involved received cultural stereotypes, as most scholarship would expect; but it was also the result of typification work, achieved after multiple years and locations handling feet. (Venus worked for Inditex—owner of ZARA—for years as a technician developing their lasts for multiple markets, the rare case of a female technician.)

Unlike the rest of the companies, designers, and technicians covered in the book, Venus's small line has a different challenge: to triangulate production, fit, and development between South China and New York for a consumer at a third, relatively new market. Her work of bracketing—while recognizing niche standardization so as to make the "Mexican" standard possible—revolves around constantly comparing the "Mexican" Chinese fit model (the company had to do a special casting in order to find her) and the "US" Chinese fit model (who works with her in most other lines, and who sometimes tries shoes on if the first model is unavailable) with the US fit model. If a shoe looks a bit loose on the "US" Chinese fit model, for instance, the shoe will get approved for development.

Regardless of which of the Chinese models is being used, if the instep is tight it is OK for the Mexican market—but wrong for the American one; on the other hand, if the US model in New York reports that a shoe is too tight

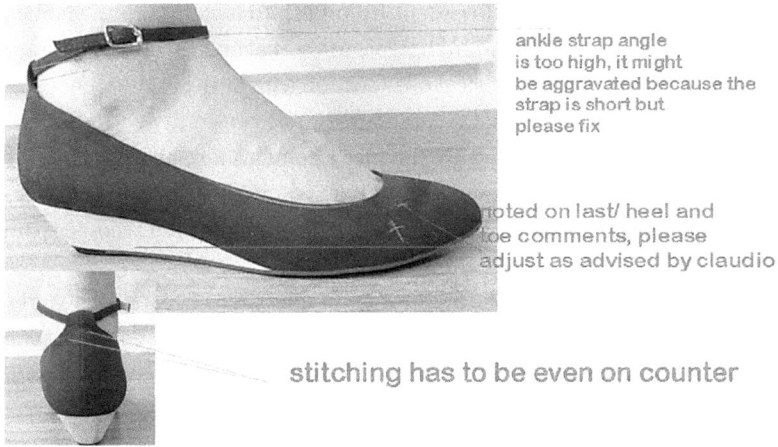

ankle strap angle
is too high, it might
be aggravated because the
strap is short but
please fix

noted on last/ heel and
toe comments, please
adjust as advised by claudio

stitching has to be even on counter

Figure 5.2. A development image for a sample featuring the "Mexican" model in China. Notice the high instep.

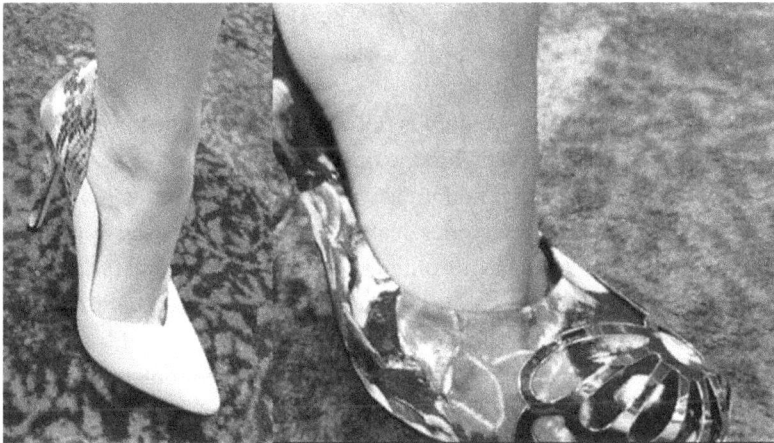

Figure 5.3. The US model in New York trying on shoes for the Mexican department store. Notice how loose the instep is in comparison to the previous image.

on the instep, it means it needs to be modified to be loose on her. The measurements of the ball and the girth of the heel present similar issues, with a Mexican shoe needing 46 millimeters of ball circumference, which would be too narrow in the US. Hence, if shoes are too tight at the ball level in China they would not be OK for the American market but would work for the Mexican consumer. Unlike other industries, replication and transposability here are not the product of the movement from flesh to metal, from the bodies to an outer bar, since all standard holders are actual bodies; rather, they are products of the meeting of flesh at one location with flesh at a different one.[8] Given that there is a potential for standards to be constantly corroded, the work of surveillance to make sure the measurements are the right ones for the market in question is a continuous endeavor; it's not about disembodying embodied features but rather about the constant dis- and reembodying of measurements and quirks.

The standardization-producing strategy of the export shoe industry works combining two styles of modelization that are at odds in other fields that use humans to produce generalizable results. The first style is universalization, wherein a whole infrastructure works around and brackets the peculiarities of a particular foot to conform to an abstract and idealized measurement scale, and in doing so it always using people from one nationality to represent multiple ethnonational differences and generalize from them, so there are "Russian," "American," and "Mexican" Chinese models.

The second style is niche standardization (Epstein 2007) and surrogacy (Bolker 2009; Friese and Clarke 2012), as fit models are stand-ins for a particular segment of the population broadly conceptualized—US women—and the work to maintain the standard is not about adapting the infrastructure to the fit model's foot but rather to the imagined consumer's foot. This relationship between particular and universal structures the industry at large, as trading companies and factories deal with this by segregating workers by ethnonational standards, having different teams of models and technicians working for different national markets. What I've described here, zoomed into, and shown is the actual work of translating Chinese (and sometimes Brazilian) feet and legs into objects that anticipate the problems expected when aligned with one market, in this case that of the US. But what is the US market? And what do American feet look like?

"IN OHIO THERE IS A SEA OF PRODUCT"

These words, uttered by Saskia, a British freelance consultant who worked in every shoe market included in this book, when trying to explain to me how the US market works, were part of a longer soliloquy in which she discussed the larger and sometimes undifferentiated volume of production with respect to Europe. They also put in perspective previous conversations and interactions, providing wording for two intertwined phenomena I had witnessed all throughout fieldwork: the division between how New York and the rest of the country are imagined and marketed to (to quote Saskia in full: "You have America and you have New York. In Ohio there is, like, a sea of product"), and how the feet (and the bodies) of the rest of the country are imagined not only in design but in shoe development and fit. After the brutal way that she linked the size of the market with the body types of people outside of New York ("It's not only the size of the market. It's the fact that you have to be able to make shoes to carry heavy weight over there") I had a reference to point to when trying to make sense of why OM designers discussed the corrections to a sample boot, having in mind how they would zip, making sure it wasn't in a way that would make the consumer uncomfortable—especially when thinking of ankle booties, which require wearers to bend over and push the foot in. I was better able to appreciate why those designers commented on the increasingly wider calf boots they have had to sketch and sample, and on the augmenting number of calf boot styles they are asked to develop. I could better understand a conversation between Josemir and Oscar at a development meeting when talking about whether to incorporate elastic straps on a sandal for a comfort brand usually catering to relatively older and larger consumers; or fully comprehend Venus's decision against making a smoking loafer—they had already developed one for the Mexican market—for the US, as it "would not look good on a wider or fuller foot, with heavier ankles."

When discussing the female shoe market in the United States, and despite all the work to make sure sizing is done right, one size does not fit all. The work of producing one set of standard measurements gets complicated when considering regional variation. If the work of trend-forecasting and the ideas generated through shopping in cosmopolitan fashion capitals had all used as an implicit reference a woman who to a certain extent replicated the designers' persona—women in their mid- to late twenties and early thirties, with an eye for combining clothing items in new ways, adhering to a slim horizon for their bodies and selves—the discussions captured within the idea of "the Midwest" made visible a population that could otherwise be imagined as overcoded and invisible (Star 1991) when producing shoes standards from New York: an older and larger population, which needed comfortable shoes that are still fashionable, and the resulting variation in construction as well as the generation of wider sizes to cater to it.

The continual reference to Indiana, St. Louis, Minnesota, Cleveland, Wisconsin—mixing up states and cities in conversation—made sure those involved in development brought into existence an object that took those body variations into account.[9] The "muscular" and "larger" foot that Marshall described gains definition and contrast when attending to the interactions I pointed to. The reference to the Midwest also allows us to find a more refined level of variation than the ethnonational differences involved when looking at the process from Dongguan and from the local fit models' vantage point. When opening the lens and painting a wider canvas the US achieves a more granular level of detail. If the idea of the Midwest appears still as vague and all-encompassing non–New York other (one of the designers, for instance, could not identify where Wolverine—the matrix house for Hush Puppies and Merrell—was located, despite having recently interviewed with them: "Was it Wisconsin? Minnesota? Michigan? All those places are the same to me"), ideas about the South are instead colored by the US's parochial ethnic and racial classifications, which in this case have profound consequences for how shoes are presented to potential buyers, as well as for the sizes that get promoted and eventually sold to boutiques.

I do not pretend to generalize from one small trading company and its designer in the paragraph that follows—just to show one particular instance in which further translation work is made explicitly evident in a way that would be harder to see—or get access to—when thinking of larger brands that cater mostly to national department stores like Nordstrom. As I hint at it here, there is translation work every time the immovable feet are moved (to offices, to fairs, to shows, to other locations).

Smaller trading companies attend multiple fairs during the year to meet potential customers and place their products. When talking to Venus about her experience at two smaller regional fairs (Atlanta and Miami) I was surprised—having met both her New York fit model and model for advertising—when she explained to me how in both cases, she hired freelance models. For Atlanta, where she usually dealt with African American boutique owners and potential customers, she hired a black model for the show, hoping to show her shoes could align with that particular population. For Miami, despite both her usual models being Hispanic, she "hired a chica Latina who had a great foot for showing" and who should also be able to help in producing the desired categorical alignment, as buyers there come not only from Florida but also from multiple Latin American countries. This is how she ended up with the big Mexican department-store account, for instance.

Another way in which the "south" translation gets enacted is when completing the orders for some of those boutiques (which go usually not for comfort shoes, as in the Midwest, but for more outlandish items). She unilaterally decides not to send sizes smaller than 8—the usual orders are from 6 or 7 to 11—to boutiques in the South she envisions to cater to white women, saying that she "know[s] how women are like in Georgia, and the sizes they carry; nobody over there is wearing a 6 or even a 7."

IT'S TOO GOOD OF A FOOT! ON
THE PERILS OF BEING UNIQUE

This second translation underscores the nuance of the cultural work involved in producing classifications that are supposed to be universal. Recall that it's not uncommon to hear conversations in which designers and line builders worry about how beautiful an ornament looks on a sandal the fit model is trying on given "that someone in St. Louis has to wear it," or how thin her ankle is in comparison to "the muscular foot of someone in Cleveland." While I focused the previous section on the imagined body of the consumer and its limitations vis-à-vis the standard, I want to emphasize here the second part of the equation: that fit models' feet—with no blemishes or bumps, manicured, taken care of, constantly surveilled, with measurements replicating the standard for the brand—might actually be *too* good and, because of that, unique in a bad way, since they are unable to generate the sympathetic replica designers and technicians need. In the tension between singularity and universality embodied by the fit model, being "too good of a foot" emphasizes neither the generality nor the diversity produced by the replica but its untranslatable character. From a semantic point of view, being the best in this case means being unique in a disqualifying way, at odds with the standard and the general.

"Too good of a foot" happened when the OM designers decided against an ornament on a sandal, though the ornament looked great when tried on the fit model, and the justification by the head designer was that "the front of her foot is beautiful, no bumps or anything, so a lot of sandals, straps looks fantastic on her, but bad once they are tried on fit models in the US. Imagine what it would look like on an actual consumer!" A foot is too good when—as the line builder for a hip Brazilian women's sneaker and sandal brand out of Sapiranga explained to me—

> Our fit model has a perfect 35—they produce mostly for the domestic market—but even if we use her to check at the factory, given that we mostly commercialize after 36, sometimes we use one

of our partners, who is a 36 and has a more "normal" foot. The fit model has too much of a perfect foot (*muito, muito perfeito*), and so we like using the other one sometimes, it has some bumps, it allows us to fit the smaller size we commercialize and to already better imagine how our customers will look when they wear them.

The tension between uniqueness and standardization can also be observed in one further scenario, outside the development room and the factory, when shoes are presented to potential buyers and customers. What is the relationship between fit models, models for trade shows, and fashion (commercial) models? What does it say about the limits to the irreplaceable character of the fitting feet?

WHEN BEING STANDARD IS NOT UNIQUE ENOUGH

In August 2015, the creative director of a brand within a large US company wanted to change the fit models she had, fire them, and replace them with "women who actually look like models," as the brand she worked for staged runway-like shows for big department-store clients where all of the sale samples got shown. The designers from the company explained that these are two different functions, and that the shoes would look too baggy on actual fashion models, usually 5'10" and size 9 or 10 in shoes, who would be unable to fill them up. Around the same week, Venus did her own sample sale for one of the large trade shows in New York, and though she had her commercial model at hand—a tall and slender Colombian woman who wears a size 9—she chose instead to have one of her usual fit models show them since she had a fuller foot and a higher instep (*el empeine más lleno*), after a clothing designer appeared who wanted to have her shoes be a part of his fashion show. The Colombian woman was too tall, and her feet were too bony, Venus said, to do a good job presenting the shoes.

These two similar yet contrasting scenes, at two very different organizations in terms of the scope of their production and the numbers of workers involved, underscore the confusion, tension, and slippage between two relatively distinct positions: that of fit model—with its emphasis on privileging how the shoes look and behave—versus that of fashion model, who is there less to present the product and how it might look to potential clients and more to present the brand and produce a particular kind of look (Aspers 2006; Mears 2011; Wissinger 2015). This continues also on social media, where the

Instagram accounts for most brands use commercial models to present their products directly to potential customers. In those cases, the standard character of the foot, and of the fit model in consequence, is not "unique" enough.

This conflict has been solved in trade shows by the hiring of freelance models, who are fit models—in terms of size they are either 6 or 7—but who have a look ("They have to be beautiful," Clint said) that is more similar to that of a fashion model, with a slimmer foot (a shoe looks good on a slim foot as long as it does not become a skinny one, Clint explained) These models have developed the necessary skills to become a different kind of spokesperson for the shoe: one who knows how to feature the shoe ("Never stand straight on, never show the inside of a shoe, stand a bit off, show the outside of a shoe, never bend the shoe, never stand like wearing heels if flat," was the list Brace gave me); understanding how to get dressed for the presentation depending on the buyer, how to dress to give a certain look to the shoe, how to align with the "personality" of the brand. They must do all this while knowing how to talk about shoes to customers.

The tension between the three positions underlines once again the friction between the functional character of being a standard and the beauty standards for being a different kind of model: a fashion one (even if one from the lower-status trade or commercial circuits). The scenes with trade-show models working the shoes also brings to the end the sequence of how the shoes are designed, developed, and sold. One of the key lessons from this part of the book is that even though at the beginning of the cycle shoes are pure ideas—disembodied abstractions made out of trends and preexisting designs, ornaments, and lasts, rendered on paper as almost pure form—they always have to be tried on in front of interested parties, regardless of whether these are designers, technicians, factory managers, potential buyers, or the higher-ups from the company. There is a need for fit models to be there as to make sense of how the shoes "actually" look. This worked almost as a mantra ("it looks good on, it looks good on" they repeat; "you have to see it on") all throughout fieldwork and is declined (as in a linguistic declension) differentially depending on the context under which it happened.

CONCLUSION: STANDARDS ARE NOT STANDARDS, ARE NOT STANDARDS?

How models have been characterized dovetails with the entanglement between typical, ideal, and average measurements that Daston and Galison

(1992, 87) discussed when talking about the representation of objectivity and how they have been classified under criteria that was deemed to exclude subjective judgments. Going through the part these three monikers play in the role of a fit model is a good way to also think about their worth. While the first and third labels emphasize their activity's mundane character, and more than anything the finality of what they are there to do—produce typical measurements for a market in which the they are not the average but in which the average will follow from a gradation of it—the ordinal ideal is precisely where we see the displacement into a universe of semantics organized around ideas of uniqueness or of being the best.

What the best foot is and how it relates to the standard for the market produces changing configurations; sometimes "being" the standard results in particular privileges—something usually not studied in the literature, too focused on how standardization produces subordination. At other times, inhabiting the standard is not good enough, or too good—and, as such, unique—for its own good. The malleability of judgments about what is standard, what is best, and what is unique points us to the relationship between nominal and ordinal judgments (Fourcade 2016), showing how certain "types" of foot (are they "Mexican," "Chinese," or "American"?) are put to work to produce sameness and generalizability (and sometimes specificity) where there was mostly difference at first—as we saw in the first chapter of this part. Looking at standards semantically allowed us hen to see the work of translation that enables products to continue down the production and commercialization cycle. Every time the immobile feet (the "type") are moved we see the amount of hard work done, the multiple sacrifices of detail and context that were made (on this see Timmermans and Epstein 2010). Women—their bodies—are made to speak for their feet and to stand for cultural characteristics tied to gender and nationality. The information they provide becomes simplified and miniaturized, allowing agents down the chain—technicians, designers, production managers, buyers—to model the heterogeneous and distant universe at hand, make it domestic, closer, erasing in translation those cultural differences inscribed in the final objects.

These last two chapters have produced an inversion of how infrastructural work is generally perceived and made visible what usually remains undetectable. In doing this, it ends an arc that began in chapter 2 in which the global scope extends and progresses, even if still seeing the everyday work of making sure both shoes as artifacts *and* the global scale stay stable. In the line that goes from chapter 2 and this one, we switched from design into development and witnessed the multiple agents involved, and the tasks and routines they engaged in as well as the techniques and devices they utilized. But the third part of the book is about an issue that is at the same time opposite and complementary to the maintenance of the global as a scale: what happens when things stop being sustained and start to unfold (in the case of the Taiwanese families who modernized the South China shoe cluster, discussed in the interlude), or have already unfolded, or—to be brutal—collapsed? That is the case of what happened in Novo Hamburgo, at the Vale do Sinos region of Brazil. If the first two parts of *The Perfect Fit* were about the scale-making practices and agents through which the global is *done*, the interlude and chapter 6 show how globalization *becomes undone*.

PART 3

The Global in the Rearview Mirror

Interlude

A LANDSCAPE OF FACTORIES

SIMON

Lunch had just finished.

As I have done before when visiting a factory or a development room, I had accepted an invitation by the production managers and the technicians to eat with them. We were coming back from finishing a stew on the upper floor of the factory, from where one could observe other factories as far as one could gaze. There was a small kitchen in it, where Simon—the owner of the development room—had cooked. As soon as we walked downstairs, he started complaining about the food he himself had prepared: "They did not put so many seafood inside, it had too much cabbage. They put in some pork, some noodles, but I like this kind of seafood, the soup will be more nice. . . ." Simon and the son-in-law of one of his friends—from whom he was now renting space after disbanding the large factory he had and making it into a development room—were in charge of the stew and had been kind enough not to put too much spice in it. Despite it being only lunch—like in other many exchanges with "shoe men" regardless of whether they were Chinese, Taiwanese, Brazilian, or American—they also served Black Label Johnnie Walker, and expected me to drink it too.

We had started the interview before lunch, but we lasted a nary fifteen minutes until Simon was called upon to put the finishing touches on an already-prepared stew. The scene I witnessed was familiar in the double sense of the word: I had been there before, but also all of the people involved were linked to each other by kinship ties. There were Simon and the son of his old buddy from Taiwan, as well as Simon's son-in-law—Grace's husband—and Simon's other son, who worked as production manager. Later, our interview was interrupted a few times by Audrey, Simon's three-year-old granddaughter, who had been there every time I visited their offices. She arrived every morning with Grace and played in a room adjacent to the main office, where Grace and her husband answered emails, checked samples, received clients, and conducted most of their daily operations outside of checking the development room or going to factories. Sometimes Grace's mom would arrive with Simon and be able to play with the toddler and take care of her, though from time to time Audrey would drop by the different rooms just to interact or be entertained by the "office girls," or in search of her mom, dad, or grandfather.

This particular lunch and interview happened in December 2016, within the confines of a sample room whose team I had visited and seen at work a few times since my first trip to Dongguan in 2014. Given that this was one of the first rooms and factories I had visited, I just assumed most other places I'd visit would work in similar fashion, made out as an intermediary space between family, home, and business. While that was true of how Taiwanese families had first structured their operations (see Hamilton and Kao 2017, the elders I had been able to observe at work and interview had a different story to tell: one of issues with intergenerational knowledge and business transmission; family members between twenty-five and forty who were blasé about taking over the shoe factory from their parents; and factories that folded as the older generation was uninterested in venturing further inland.

Even when shoes had been part of their kin's life when they were kids, lots of the children took advantage of the older generation's upward mobility to go study in the US and were uninterested in returning to the fold. Even those like Grace, who did return, studied in the US for a time and mulled whether to come back to work with their families. Both Simon and Tony estimate that 70 to 80 percent of the twenty-five to forty-year-olds have chosen not to work in the industry. When comparing current family situations to his kids' life, Simon is clear: "Grace used to come with me to the factory. As soon as they came from school, they would come into my office . . . then they would start in the showroom, would go to everything. It's different. They touched the shoes, since they were little, that's why they know about shoes."

Taiwanese entrepreneurs had been key in putting together the shoe industry in South China, moving it from Taiwan and Hong Kong, first with loafers and injection shoes, and later on with better-quality shoes that tempted
US buyers to make the jump from South Brazil. But during my fieldwork
they were being displaced geographically, to the point that some of them
returned to Taiwan and left the industry. Explanations of why the shoe industry made its way to China emphasize, of course, how the economic reforms
implemented by the country since the 1980s, and the deindustrialization of
Western countries, have clearly been the main engines behind production
taking place in China.

Past knowledge also plays a role. Many of the factories that are in contact with US shoe-production companies are owned by Taiwanese families
who have owned the factories on Taiwanese soil in the 1970s (when "Made
in Taiwan" was in every piece garment you could get your hands on) and
later the ones in South Korea, during the early round of the globalization
of sneaker production.[1] As production costs lowered on the mainland,
Taiwanese entrepreneurs invested in Dongguan—partially taking advantage
of the common Han ethnic ancestry with government officials (on this see
Cheng 1996; Hamilton and Kao 1990; Cheng 2007). It was common while in
Guangdong Province to meet with agents, quality control officers, and technicians who were all of Taiwanese origin. It also became frequent—as this study
progressed—to find out that factories had closed or slimmed down, that people I had been in touch with—the technician at OM, the production manager
at the first sample room I had access to—had decided to return to Taiwan.

The tone and the tenor of Simon's story transmitted some of his feeling
of loss. His was a history of upward mobility, going from being the inspector
of factories back home to the owner of factories on the mainland, but also
one of slowly closing shop in the last few years. The first time I met him he
had been in Guangcheng (or Tangla)—a relatively posh neighborhood for
Dongguan—where he had a factory with barracks and a sample room, with
enough workers to fill up three assembly lines. During my next visit they
had started sharing that space with a Dutch company that specialized in
personalized orthopedic shoes. By the third time I visited they had moved
the sample room to Houjie, into the heart of industrialized Dongguan, in an
area mired in traffic and relatively far from Dongcheng, the "international"
district where designers and visitors preferred to stay—and where a lot of the
owners and managers also lived.[2] The sample room and quality control unit
they maintained there (on top of the office services) occupied one of the three

Figure I.1. The view from Simon's factory.

floors of the factory I had lunch at, which was owned by Tony, Simon's old pal. In the three years I spent doing fieldwork with them the company had both gotten smaller and been displaced geographically from one local area to another. The relatively small movement mirrored the larger transfer of the industry at large, with the birth of export production in Dongguan related to the movement of US buyers from South Brazil to South China, and the current exodus from Dongguan expelling generations of factory owners and specialized workers, uninterested in moving themselves and their families closer to where the cheap labor is.

That wasn't the only time I ended up in Houjie. While during my first trips I'd only go there to visit its market with different sourcing teams, little by little I started visiting more agents and trading companies that had their home there. The area had also become better connected to the rest of the city, thanks to a new subway line that made it easier to gain access to it from Dongcheng, and so I slowly ventured into it without the need for a car. Most of my last two visits to Dongguan happened with me going almost daily to Houjie, navigating among a landscape of factories, plazas, and other structures that were hard to distinguish.

On those other visits, instead of listening to the swan song of Taiwanese entrepreneurs, what I witnessed were the life stories of Brazilians and how they ended up making their livings in China. Juxtaposing these stories is a significant choice. The link between them became obvious as I spent further time in the area and inquired about Brazilians' lives and roles in the industry: they were there to replace the technical expertise that the Taiwanese failed to reproduce intergenerationally, and that the Chinese had not been able to develop yet.[3]

OSCAR (AND MARTIN'S)

I met Oscar when he took me for lunch in June 2016 to Martin's restaurant, which serves German food but is owned by a Brazilian and favored by most of the people from Vale do Sinos whom I met in South China. Even though there was a Brazilian-themed bar in the same strip, I'd end up going to Martin's several times, thanks to the invitations of some of my Brazilian informants in Dongguan, and never to the other bar, Botego Brazil. Once at Martin's, I'd run into people I had already met, and I could observe how tight-knit the community of Brazilians in the area was. Instead of moqueca or feijoada they ordered from a menu full of schnitzel, sausages, and sauerkraut.

Oscar is in his late thirties and talks fast; he is meticulous in his descriptions and generous in showing me around. I'd end up going to his trading

Figure I.2. Martin's ad on Bar Street.

office, to some of the factories and sample rooms he worked with, and to the Houjie market, looking for laces and some fabrics. His life story has some similarities to those of others I ended up meeting through my research: he arrived in 2011, a few years after the 2004 crisis that revalued the real (the Brazilian currency) against the dollar. He waited until the last minute to come to China—once he had exhausted his life chances in Novo Hamburgo—and had had experience working in shoes before coming to China. He had studied at SENAI; in fact, he had Josemir—who, the first time I met him, was working for Oscar as a technician and developer—as his teacher. To leave the country, he had accepted a job as a sales manager with a now-defunct small Brazilian trading company, hoping that this would only be his entry point into the South China realm. To do so, Oscar had used contacts he had from before leaving, as the number of *Novo hamburguenses* in the area had grown exponentially, to the point where, in the period of my research, there were between four and five thousand specialized workers living in the area.

At the time of our lunch interview his gambit had paid off. That company had paid him around US$1,500 a month, but the job proved to be his launching pad to something more ambitious: his own trading company, where he developed shoes for multiple markets, including the UK, Brazil, South Africa, Australia, and the US. In fact, I met Oscar thanks to a Brazilian designer who had worked for the most important brands in New York, and trusted him to develop shoes for the small boutique brand she was working for then, thanks to their time together in Novo Hamburgo. Depending on the fluctuations of currency, he mobilized his contacts to develop and produce his prototypes, samples, and shoes sometimes in Brazil, sometimes locally in China. Much like other diners at Martin's, Oscar found some of his clients at international fairs, and either developed shoes from scratch according to their instructions or offered finalized products (what shoe people call "private label" and "first cost") for their brands just to put their stamp on them.

BAIRON'S LAST

I met Bairon thanks to one of his friends, whom I had interviewed in Novo Hamburgo in the summer of 2016.[4] He had arrived in Dongguan in 2011, following the loss of his job in Dos Irmaos, some ten miles away from Novo Hamburgo, and after mulling multiple times against moving across the world. He had been working in the shoe industry for over fifteen years, since he was sixteen. Like most of the Brazilians in the area, he had studied at SENAI, his stipend paid by one of the largest factories in Dos Irmaos. He held off many times, but when he was laid off and felt like he had finally run out of chances in the Vale do Sinos, he took advantage of an invitation by colleagues to move to China. He started by working in a large multinational company that, like many others, had its own developing office there. He had changed jobs a couple of times since arriving when he was twenty-five years old, including one short stint at the company where Oscar and Josemir had found their first stop in Guangdong Province. Bairon proudly claimed to be sixth-generation German.[5] By the time of our meetings he was working for a company for the US market and was in charge of production as a technician. I interviewed him formally a couple of times and went into his sample room, where he discussed his work and the operation of design- and sample-making by his current company.

By the end of my third time with him Bairon reflected on what he saw as a key material difference between working in Brazil and in China: the quality of the last. The making is the same, but in Brazil the last is done with wood instead of plastic; that, in combination with preexisting skill, means that technicians can adapt them, even making suggestions for improvement when they receive an "original" last that technicians deem faulty and in need of correction. For him, the last is a marker of how "in Brazil we do things better." Wood's "natural" character points to having the "feeling" and "skill" necessary to make small adaptations and changes. With plastic this is harder, as things come straight from a machine, he contended. And unlike wood's noble character, plastic has to be supplemented for corrections—especially when trying to add volume—with sawdust and glue, which look far less elegant.

While of course there are differences in how a last works depending on its material, those differences are charged with layered distinctions about what distinguishes and separates the work of Brazilians from that of Chinese technicians. The emphasis on skill and adaptability contrasts with how Bairon—and Brazilian technicians at large—perceives the work of local experts in the industry. For him, *Novo hamburguenses* like him know how to relate and coordinate with others, are aware of the many procedures involved in making a shoe and how to adapt to others working on it.

On the contrary, Chinese technicians—regardless of whether they are patternmakers, last builders, developers, or production managers—are "good soldiers," following orders and executing their own work, but unable to relate to and coordinate with others and to anticipate problems (and solutions)

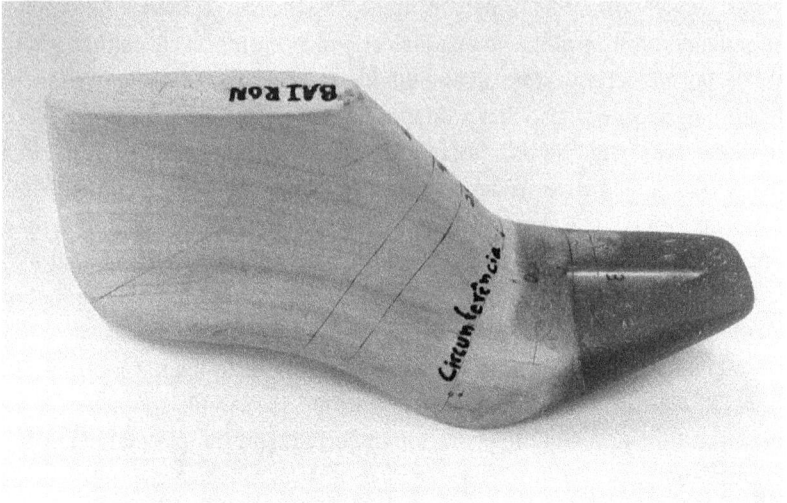

Figure I.3. Bairon's last, kept in his office. in Houjie.

in consequence. Moreover, the lack of trust in those skills is presented by many of the Brazilians who have stayed over five years in Dongguan as the evidence for why they are there. According to Bairon, "Brazilians are here because Americans do not trust Chinese." In his narrative, Brazilian know-how is presented as the glue that allows regimented actors, with little impro-visational skill, to be coordinated. And it replaces in the middleman position, the Taiwanese shoesmakers who are slowly leaving the industry

The distinction against Chinese—but also Taiwanese—technicians is explained by how they learned their trade and the structure of design and development in each region. As I've shown throughout, there is a separation, both geographical and of companies, between the different tasks and steps in-volved in the generation of a shoe. Brazilian companies used to do everything in-house (design, development, production), hiring personnel who acquired practical knowledge in the making—usually as interns who studied on the technical school, getting a fuller understanding of all the tasks involved in shoemaking as well as their role in it. The only task that was not executed in-house was last-making. While Bairon took a fifty-hour course on it, he had to leave the German-named factory in Dos Irmaos he worked for and intern at Formas Kunz to do so.

He admired that company so much that he kept his training last as a memento—and used it to contrast with the local procedures he described to me—in a drawer of his office at the sample room. Much as had happened with Oscar and at Martin's, Bairon's reference to Kunz was as much a nod to the differences in procedures in the two parts of the world as an indication of the cosmopolitan skill tradition Southern Brazilians saw themselves belonging to. The Kunz last-making factory personalized its lasts—each firm had its special code and assigned technician—and that personalization was a marker for last- and boot-making in general that *Novo hamburguenses* abroad recognized as their own. Moreover, the mention in conversation of the famed factory was not only a confirmation for technicians of their own importance—given how lasts could give shape to the shoes during the production process—but also a point of pride, as the facility was usually discussed to point across the Atlantic to Fagus, the legendary German factory building designed by Walter Gropius and the Bauhaus, of which Kunz was a replica of sorts.

MATEO: CONTROL AT A DISTANCE

Mateo received me in his office. Unlike at most of the other companies and development units where I had visited Brazilians, he seemed to be the only one from South Brazil there. He and his wife had been pioneers in moving from Vale do Sinos to China. He came in the early 2000s, when a Brazilian company that used to do production for big US buyers in Novo Hamburgo decided to try its luck partnering with those big buyers to develop and produce shoes there. The company had a small commercial office in Taiwan and moved to the continent in 1998—more precisely, to Shenzhen—but just to operate commercially, offering expert services to Taiwanese companies and to do import and export of some key materials.

To a certain extent one can think of said company as the original sin of what I witnessed both in Dongguan and back in Brazil too: the movement of production from a place with skilled workers to one with a cheaper labor force, and the consequent necessity for expert labor that could help facilitate and coordinate at a distance. Once the now-defunct Paramount established itself in Dongguan, it became a vortex that sucked in technicians and managers, not only in lasting but in all steps of the production chain, including cost, sourcing, the interface with sample rooms, and factories. Much as it had done in Brazil, the company had both sample rooms and a huge factory, consisting of over twenty full assembly lines and four thousand employees during its apex in 2008.

Other companies followed suit and slowly started recruiting Brazilians. Some of those I had spoken to were tempted after seeing that some of their less-skilled coworkers had escaped the waves of bankruptcies that engulfed a lot of the large factories in Novo Hamburgo during the early 2000s. Many of the production managers and technicians I interviewed came to smaller Brazilian-owned companies that paid little at the time (US$1,500 for a technician) but were perceived as entry points into the network of firms in Dongguan. Slowly but surely, in the top firms Brazilians occupied the roles that historically had corresponded to Taiwanese expert workers: they were production managers, developers, technicians for leather and lasting, and quality inspectors, making up all the positions that involved trust along the chain, including the relationship with buyers. In a matter of ten to fifteen years, those who had worked in Brazil during the mid-1990s for large US buyers were doing the same, but in China.

As the company expanded, Mateo played different roles, mostly in the commercial area, focusing on cost—since he had studied economics in school (at UNICINOS) and learned there about development and sourcing. Though he started in Dongguan, he eventually moved to Chengdu to be the person who would guarantee the quality of the factory his boss had established there to reduce cost on the operations that needed less expertise, like stitching or cutting. He returned to his apartment in the New World Garden complex in 2010 and stayed at companies associated with his Brazilian boss until 2016, when the factory that had started it all had to close—because the large US buyer that had *also* started it all had decided to develop its shoes with a competitor.

After the demise of Paramount, he predicted that Brazilians would stop going to South China. In his case, instead of yet another company run or owned by co-nationals, he ended up working at the largest Cantonese conglomerate, where he was a manager when I met him, developing shoes at a low price point for well-known US brands. When asked about how he ended up there, he said bluntly: "China is now the center of the world. And yet some European and American people built trust with Brazilians and demanded for those people to stay in place . . . as top commercial, technical, and managers for production." His story is one where being Brazilian is a way of establishing and stabilizing trust at a distance—at first for companies mostly run by Brazilians themselves, and eventually for Chinese companies, who see Brazilians as an in between them and US (and sometimes European) buyers.

TRAITORS, TURTLES, NATIVES

The literature on infrastructure has repeatedly underscored the amount of control at a distance necessary for undistorted communication to happen and the surveillance procedures that have to be in place to transfer information. As Hetherington and Law (2000, 41) wrote when discussing the relationship between the global scale and local materialities, one of the main issues has to do with delegation. For them, one could ask those key in-between players: "Will you act as my agent at a distance? Will you stay reliable? Will you hold together? Or will you turn traitor, turn turtle, or go native?"

Those were of course questions not necessary when all of production was done under one roof, as in the Brazilian case; or when co-ethnics managed the industry, as happened with Taiwanese entrepreneurs early on in Dongguan. But it is a question asked over and over by buyers, sample room managers placing factory orders in far-flung places, and factory managers and quality-control inspectors trying to reproduce the quality of the product. Some of the questions are about price point and skill—as in whether they can really do what they said they would do and allow the profit to stay the same. Some of the questions are about copying—as in how much trust and information one can give the sample room about uppers and lasts until they start using that information to develop similar shoes for a different company. And some of the questions are about being replaced—as in, how well should a technician train a local assistant, given that in the future they can perform the same tasks cheaper.

The relationship between distance, trust, and control is highlighted repeatedly because of the geographically dislocated character of shoe production, always moving in the search for cheaper labor, while making sure there are expert cadres not so far away be able to reproduce standards. In this case, part of the explanation has to do with the lack of technical expertise among the local population; part of it has to do with the issues with intergenerational labor reproduction among the Taiwanese families who dominated the industry early on. And another important segment of it concerns importing specialized knowledge from preexisting clusters, accelerating how quickly those clusters are put together and made to work.

At the level of craft this means dealing with the tension between tradition and how standardization can be produced; it also means interrogating what happens when the face-to-face and *in situ* process of apprenticeship is replaced by other means (on this, see Polanyi 1958, 53). This interlude hinted at what happens when one tradition replaces another. In the last part of the book, I explore not so much what traveled from South Brazil to South China—to a certain extent the last three sections of this book have thematized that question—but what was left behind in Novo Hamburgo once the export industry left.

Chapter 6

THE RUINS
AND RUBBLE
OF NOVO
HAMBURGO

Skill and Melancholia in a Global Shoe Town

The rough, skewed constructions seemed to have been
erected that morning with the sole purpose of being taken down
at dusk. New but precarious, as if decrepitude had been built
into them, the houses seemed eager to become ruins.

Hernán Díaz, *In the Distance*

WASN'T THIS A FACTORY AT SOME POINT?

During the Southern Hemisphere winter of 2016, I stayed in the Vale dos
Sinos area, as my many Brazilian informants in Dongguan and New York
had insisted I should, aiming to see what Brazilians had brought with them

to the global shoe industry. I visited multiple sample rooms and factories, did my share of interviews, gathered as much visual evidence as I could, and collected life stories and archival materials. During that stay, I made the taxi trip from the downtown Novo Hamburgo hotel where I lodged to nearby Sapiranga a few times. Each time, the driver assumed that I was doing work related to the shoe industry and picked up conversation with me in Portuguese. On my first trip I went to Paquetá, a factory and sample room that had been mentioned by lots of Brazilians—either in South China or in the Vale do Sinos—and where lots of well-known brands for the US market were developed. The driver shared with me how many more trips he made in June than in other months and recognized immediately the address I was going to. Once I got to the six-lot behemoth the first issue arose: the main entrance on Avenida 20 de Setembro was for employees, and so I needed a card to get in.

I took advantage of the small setback to walk around the perimeter of the factory and see what was next to it. As I made it to the other side—Avenida Vasco da Gama—I could see we were surrounded by a few empty lots. So much that the street there was the semipermanent structure of a circus in place, the white monotony of the tent cut by strident orange-and-green figures surrounding the hyperrealist attempts to draw a couple of clowns.

As I made it to the back entrance the guard announced me and allowed me in. I entered a large lot with a sign for a brand the factory is involved with. It felt eerily empty, and a secretary walked me to a small windowless room where I'd meet André, a production manager who had agreed to talk to me thanks to his friendship with multiple informants both in Brazil and in China. Our interview was very cordial; André described how he had recently relocated after working abroad, first for an international company and then for the factory itself, as they had moved production to the Dominican Republic in 2011. As the interview waned, I asked him if he would mind showing me the warehouse next to us, where I imagined many assembly lines in place. The space was one of four similar ones on the property. Once he opened the door, I was able to take a few pictures of.

The four factories, previously full of assembly lines, had then—by summer 2016—been converted into two empty spaces: a warehouse for materials and a sample room for higher-end US brands. Labor had slowly been relocated, first within the Rio Grande do Sul state itself, moving away from the expertise of the Vale do Sinos and a couple of hours away into Teutonia, where the workforce was less qualified but cheaper. Later, it went into the northeast—where most of the domestic-market production took place—to

Figure 6.1. One of the empty assembly-line spaces at the Paquetá factory in Sapiranga.

places like Bahia or Ceará. The export industry made a longer trip, moving in 2011 from Sapiranga in Rio Grande do Sul to the Dominican Republic, leaving behind only expert workers, who do research, development, control, shopping, and administration.

What happens when a skilled industry leaves town? What happens to those who have acquired embodied skills when the industry goes in search of cheaper labor? How much can they still perform their specialized work *in situ* while codifying and reproducing it electronically? And how does the departure affect those who leave versus those who stay? This chapter aims to answer these questions by looking at the global shoe industry and how Brazilian specialized workers in Dongguan (China) and Novo Hamburgo (Brazil) cope with the movement of their export trade from South Brazil to South China, looking at their strategies for memorialization and remembrance.

As I've discussed, shoemaking exists within two logics: the search for skill and the search for cheap labor. For some twenty years, from the 1970s until 1995, those two searches coincided geographically in the Vale dos Sinos in South Brazil, where a successful industry exported a big part of its production to the US. The following pages explore the memories of the manufacturing boom, what have been the strategies by those staying in business since the almost-complete demise of the export industry in 2004, and the role that family and regional identity have played in this. It also scrutinizes the tension between nostalgia and melancholia attached to the embodied skills needed to produce shoes, and how that tension is inhabited—through multiple material artifacts—by Novo Hamburgo at large and by people who have left the industry, those still in it, and those who have moved to Dongguan, South China, to keep working in the trade. Based on archival work, ethnographic observation, interviews, and oral histories, the chapter shows the variegated landscape of mnemonic material practices and spaces (ruins, rubble, monuments, mementos) and how they communicate the distinctive relationship of skilled workers with respect to Brazil's future and their personal roles within the global shoe industry.

"CEARÁ É A CHINA DO BRASIL"

Said André, and this statement captured the complexity of how unevenly development impacted shoe making, with the industry almost inexorably leaving the expert clusters in search of cheap labor—where eventually infrastructure might also be developed as well. The departure of the shoe industry for China and the *Nordeste* begs one question, though: how did South Brazil come to have a supercluster dedicated to the export of leather shoes?

This section offers a compressed answer to this query, giving an overview—based on secondary sources—of how Novo Hamburgo became the national capital of shoemaking. Part of the answer has to do with the German character of migration to that area, part of it with the subsidies provided by the federal government once the cluster was established. The subsequent transformation of the local regional economy—from depending on small agricultural colonies to the factories and shops associated with the export boom of the 1970s and 1980s—led to Novo Hamburgo's becoming a shoe capital, as did the slow departure of factories, first to other parts of the Rio Grande do Sul province, and later to the *Nordeste* and China.

The consensus (Da Costa and Passos 2004; Schneider 1996; Schmitz 1995; Selbech 1999; Bazan and Navas-Aleman 2003; Schemes et al. 2005) is that the establishment of Colonia Sao Leopoldo by German migrants in 1824 is where we can find the beginning point of the supercluster of the Vale do Sinos. Some of the German migrants—mostly peasants from the Hunsrück area—brought with them shoemaking skills and promptly established small workshops, with low capital accumulation and no division of labor. The presence of cattle in the region meant that shoes were produced using leather, though it wouldn't be until the 1870s—because of the war of Brazil, Uruguay, and Argentina against

Paraguay—that shoes became manufactured following something closer to industrial practices, including steam machines. The advent of the train to Porto Alegre in 1876—and of electricity in 1875—catalyzed the establishment of proper factories late in the century. The last names of all the protagonists with major accomplishments point us to surnames not as common when we think the Portuguese and Creole last names associated with Brazil's history. The first tannery—central to the shoemaking infrastructure—was established by Nicolaus Becker; the first shoes were commercialized by August Jung; the first machine to make leather saddles was put together by Nicolaus Schmitt; and the first official factory (in 1898) was started by Pedro Adams Filho.

While the last names give us a sense of the German presence, they pale in comparison to the two hundred thousand migrants who came into the area; self-ascribed descendants of German origin number around three million, or more than five million when combined with descendants from other European migrants into the area, like Portuguese and Italians. About half of the state of Rio Grande do Sul claims German heritage. Unlike in other parts of the country, the self-identified white population of the state makes up a large proportion of its inhabitants: 87 percent, in comparison with the 56 percent in Brazil as a whole.

The industry stayed relatively stable from the 1920s until the 1960s, with an organizational structure in which most companies were relatively medium or small, with a high artisanal component, low value of entry and exit, as well a labor-intensive process. On average, firms had less than twenty employees until the 1970s. Then, the export boom transformed the industry in size and scope. There were over three times as many firms in 1975 than in in 1960 (forty-seven thousand versus thirteen thousand), and firms had an average of fifty-five employees. Myriad factors contributed to this—which shows the political-economic complexity behind the establishment of an industry at the global level. Even if the most obvious one is the establishment of what scholars call a supercluster in the region, this would have not happened without three developments at the national, regional, and international levels.

At the national level, the Brazilian state started to play a significant role in the development of manufactured goods. Most goods suffered what Oliveira (1988, 73) has called a "realization crisis." The local population's low purchasing power resulted in policies at the national state level to incentivize industries that depended on the consumption power of the working class (shoes, clothing, and textiles at large). The local shoe industry benefited largely from this; it started its expansion by exporting women's sneakers—these made up over 90 percent of early-1970s exports—mostly for the US working class, with low variation in the quantity of models and colors. The conquest of this particular market segment transformed the technological base and the productive structure of the industry, starting a period of expansion.

At the regional level, the agricultural transformations of that decade pushed the German *colonos* into Vale do Sinos (where I did archival research and interviews) as well as Encosta da Serra (around forty miles away), turning farmers into factory workers, providing young bodies to an expanding industry—bodies ready to be exploited outside the traditional way of living and the productive structure of the farm. The disarticulation of family-based agriculture made a new working class readily available. *Colonos operarios* (as Germans but also workers of Italian descent were then known) brought to the new organization patterns related to the German agricultural past. Many scholars have pointed out how even in shoe-related work the new laborers brought with them the *colono* work ethic (Rodrigues Kanaan 2013), as well as how the older workers reached an alliance with the new factory owners to administer the work in the expanded factories. The old family structure was also important, as the expansion of the industry was based partially on the geographical movement toward farther regions of the state—first, between 1985 and 1990, to Vale do Rio Cai, forty miles away; and then to Vale do Rio Tacuari, some sixty miles away. Subcontracting was another contributing factor, with families setting up small shops and ateliers, where they would execute some of the menial parts of the shoemaking process.

National subsidies were complemented by policies at the local level, like the establishment of a technical institute (SENAI) and an annual fair (FENAC) to showcase the region's products. But an account of the process of consolidation of the supercluster would be incomplete without noting the role that US buyers played in its expansion. Brands like Nine West moved from buying shoes in Italy and Portugal to Brazil in the 1970s. If sneakers paved the way during the 1960s and 1970s, women's leather-shoe exports exploded in the 1980s and 1990s. The area went from exporting about a half percent of the world's leather-shoe exports to over 12 percent, though most of it was concentrated on a few American buyers. The numbers of production increased as well, as it went from twenty-three to one hundred million pairs, of which thirty-two million were exported. The figure of the export agent became central, as the key person who matched foreign buyers with local factories, ateliers, and shops (Schmitz 1995). According to most testimonies, the 1990s saw a real "gold rush," with shoe people rushing to set up export agencies. If Rio Grande do Sul was known for being a "frontier" state (Oliven 1996), fueled by a distrust of the federal government and by the expansion of cattle—always the sister industry of shoemaking—this was the third way the province semantically resembled the US West of the late nineteenth and early twentieth centuries.

But the boom had its bust in the mid-1990s when those same buyers—scared away by the loss of profit margins because of the reevaluation of the local currency against the dollar in 1994—allied with the owner of Palladium and the Chinese government to open a factory in South China in 1996. The crisis from 1994 to 1998 shrank the number of workers in Novo Hamburgo from twenty thousand to six thousand. The industry would suffer a more permanent blow after 2004, because of a second reevaluation of the local currency, thanks to President Lula's progressive policies.[1] Just to give an idea, in Sapiranga in the period immediately afterward (2004–2007), over thirty factories closed, and the number of workers went down from thirty-five thousand during the apex of the 1990s to sixteen thousand in 2007. As Rafi—one of my key interlocutors in the Vale dos Sinos—dramatized it through the factory that opened this chapter, so I could understand the poignancy of the process: "In 2007 Paquetá fired over eighty people a day; it was heart wrenching."

The migration of production to China, coupled with the transfer of the cheapest part of the production process to the *Nordeste*, resulted in a devastating picture for a place like Novo Hamburgo, which depended on the industry for up to 70 percent of its city budget.[2] The current picture is such that the value of women's shoes exported to the US market from Brazil pales in comparison to that from China (64 percent to 1), and in the Rio Grande do Sul area produces only 12 percent of the shoes developed for export, against 41 percent by the northern state of Ceará—when as recently as 2000 the percentages were 80 to 9 percent in favor of the *gaúcho* state. And of course—as we saw in the preceding interlude—all these numbers have resulted in the emigration of skilled labor from the area to Dongguan, where approximately five thousand Brazilians from the region lived when I was doing fieldwork.

This short travel through the history of shoemaking in the region is set up to understand some key characteristics of how the industry was established, as well as what the key constitutive elements of this particular assemblage were: the attachment to a central categorical identification (the German agricultural past), the honor and ethic that go hand-in-hand with craft practices and the knowledge they produce (seen in the multiple generations of designers and technicians who worked not only in the area but also in China and the US), and the family firm as a central component of what made the industry work. When this was not the case, the pride attached to the practice was somewhat related to the interviewees having parents who were "shoe people" as well, the "normalization" of what had been in reality a relatively short expansionist period—the export boom—as the horizon of expectations about the scale and scope of the enterprise.

Before I expand and elaborate on the relationship between the desolate and liminal landscape of objects that have been and no longer exactly are what they once were, and how they are represented and described, in the passages that follow I show how the boom was presented as the frame of reference against which the current situation is compared.

MEMORIES OF THE BOOM

I started at SENAI in 1986; it was three years, morning and afternoon, and then a stage at a factory. [From] 1984 to 1986 I worked during the holidays as part of my fellowship. From my home to the factory it took ten minutes walking, but so you have some idea—when people had to leave work for lunch they had to do it taking turns; there were so many people that you couldn't leave everyone out at the same time. It had to be 11:30, 11:40, 11:50 in order to have some space. You could not get through with a car, today you could drive through with a semitruck! Don't know what happened to all that people . . . the city must be kept up by remittances.

This testimony comes from an interview with Denilson, a professor at SENAI since the late 1980s, the technical school established in the late 1960s to foster the standards of the industry. The narrative establishes a golden era that coincides with Denilson's entrance into the labor force, as well as linking that past of opulence to the present, in which the city is basically a ghost town.

Our conversation happened in his offices at the institute, where he gave me a tour of the facilities as much as a historical walkthrough of what had happened to the industry. The quote I reproduce at length, where he discusses via numerical, spatial, and time-related figures the size of the workforce, gets complemented by his evaluation of one of the key specialized role: the technician. When discussing how during the mid-2010s there wasn't a cohort of technicians graduating from the Institute—a kind of learning that was subsidized by the industry, as factories paid for the training or hosted the students in paid internships as they were going through the program—he pointed in contrast how in the early to mid-1990s the school had three shifts of apprentices aiming to learn the skills, with twenty students in each. In 2016, when the interview took place, he had—together with other local developers—managed to recruit a cohort for the first time in a while, but it was only one shift consisting of fifteen students. Earlier that year in Dongguan, I had met Marcio, a quality-control director for a large transnational corporation, who claimed to have been "one among the last cohort of technicians in the 2000s."

Talking to shoe people over forty years old about the industry meant always talking about the relationship to its past, even if I never prompted for it on my interview guide, which was mostly about work routines. This recall of the past was not made of revelatory moments or serendipitous stories. Rather, it was a rich tapestry, dense and tightly woven, saturated with history. The tropes for describing the present and the past were common in different points of the industry. So Zeke, a representative at the shoemaking union, described how "during the golden era, you had on one street, sometimes even on one block, something like five thousand workers ready to work on a factory. Today the whole city has six or seven thousand, tops." And Victor, a matrix specialist from Chile, who like others from the Southern Cone had come to try his luck at the Vale dos Sinos cluster painted the following picture:

> During early 2000s everything collapsed, we began to work ten
> times less. Some firms produced millions of pairs; a company
> like Reichert could produce 180,000 pairs a day! The demand was
> huge, and they had the capacity to expand production rapidly, via
> outsourcing to smaller units. There was a gold rush [*febre de ouro*]
> with exports. The '80s were the best: credit was cheap, the dollar
> was high, it was a fairy tale. Brazil was a wonderland. Then the
> factories closed, there was a horrible surplus of workforce, nobody
> knew what to do. Novo Hamburgo is a ghost town!

Lucas—the technician who took me to see Victor—personalized the temporal narrative, discussing the ebbs and flows of his own trajectory and the fate of those close to him. He talked about how during the apex of the export era he had actually owned a factory, and how by the time of our sojourn together into his daily routine, although he had already formally retired, he continued working as a technician, pushed both by his love of shoes—"once you smell the glue, you are hooked for life," he declared—as well as by economic need. He described how well he was still doing in comparison to some of his former colleagues, who "used to make US$15K a month" and now call him to ask him for work.

As much as these narratives have a common structure—the subject of the doing, a temporal arc with a clear normative division between past and present—they have a second commonality: they were all uttered at work-places that had been physically affected by the export boom, so the pride instilled by the continued work contrasted heavily with the reality of the material landscape and the remaining infrastructure. If it is true, as Ingold (1993, 152) contends, that the landscape tells a story, what kind of history does it reveal? Denilson's office, for instance, seemed stopped in time, a combina-tion of details from the 1970s and the 1990s, the paint on the brick wall faded green. His room had old machinery—so much so that students were unable to work with synthetic materials and polyurethane instead of leather—mixed with the new. The traces of the boom could also be seen in the use of the Braddock machine for measuring, which followed the standards of the US instead of the "Paris point" that was used for shoe sizes for the local industry.

The place where I met Victor makes the disparity even more salient, as we stopped by in a vacant lot to meet with him. I was at first confused as to why Lucas had stopped his car there, but the empty space helped Victor to work the heavy machinery he had invested money in to develop the matrixes. He did not need a whole factory to do this, not even a small workshop, just a space where to store the orders of shoe matrixes that would then be picked up by his clients. The unkempt character of the space—a combination of dry barren land, barely grown abandoned plants, and some mud, located in a nondescript residential neighborhood—made the contrast with the archi-tectural infrastructure of the past even more salient.

The previous paragraph previews in method and content the principal contribution of the chapter: to give a full account of how is the life of those who inhabit a world they perceive as degraded, and the push and pull be-tween nostalgia and melancholia. Historical sociologist George Steinmetz (2008) mobilizes the Freudian distinction between melancholia and nos-talgia to analyze the contrasting responses of white people in Detroit and Namibia, respectively, in making sense of the ruins of a more powerful past. Ruins work as evocative objects, and the memory regimes they invoke must take into account historical context, he argues. Detroit inhabitants engaged nostalgically with the industrial rubble of the automotive industry, whereas white Namibians oriented toward the leftovers of the German colonial past with melancholy, acknowledging the end of the colonial relationship while longing for its restoration.

The case of Novo Hamburgo seemed in between, with specialized workers who neither have fully mourned the passing of the industry nor are thinking of a potential restoration; rather, they are focusing on how to make do with the scraps of what has been left behind. The result was a leaner industry in which the cost of labor was less important and skill more salient; it operated in a more craft-like way for a higher-end market, with more expensive final prices than what was produced in the export era. Every exchange was an opportunity to lament what was and compare it to what is, inhabiting a liminal world in which some of the dispositions of the past were restored—the skill, the hard-work ethic of the *gaucho* way of doing things—while others could not give meaning to the degraded landscape they lived among. In the remaining sections of the chapter I disentangle this proposition in detail by showing the multiplicity of shoe-related spaces in different states of conservation or disappearance, and the variegated strategies (are they ruins, monuments, objects of affection, plain rubble?) that subjects have used to memorialize the past and make sense of what is and is not there.

WALKING THROUGH CREATIVE DESTRUCTION, OR THE CANUDOS NEIGHBORHOOD

No section of the city had been as physically affected by the demise of the shoe industry as Canudos, a central neighborhood next to the old core of the city. When with Francieli, my research assistant during my time in Brazil, we started putting together maps with all the detailed info she had solicited from the shoemakers' union about factory closures; it became evident that it was worthwhile to walk around the space and try to experience and document it ourselves. During two afternoons we spent time not just walking around but also taking pictures of what had become of those former factories. The landscape alternated between those spaces that had been converted for other uses; those that were still in place but had closed, pointing to a time that had ceased to be; or had simply been erased from the geography. The geography of closures showed us how, in a radius of less than eight miles, over thirty factories had closed between the 1990s and the late 2010s, though most of them were gone by 1996 (see figure 6.2). In Canudos, we were able to identify thirteen factories that had closed within one mile of each other (see figure 6.3).

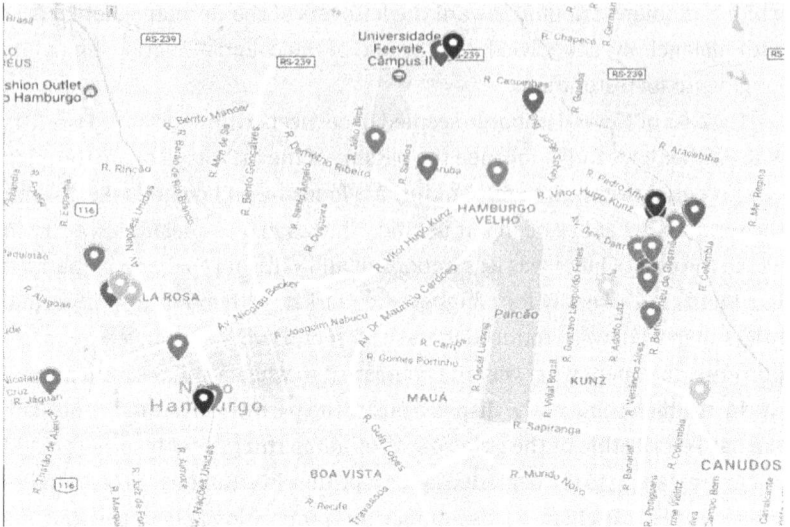

Figure 6.2. Map of closed factories in Novo Hamburgo.

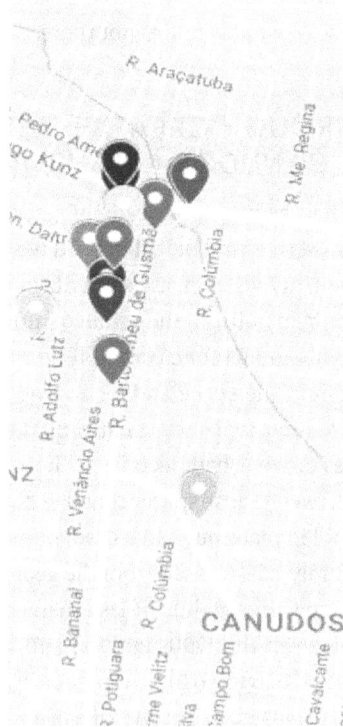

Figure 6.3. Map of closed factories in the Canudos neighborhood.

Figure 6.4. The former factory of Calçados Eneri.

Figure 6.5. Inside detail of the school's basement, where Calçados Eneri used to be.

The first stop in our landscape of debris was the building that formerly hosted Calçados Eneri, a medium-sized factory that had been established in 1968 and closed by 1996. Much like in other places, the last factory on record was already a palimpsest established over preexisting firms, Sucessora and Ecel. The factory, which had four hundred workers when it closed, sits on a relatively busy commercial corner on the border between Canudos and Novo Hamburgo Velho. The structure had been recycled and turned into a school—which my research assistant's then-fiancée had attended—and a

Figure 6.6. The former factory of Calçados Kinkol, now a Pentecostal church.

Figure 6.7. An inside detail of the church.

series of small shops for décor and clothing. Even then, there were some marks of the past, beyond the obvious regimented and nondescript look of the structure. We took pictures of the basement of the building and found—in what probably had been a deposit for materials—a piece of paper attached to one of the walls that read *Camurca* (suede), indicating what had been stored there over twenty years ago.

If the use of a former factory as a school is not surprising, given the architectural homological family resemblance between institutions focused on surveillance, discipline, and productivity, its conversion into a church while counterintuitive, makes a lot of sense when taking into account the expansion of Pentecostalism in Brazil—the most Catholic country in the world. Pentecostal churches do not need the elaborate décor of their more-established counterparts, and priesthood is usually achieved locally, with small groups splitting from previous congregations and establishing their own temples elsewhere. The pictures that preceded are from what used to be Calçados Kinkol, another medium-sized factory, which had four hundred workers and closed in 1992; we also encountered two other, smaller factories on our walk that had been turned into Evangelical churches. The detail from *Encontros de Fé—snapped* through a broken window—gives us a view of the inside: white plastic chairs sprawled like the foam on a sea of gray.

Seeing factories turned into schools and churches is of course more unexpected than seeing them become factories for other commodities (like the Tramontina cutlery factory that occupied a part of what used to be one of the largest shoe-making establishments in the area) or just used as warehouses for other industries (this happened to Calçados Graziela, a small factory that became a deposit for paving machinery).

The case of Irmaos Muller is telling about the transformation of the shoe industry in the area. It was one of the largest factories; before closing in 1995 it had a thousand employees. The property was by the time of our sojourn occupied by a smaller company that specialized in a chemical-treatment plan for plastic components for shoemaking. Instead of a large factory composed of both skilled and cheap labor, which was fully vertically integrated, what we have is a specialized firm that is part of the supply chain for cheaper domestic shoes, dependent on PVC instead of leather. The space that follows embodies even more the Brazilian shoe industry's role in the global division of labor and expertise.

In chapter 4 I discussed the fitting practices of an export company that does line building in Campo Bom and Dongguan, with meetings in New York by designers and the fitting done on alternating feet by the owner's wife. I mentioned that the office where they meet in South Brazil is located in what used to be a factory. Elaborating further on that allows us to see the transformation of the local industry, and to better understand what had been left behind in terms of work routines. The company set up shop in the factory in 2006 to export a higher-end line, only to have to fold by 2009, while keeping its sample-room operation in South China as its main development hub. They've organized the structure of the factory into a hub of multiple coworking spaces, a creative hub like those that exist in many capitals of the Western world. Given the company's prestige, my arrival for an interview with the head designer—to an address at which I was hoping to find, if not a full-fledged factory, at least a sample room—was not as shocking as the vignette that opens this chapter, but it's close enough. The only recognizable sign of a shoe company existing there, paradoxically, were the statues of Buddhist deities on the desk at the waiting room. I had seen them both in China and in export offices in Brazil, as icons to ask for prosperity, and the odd marker—here—to the shoe-related character of the nondescript space.

The firm had kept a big part of its expert labor locally, who engaged in some of the routines of their counterparts in New York (like shopping trips or assistance at international fairs) while working on producing shoes for a relatively higher market segment than what is usually produced in Dongguan. In its China offices—as I'll show later in the chapter—they have established a team of Brazilians, a beachhead operation that resembles the work the firm used to do in Campo Bom but had stopped being economically viable. And I'm not referring here to a production factory—which they subcontract for large-scale runs—but rather to the sample room where they develop their own prototypes and samples. The office in Brazil consisted literally of ten people when I stopped by, which was consistent with other trading companies I visited in the area.

Marxist geographers have used the Schumpterian term "creative destruction" to refer to how capitalism revolutionizes the economic structure of a society from within, destroying the old one, creating a new one. One of the ways this can be seen is in the new uses found for the structures of the older economy. The investment in fixed assets has been signaled by David Harvey (1995), for instance, as a way out the periodic crisis of overaccumulation, as capital gets spatially fixed in buildings and infrastructure. This "spatialization of capital" can in the future, though, constitute a limit, instead of the crisis displacement that it helped to generate at first, since it freezes productive forces into a fixed spatial form. Given the drive to relocate to more advantageous places periodically, the intersection between the destructive power of the international and territorial division of labor and the attempt to fix production in infrastructure can be best observed in the built environment—or, as I called it earlier, the resulting landscape of debris. The follow-up to a golden era of infrastructural expansion resulted in myriad strategies for reusing preexisting structures, but it can also turn the area into rubble or, when memorialized, into ruins.

A SHADOW YOU SOON WILL BE

In the previous section I showed spaces that were refitted and as such resignified, given a new purpose and function. But what happens with "stuff" that has stopped behaving like an object, legible from the outside, without a clear set of indications about how to be read, and has not yet become a new thing?

This liminal space of indecision, between an identity that was and one that has not arrived yet, can be explored by touring places like Calçados Padova. By the time of our visit, Francieli and I could not find information on whether the factory was open or closed, though from the outside it looked as if it wasn't engaged in production, hidden under bars in its windows and padlocks in the doorways. A peek inside revealed probably one of the most poetic visual pieces from this research: a place reduced to its minimum expression, still open but in-between human labor and nature, frozen in time. The lasts were all boxed, waiting to be picked up; the scene showed the absence of people, of work. Scholars of how ruination happens have all underscored that the ruin is a conceptual invention of modernity, presented as a break from the past, marking in the preexisting built environment eras that had ended and thus had to be explained and foretold. Understanding ruination as an activity—as a process that hinges on the destruction of past ways of living and their memorialized recreation—is a powerful way to highlight the active forces of destruction, be it from capitalism, development, or the force of empires (on this see, for many different contexts and historical periods: Gordillo 2014; Stoller 2008, 2013; Hell 2018; Keane 2003; Steinmetz 2008; Zukin 1993; Tsing 2005; Grandin 2009). In this case—given Padova's frozen-in-time yet not memorialized character—it has the ability to, as Simmel (1958) wrote when discussing *The Ruin*, "make us think of the past that could have been and the future that never took place."

Calçados Centenario was one of the key large factories in Novo Hamburgo, with over 1,300 workers at its apex. Built in 1936, it was in the core of Canudos, and one of the most fundamental pillars of its development as a spatial nexus

Figure 6.8. Calçados Padova.

Figure 6.9. The former factory of Calçados Centenario.

for shoe production. Its significance was such that its existence was memorialized in a square (Praça Centenario) inaugurated in March 1993 by the city prefect. The square was at the same intersection of the roads that also crossed the factory, and it served to mark not only the factory's existence but also its importance for the golden era of shoemaking.

The picture in figure 6.9 shows the state of Calçados Centenario in July 2016, across from the square built to memorialize the factory and allow workers to take a break. Ironically, the factory closed in 1994, only one year after the inauguration of the park with its name. In 2019 the property was demolished after two decades of being abandoned with padlocks on the entrance—padlocks that became every time more ridiculous as the building deteriorated enough that was slowly giving way to nature; it stopped being a bounded entity needing to be defended from the outside. It took over two decades of decay for the structure to look as it does in the image, while being surrounded by a square where people took their kids after school, a bus stop, and a few small commercial shops. Pairing the—albeit moderate—activity of the street with the slowly corroding factory gives us a better understanding of why, to quote Stoller (2013), we turn to ruins to know what people are "left with": to what remains, to the aftershocks of development, to the material and social afterlife of structures, sensibilities, and things.

But some traces of the golden era are harder to find. They are neither monuments nor ruins. The most confusing part of our walk was when Francieli and I were trying to find Calçados Fibra, a factory of 1,200 workers that closed in 1995 after its owners decided to invest in real estate instead. We walked around for a little while looking for it, trying to guess whether a large house slightly off from where we had placed it in the map was it, if the construction site across from the house was actually where Fibra had been. We also asked a couple of people who were walking with their groceries, but they had no idea—the area was mostly residential. We finally found it after a few workers from the neighboring construction plant asked us what were we looking for and confirmed to us that the large, empty lot full of weeds we had been dancing around was indeed its actual location.

Argentinean anthropologist Gastón Gordillo (2013, 2014) has coined the term "rubble" to refer to those instances in which we can see the material sedimentation of destruction; the term deglamorizes ruins by showing the work of destruction and construction next to the word "heritage." If the empty lot of Calçados Fibra was an obvious instance of traces that have all but disappeared, there was another hidden-but-pervasive presence in the Novo Hamburgo environment. In the newspapers, in official records of the municipality, and in expert documents, there were reports of large amounts of leather still sitting underground (Penteado 2011). If this was a priori an environmental issue, it affected the lives of local poor inhabitants even more, as it made impossible the establishment of low-income housing, on a project that had been promoted by the municipality. Those most punished by the industry leaving town—Novo Hamburgo is a city that depends on

Figure 6.10. The lot where Calçados Fibra used to be.

remittances for almost 70 percent of its economy, with rampant crime and unemployment—were at the same time those most penalized by its history, the city's sedimentation operating almost as geological layers that hinder the architectural foundations of a potentially better present.

Locals are trapped between all these ghosts from the past, equally presence—as in the obvious case of ruins and buildings with new uses—and absence—the traces that are there only to call our attention to what once was. Some of them lend themselves better to being memorialized, becoming an identity that can be mobilized by a museum or become capital to construct the present and the future as anchored in the representation of a golden local past. Some others are just debris, though, impossible to be integrated as memory and ruins.

Thanks to object-centered sociologies we know that things are an active part of the explanation; as with dead labor, previous interpretations are already incorporated into the object, interacting in affording or constraining meaning. To put it in pragmatist parlance, objects are the felicity conditions of certain interpretations. We can see this in how previous interpretations aim to capture new objects, attempting to reconstruct—at least partially—the older equivalent chain that was used to frame what they did and how they thought about it. So how do locals actually make sense of this past? How do people still working in the industry talk (and act) about the export industry in its apex in their everyday lives? And is there any relationship between the

tension between ruin and rubble and the differentiated work of remember-
ing encompassed by nostalgia and melancholia? The remaining sections aim
to reconstruct the variegated regimes of remembrance under which *Novo
hamburguenses* reconstruct their experiences.

OF PIONEERS AND DEBRIS

I believe there are some things we've lost forever.
In fact, I believe we are more the things we've lost
than the ones we actually have.

Milena Busquets, *También esto pasará*

With schools, churches, studios, and factories reutilizing the spaces that
would have otherwise been rubble, the material traces of past *Novo ham-
burguense* life was slowly erased. The very memory of its history, one could
argue, was gradually effaced. How do people cope with a landscape made
of debris and rebuilt and repurposed infrastructure? How does the past in-
form their understanding of space? And what preexisting official structures
ensured that the history of the export boom was not totally lost? And among
those in the industry, what are the strategies to make use of this history as a
legacy? The following section shows the variegated landscape of mnemonic
material practices and spaces and how they communicate the particular relationship of skilled workers with respect to Brazil's future and their personal
roles within the global shoe industry.

While I talked to multiple officers, managers, developers, consultants,
and technicians in Brazil, I enjoyed cab drivers' reactions to my presence,
always assumed to be about the *industria calçadista*. They gave me the pulse
of what the industry meant for people no longer in it—its past importance,
ghostly overwhelming presence, and the liminal character of its unfinished
disappearance. On one particular trip, as a driver took me down Joaquim
Nabucco—one of the city's main thoroughfares, where a lot of developers and
factory owners who had made their monies during the export boom of the
1980s and 1990s lived in gated towers—he insisted on discussing his life as a
factory worker. He remembered when there were so many factories competing for bodies that scouts would camp out in front of where he worked trying
to entice him to work elsewhere, or to "steal" him (*o roubar* as he said)—as
well as the many spots where factories used to be located. He pointed during
that trip to a *loja de lujo* (small luxury shopping center), mentioned a small

church, and made sure I looked toward an unmarked space he said was a factory that had closed down. He later mentioned that the old factory for Azaleia, an iconic domestic brand, had been abandoned since 2014.

Every taxi ride—since I was taking them to go to a few of the places still extant for the industry—was at the same time the chance for an almost automatic map of places that had been. A mnemonic trigger that signposted the feeling of loss and relative grandeur that pervaded the *Capital Nacional Do Calçado*—as the entrance to the town from the parkway announced. The architect Aldo Rossi (1982) gave the name "object of affection" to those spaces that could involuntarily work as the traumatic marker of loss. Following the Benjaminian distinction between the work of recollection and of involuntary memory, Rossi highlights how those fragments—the closed factory, the church, the mini-mall—are not just an amalgamation of debris. Rather, they indicate a certain order: the fragments are always fragments *of something*; they refer to a lost feeling of wholeness, its form still obliquely remembered.

In contrast to the involuntary shock of the past mobilized in each encounter during fieldwork, the city itself pointed in different ways toward how it has been built on the legacy of the shoe industry. The name of The Pioneers (*Os Pioneiros*) appears on street signs all over the historical center and the Canudos neighborhood. Regardless of the name on a corner sign, we are constantly reminded of how the history of the city is at the same time the history of shoemaking and its associated enterprises. It is not just the names—after all, maybe the current local population does not have to know who Nicolau Becker, Victor Hugo Kuntz, August Jung, or Pedro Adams Filho were—but that each street sign is accompanied by a legend underneath that makes sure those reading it know that the person the street was named after was "a pioneer of the shoe industry" (Pedro Adams Filho), "the pioneer of tanneries" (Nicolau Becker), or a "leader in wholesale trade" (Julio Kuntz).

Unlike other places where experiences get memorialized after the fact, once history has achieved closure and is reflected upon, most of the street names here were chosen in parallel to the growth of the industry, to celebrate the city and shoemaking as concurrent phenomena. For instance, the Avenue named after Pedro Adams Filho already had that name by 1936; uniting the main square with the town hall, cementing the symbolic anchoring of the most important spaces in the city through one of "the Pioneers." The official mnemonic intersection between Novo Hamburgo and *calçadistas* continued over time, with the *Monumento a Sapateiro* opening in 1979, during the apex of the export boom (see figure 6.11). The monument, designed by renowned

Figure 6.11. *Monumento a Sapateiro*, sculpture by Flávio Scholles.

local artist Flávio Scholles, is a celebration of factory workers. Each of its six humanlike figures is crowned by a watch, explicitly representing the days of the week they worked to make shoes. As can be observed in the picture, the work of art stands next to the main train station, which links the city with Porto Alegre, the capital of the Rio Grande do Sul region. Whether walking the main thoroughfare or arriving via train or by car, it is impossible to escape the official identification between city and *calçado*.

If monuments and street signs are part of the paraphernalia that makes sure we understand the representational power of memory (against the landscape of debris), then the logic that binds past and present—less through unexpected bodily sensations and more through a clear narrative of how the city and industry go together (or went together?)—is clarified at the Museum (*Museu Nacional do Calçado*). The museum, established in 1999 and located within Fevale University, links the pioneers of the industry with the virtuoso skills of craftsmen, but it also emphasizes the design component that modernized shoemaking and highlights how the work of design put the industry on the map and made a nationally recognized endeavor out of what had been a regional affair. The story that it presents of its past is one that makes sure the audience understands what is unique about it, and what from it can be projected into the future. The museum reveals the Janus like character of modern temporality, looking both backward and forward. On the one hand, it draws heavily on the origins of the industry; on the other, it indulges in

Figure 6.12. The atelier of Nestor Erni Dullius, reproduced at the Museu Nacional do Calçado, Novo Hamburgo.

modern visions of life, showing how the designs by the *Novo hamburguenses* masters were worn by personalities such as the "queen of Brazilian TV" and the wife of writer Jorge Amado, as well as—or more importantly—by the *paulista, gaucha* and *carioca* elites.

As in every other mnemonic device about the history of the city and of shoemaking, Pedro Adams Filho played a central role. His presence is memorialized by showing the key to his famed factory, the *Fábrica de Calçados Sul RioGrandense*. Recall that he worked to modernize the industry by hiring Italian technicians, established one of the first tanneries, and pushed for the construction of an electricity company to bring power to the factory and the city as a whole. In all of his enterprises the names Hamburgo and Rio Grande were prominent.

A central piece of the exhibit is a full (albeit small) atelier, in which we can observe all the tools of a craftsman going by his trade. I inquired about the workshop's precedence and importance and was told by one of the museum attendants that this was the odd case in which they had a complete tool set; the family of Nestor Erni Dullius had donated the collection in 1959 after the closure of his firm. The piece makes the craftsman—with the sketching, sampling, cutting, modeling, and sewing operations all at his hands' reach—a synecdoche of the work done at the factory (which in some cases had over a thousand workers) and reaccentuated the link between the trade and German ethnicity. On the wall next to it, the museum also introduces to the audience a work of art functioned as another synecdoche-like, pastoral representation of how shoes were made: *The Shoemaker* by Ariadne Decker (which, as we'll see, later traveled from the museum walls to current workshops, development firms, and sample rooms).

The last picture from the Museu is of a shoe designed by Ruy Chaves, a local designer who rose to prominence in the 1960s and is considered—with others like the Spaniard Carrasco Mena and the Italian De Nicola—the "masters" (*os mestres*), and presented as such by the museum, the local association of shoe producers (FENAC), and the press, all of whom are seen as modernizing design for the industry. The indication of the last names and their precedence highlights the linkage between ethnicity and the elision of

Figure 6.13. Shoe by Rui Chaves, Museu Nacional do Calçado Novo Hamburgo.

the "Brazilian" dimension of what was accomplished. In all of the stories, the bond is built between the local and the cosmopolitan character of those involved in the industry, with nary a reference to other shoemaking clusters like Franca in São Paulo, indicating always the jump over the national scale, celebrating the craft's regional and foreign character. The centrality of design and the "upgrading" capabilities of the local cluster were underscored by the twentieth-anniversary museum show celebrating the pioneers—yet again that word—of design in Novo Hamburgo, which featured the *mestres* in full (including Carlos Gilberto Simon, another local modernizer less-present in the permanent collection).

RE-PRESENTING THE PAST AS COMPETITIVE ADVANTAGE

> I also wonder about the invisible ghost museum lurking in its margins, with vast halls full of all the objects people couldn't stand to part with.
>
> **Leslie Jamison, "The Breakup Museum"**

Looking outside the official museum—as Leslie Jamison asks us to do—resulted indeed in a second, invisible ghost museum, full of objects that referred explicitly to the golden past when trying to present what was unique about the local industry in the global context. What I found instead of the critical power of ruins—emphasizing its destructive and discontinuous character—was a regressive engagement that presented the future and the past in a continuum and the heroic figure of the craftsman as the comparative advantage the Southern Brazilians still had over China. So, for instance (see figure 6.14), the entrance to a shoe company I'll call Guerra Shoes had an old sewing machine welcoming visitors, and above it the same painting by Ariadne Decker I had seen at the museum, as well as a second work of art by the local painter called *Sapatos Bandeira—*, part of a larger series presenting shoes in a colorful way, emphasizing their texture and depth.

If the affiliation with the past via tools and art made sense at a small company, run by two men in their thirties, starting from scratch (still with a family investment from one's father, who had been involved in the export boom), as a card to present themselves for what they did not have, I was surprised to see a replica of *The Shoemaker* painting at the Dongguan office of the firm that had closed its factory in Rio Grande do Sul and made it into a shared workspace. Moreover, according to the office manager, the painting had not been brought from Brazil; rather, its specifications were sent to Hong Kong's

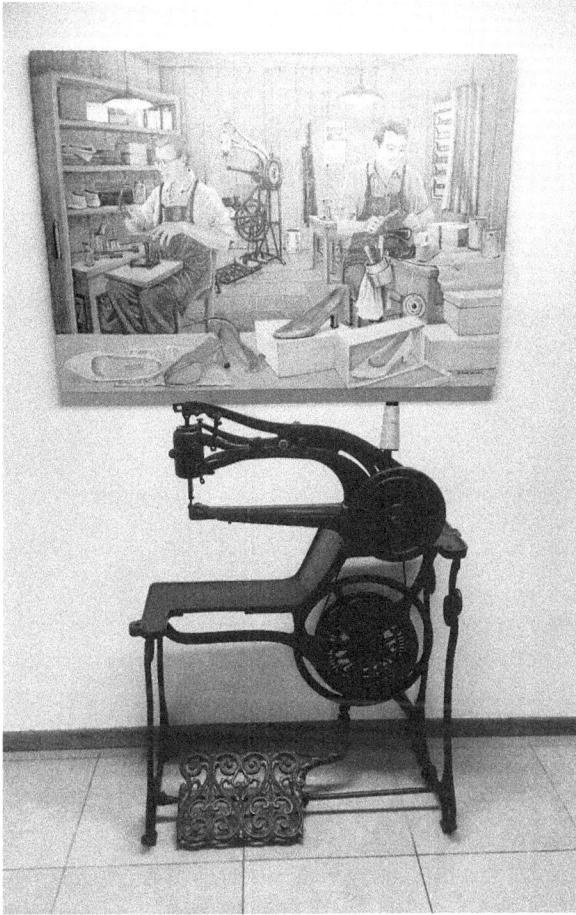

Figure 6.14. *Sapatos Bandeira* by Ariadna Decker.

Stanley Market to make a copy to be displayed in the South China office. So once again we witness the paradox of a firm that had all but emptied out its productive capabilities in its home country, designed its collections thanks to the encounters of the line builders from Novo Hamburgo and Dongguan in New York and on shopping trips to Europe, and had its main sample room in China, but memorialized itself through art, establishing a nostalgic affiliation to the craftsman trope.

The memorialized character of the craftsman past of course was not just a monopoly held by this painting; it morphed in other firms into other objects and media. For instance, at the largest shoe-ornament company in the area

Figure 6.15. Reproduction of *Sapatos Bandeira* at a development office in Dongguan, China.

(in Sapiranga), the company's myth of origin in a small toolshed in the 1970s is celebrated both in the actual shed where the company started—which has been rebuilt, refurbished, and repurposed as a break room for workers—as well as in a painting by the entrance that commemorates the small first shop that gave way to the multinational company specializing in metallic adornments. The company also celebrated itself having commissioned multiple artworks made with some of the materials it produces.

Some other times the reference was not to an abstract shoe-man from the past, or to the firm's own origin story, but to the building where the firm was located. That was the case with one of the design studios developing shoes for export to the higher end of the US market—as well as lines for the kind of market studied in this book, usually complementary shoes for an existing collection in need of a particular item. They advertised their location in a house classified as national historical patrimony. Once you arrived at the mansion, you could see the images of the many traditional (German) families who had occupied the property. The brochure that went along with the display explained "You can take a person out of history, but you can't take history out of a person," for the reader-customer to understand that while the studio had left another well-known property, the one they had moved to also had a rich history, dating all the way back to its construction in 1875 that culminated in its architectural restoration and designation as a historical monument.

In all of these examples, the nostalgic use of the past was peripheral to design, but what happens when we observe how the past rears its head during the execution of design and development? The section that follows details one case in which the past inhabits the present all the way from the business ideas and trade practices that constitute the workshop to the last sequin.

PAST FUTURES

On my first full day in Novo Hamburgo I went to the small workshop of a contact I had made thanks to a local anthropologist who had sent out a request for shoe people to be interviewed for this research project. Much like the other Brazilians I became involved with during fieldwork, the people who responded were interested in talking to a "professor from the United States" and performing their story for me. When I arrived at the first address of my stay—on Rua Carioca—I did not yet know much about the city and the area, which alternated small shack-like urbanizations with patches of grass, recalling for me a derelict area, equal parts culture and nature, much as I had witnessed in Dongguan. But instead of the city invading the countryside—as I thought in my multiple forays into South China—I thought in this case of nature slowly reappearing in between the spaces that "development" had failed to fully convert. Inside an unassuming stucco yellow house with red metallic sliding doors, I was brought into an unexpected counterpoint to its surroundings: a world of skill on a small scale.

As soon as I arrived and introduced myself, Vinicius—the designer for his own eponymous brand—quickly explained that what they were doing there wasn't at a mass scale (as he had done when working for Umbro, Havaianas, or the local subcontractor for Puma) but was rather inscribing himself in a tradition that was a hundred years old. Vinicius was in his mid-thirties, with a blond pompadour, a hipster beard, and skinny jeans, and he told me he had the idea of creating his own brand to take advantage of the heritage of "premium" Brazilian shoes after the "tsunami" that engulfed all factories post-2001. The shop took advantage of the local ecology of tanneries—they worked with one located in nearby Estancia Velha that supplied the calf and cow suedes, the cow leather, and the goat lining—to make the whole product in-house, including the elusive lasts. The brand had an office in Porto Alegre—which I visited a couple of times—where he commercialized a bespoke catalogue of handmade shoes for both men and women. By the time of our meeting he had already had moderate success doing this; his shoes were

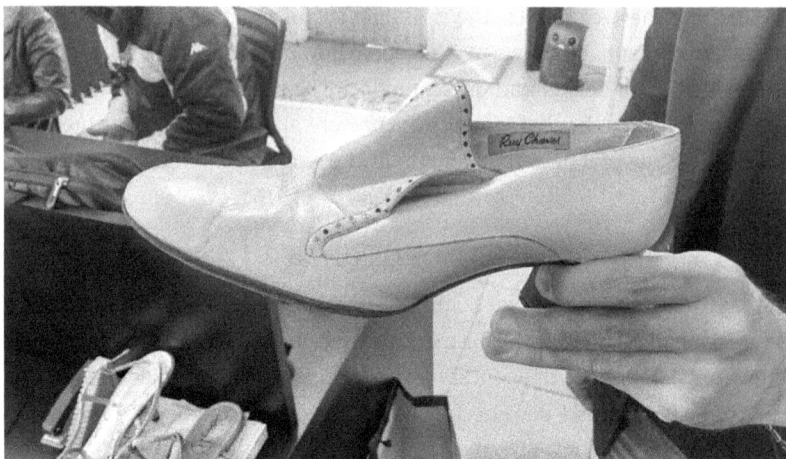

Figure 6.16. A Ruy Chaves shoe from 1967, held by Vinicius in Novo Hamburgo.

being worn by the models for one of Brazil's designers in the Paris Fashion Week of 2016.

A bespoke catalogue is predicated upon the individualized measurement of each customer, so it was not surprising when Vinicius and his right-hand man Marcelo—another thirtysomething designer from SENAI, who had decided to come work with his friend as a scale modeler—asked me to take off my left shoe and sock to measure my foot. The beginning of my fieldwork in the Vale dos Sinos area was a performance of sorts, but one that, given the history of the workshop and of Vinicius's family—his dad also worked at the atelier—made a lot of sense. Besides his father there were other veterans of the industry there: the stitcher, for instance, had worked in it for the last thirty years; the technician since 1969; the sole maker since 1980. The shop replicated traditional production dynamics, at the scale of pre–export boom companies like the one recreated on the museum. Twelve people worked in artisanal fashion—all but one had worked before with the designer at a larger company—in generating a final product via a process very similar to what I had witnessed in multiple iterations at different sample rooms around the world, with sketchers, pattern- and last-makers, technicians, and finishers all in two interconnected rooms, using one set of specialized machines for cutting, sewing, gluing, and sawing.

If this would have been enough to point at how the shop replicated some of the practices by the *mestres* from the 1960s, the connection became explicit when I was shown a shoe one of the technicians was working on: a Ruy Chaves shoe owned by a sixty-five-year-old woman who had worn it to her sweet sixteen, who wanted her daughter to get married wearing a new version of it. The technician was attempting to replicate the Roger Vivier heel, to work on the rubber sole with the procedures created by Chaves himself, aiming to reproduce even the placement of ornaments to the last sequin.

Vinicius's *horizon of expectation*—to use a concept by German historian Reinhart Koselleck (2004) that referred how we think about the future— actually looks toward the past, and what we have accumulated, incorporated, and made present from it.[3] Past and future appeared once again linked at a moment in which labor was not cheap enough to reestablish the past conditions and in consequence the export output, but in which the best craft practices—learned from the modernizing generation of designers from the 1960s—were still available and served as the horizon of a potential future for the local industry. The paradox of the link between past and future aiming toward the consumer's melancholic use of nostalgia[4] was that it all but erased what others have emphasized when discussing the experience of shoemaking in Novo Hamburgo: it almost lamented the export boom and its consequences, placing instead the golden era in the exact moment before everything exploded in terms of scale.

Others who were weary of the export scale (and of the experience of migrating to China) reestablished their place in the world emphasizing family— kinship had been, after all, central in the narrative of the gaucho craftsman—as the main frame through which to organize their new place in the shoemaking world and to connect to a past that no longer exists. I discuss them in the next section; the purpose of featuring all this variation is to show the superimposed and sometimes competing cohabitation of multiple forms of nostalgia in one region and trade, and the multilayered materials through which the past is made visible (or, in some cases, simultaneously erased and made visible).

FAMILY AS MEMENTO?

The answer is simple, like every generation before, we live in the aftermath.

Steven Jackson, *Rethinking Repair*

By the end of my time in Novo Hamburgo I went to a factory mostly focused on the domestic market. Like most of my life-story interviews, this one took place at the actual workplace. The conversation itself felt like a

classic instance of what happens once you are slowly closing down the recollection of data phase, as it saturated and confirmed most of the themes I
had figured out from previous encounters. The two men I interviewed—Rafi
and Eric—were in their early thirties, eager to show me how together they
had run the company created by their respective fathers, and much like in
previous instances of this research, they also shared their view of the region's
past and future in the industry. The dialogue was very much routine until
one of them (unprompted by me) mentioned that they had been "brought
up in the factory." They then asked if I wanted to see some pictures. Soon
after, the table of their meeting room, which had the name of the firm on it,
was covered with photos.

The set told a compelling story, one in which the relationship between
their fathers (who had at first named their company using the beginnings of
each other's names) had slowly become the history of the company, through
multiple iterations in different buildings. More importantly, it included pictures of a younger Rafi and Eric: for example, an image of all the workers
in the company, taken when they were still teenagers and worked for the
company during the summers or on holidays—much like other locals in the
area, who had also started collaborating with their parents first. Later, when
he walked me through the sample-room floor, Rafi made sure to say hi to
everybody, introduce them to me, and say they were all "like family." Despite
this, the company had a second (and larger) factory in the Northeast, close to
Bahia, taking advantage of the cheaper labor costs there for the least qualified
parts of the development and production process. The end of the story was
one in which though their dads were still working—I managed to meet one
of them in my factory visit—the people in charge of the legacy were Rafi and
Eric, as director and CFO respectively.

If the images showed the family trope in full, making of the company, its
variegated locations and architectural manifestations, and the production-
floor sociability, they also achieved further contrast if we contrapose them
with what was not in there.

The set of pictures was telling for the density of history that it left out but
which was still present in Rafi's words. He explained to me how he had gone
to South China a few years earlier, thanks to his uncle, who was the director of
the developing office for a large US conglomerate. He felt isolated and alien-
ated while there, but more importantly, being in Dongguan allowed him to
formulate what the future would look like for him as a family member: would
he want his kids to grow up there? Unlike his uncle—"Senhor Roberto"—his

Figure 6.17. Impromptu family album at a small factory in Sapiranga.

father had decided to stay put and—instead of worrying about building a firm that could compete with the trading companies—decided to focus on the domestic market and slowly build up lower-tier export destinations, like neighboring Argentina and Paraguay, or countries in the Middle East. If the decision made economic sense, it seemed to also be the rationalization of Rafi's perception of what would happen to his family if they went to Dongguan. He described how much he was always in shock when his cousins from China visited: "Imagine all those blondes speaking in Mandarin!" (*loiros falando em chinese*). He had a small child and did not want his kid to be a stranger, like those cousins who came once a year full of gifts and dressed in top brands.

The experience of those in the Vale do Sinos can be best understood by thinking about part of the epigraph above: "that all generations live in the aftermath." And the sentence resonates with both the aftermath of a shock, that of the export trade, its boom, and the infrastructural consequences once it ended; as much as with the kinship dimension related to how generations think of themselves as coming after someone who was part of the same world, but who had a different experience within it. All but a couple of my interviewees came from families who were already in the industry. It was rarely the case—only for the older ones, who had migrated from the rural periphery to the factories—that parents did not try to get their children to work making shoes. As Rafi narrated, this started early on in life, when most of the interviewees were still in high school. The story that follows details how one family kept itself part of the shoe world at the same time that it withstood the impact of the export crisis, paradoxically managing to memorialize their own family—and the "pioneers" along the way. In doing so, I aim to also present yet another way the challenge of China was understandable through extended kinship.

Didi is in his early forties, but like many of the people from his cohort, he had by 2017 already almost twenty-five years of experience in the shoe world. His father had worked selling materials but wanted him to stay away from the industry, so much so that his first job was at a bank. Still, by 1993 (he was just 19) he had started selling leather soles for the domestic market. Soon after, in 1995, he found an ad in Novo Hamburgo asking for someone to sell bonded leather in China. Once the Taiwanese entrepreneurs moved into continental China, the business expanded so much that his business partner moved to Taipei to establish a continuous presence. The local trading companies had increased their demand greatly, given the transition in materials from synthetic to leather because of the presence of US buyers that slowly transitioned from South Brazil to South China when placing orders for the women's leather-shoe market.

Didi fondly remembered how sales were a combination of fax orders and taking a lot of shoe samples overseas to show the trading companies what could be done with the suede, pigskin, and other leather styles he commercialized. The growth of the firm paralleled the growth of Brazilian arriving to Dongguan after the Plan Real crisis of 1994. The apex of his work in South China was in 2001; he had already made inroads with big clients like the Palladium factory and had many friends—both from before and newly found expats there—but at the same time he had started worrying about having a family of his own, as well as about his relationship to his parents and two sisters. By 2002 he had decided to come back to the Vale do Sinos area: "Being in China made me blue," he recalls. The owners of the company where he worked sold it and the new bosses wanted him to live there full time. He wondered out loud, "What am I gonna have, a Chinese wife? Chinese children?

I liked life in Novo Hamburgo . . . so decided to look for materials to sell in Brazil." He started to seek what he could trade locally, and he structured his life so he could travel to China just twice a year.

Once he established a viable business model—he had a Brazilian business partner who stayed living first in Taipei and then in Dongguan, putting together what was an impressive stock—he celebrated being "a pioneer in bringing specialized materials to Brazil from China." If he had in the past exported the full range of leather products—soles, inner liners, full skins, bonded, suede—what he imported then were synthetics and, to a lesser extent, ornaments. If the former had been easier, given that in the 1990s China lacked tanneries, there had also been no secondary specialized services developed, no infrastructure in place. The transformation of where shoes exported to the US were made meant that dealing with materials in Brazil involved mostly the domestic market, since over 80 percent of what was being produced in Novo Hamburgo in the 2010s was for domestic consumption— Rafi and Eric's firm was among his clients, for instance.

The house where Didi's company had resided since 2005 was, like many of the others I've discussed, a historical building located in Hamburgo Velho, which housed the city's first water well. The firm was structured similarly to other trading companies: it had a line builder, presented trend reports to clients, traveled to Europe and the US to look at "originals," and received information through trend services with pictures from fashion shows and window displays. Their main Chinese office was in Dongguan, but slowly a lot of the materials were coming from the Shanghai area instead, since the Pearl River delta had become too expensive given the development of the electronics and furniture industries in the area. The storage of materials was done in nearby Dos Irmaos, where they had rented a portion—20,000 square feet—of a 180,000-square-foot warehouse that was used by factories to store materials for export. The products were entered not through the ports of Rio Grande do Sul, given the state's higher import tariffs, but rather through nearby Santa Caterina, which had only a 4 percent trade tax on items imported for commercialization, but not as finalized products.

As told, his story belonged to the same narrative frames I've used to analyze previous cases: being a pioneer is celebrated, even if for importing and stocking materials from abroad; the reuse of multiple spaces with a history in local shoemaking is emphasized; the flow from Brazil to China is reversed; and the kinds of materials Didi worked with, from the leather that has been the pride of gaucho craftsmen as the central component of a "good shoe" to the synthetics that have become key to the production for local consumption. It even included a reference to how family guided his decision to return to the country. The last five minutes of our conversation had a surprise, though, as Didi told me about his sisters, one of them probably the most important historian of the shoe industry in the Vale do Sinos area—the author of a book from 2005 I had been chasing, herself married to another scholar of *calçados*. His other sister was married to the editor of the main trade journal, *NH*, which I had consulted to better understand the local shoe world. As I celebrated the coincidence and asked for a copy of the book, I realized something else about the story: his family had actually been one of the founders of the modern period, his grandfather having owned the first shoe-transportation company in the region. His grandfather had died, so in the book—which included audio-visual material as a CD—the interviewee was his grandmother, memorializing what had been left behind through her.

What had started as a story about the loss of centrality of South Brazil versus South China—through the disruption brought by the aftermath of the export boom—had by the end become another plot that intertwined family, craft, and regional pride, marking their continuity over time—though in this case through different cultural objects than the most obvious pictures, street signs, or artistic representations. Didi's life also highlighted the many competing ways of narrating the *calçadista* past, the periodization of its golden era—was it the craftsmen of the early period, the modernizers who expanded the industry, or the entrepreneurs of the export boom?—as well as the interpretations of what was left from it, and the strategies to still find ways to belong in it. In the conclusion to this chapter, I elaborate thoroughly on this variegated mnemonic landscape.

CONCLUSION. *E OBRIGADO PELA OPORTUNIDADE DE CONTAR MINHA HISTÓRIA!*

How do we make sense of absences? Some authors study how they are created—the history behind them—whereas some scholars focus on the interpretation of absences, how people make sense of them, what from the past and the future is mobilized. Others try to fill those absences, explaining the new uses for what was erased or left behind. And a few others try to find in the absences the evidence of acts of power, many of those accounts presenting derelict sites and outmoded material culture to unmask the illusions of capitalism as progress.

Each one of these options results in different ways of interrogating the material landscape and our ways to remember it a priori; in combination, they juxtapose the multiple layers of history, the conflicting narratives of the past, and the common frames under which common references are elaborated. While some of the spaces, for instance, obey the logic of ruins or the fetishization of nostalgia, others have already been recycled, have another function and serve as a palimpsest, with history inhabiting them but no nostalgic attachments. Moreover, a few have simply reduced their intensity, latently maintaining what is necessary to be recognizable in identity and form, between a past that was and a potential that had many futures. All this occurs as ruins become memorialized in their conversion into monuments, street signs, or works of art. What we witnessed in Novo Hamburgo was a whole world that had collapsed, taking with it—to a certain extent but not fully—its names and identities, frozen still between absence and presence.

If the juxtaposition does justice to the heterogeneous character of what has been described, I also want to elaborate on the relationship between objects and styles of memorialization, and what we can say in consequence about how skill cathexis, melancholia, and nostalgia go together (or not). Given the extensive literature on the relationship between craft and self-hood (among them Polanyi 1962; Sennett 2008; Crawford 2009; O'Connor 2005; Ocejo 2017), I underreported the intense attachment shoe folks themselves described when talking about their love for what they do. The title of this section comes from the end of a life-story interview I conducted with Marcio, a technician in Dongguan, who after almost three hours of talking over dinner ended up thanking me for the opportunity to voice his life and find recognition in it.

For those convinced of the intimate linkage between who they are and what they do, what I witnessed was what—following Freud—scholars like Steinmetz (2008) or Hell (2018) have described as melancholia. This was particularly true of skilled workers abroad, who in establishing their geographical and temporal distance with the collapse of the industry had—paradoxically—found a strategy to not fully mourn it, constantly comparing their new circumstances and work routines to those when things were better in Novo Hamburgo. As we saw in the section on memories of the boom, this was also true of older skilled workers who in deciding to stay seemed to inhabit a world of specters, in between what had been and the new, more modest possibilities to continue being *calçadistas*. Relatedly, for those who decided to leave the industry (I interviewed a few people who had), exiting was a life-altering event that absolutely redefined their identities; as one of them exclaimed, "I don't want anything to do with shoes!"

Younger skilled workers in Novo Hamburgo, on the other hand, not only had a nostalgic relationship to a past they had barely witnessed, but in fact also used nostalgia almost as a productive inspiration, a force vector by which they related less to the history of abundance and excess of the export age, and more to the smaller scale of earlier times, the work routines attached to them, and the heroic character that went into creating that world. In creating their own new world, they did so by framing themselves with the tools—both figuratively and literally—provided by representations of the pre–export boom era, taking a page from the museum and other institutionalized commemorative settings. The content of this mourned memory is not so different from remembrance—the involuntary memory that assaulted here and there former unskilled workers who had made their peace with the end of their engagement with the industry but still were able to recall a past that—for them—definitely just was, it did not continue in time. Their recollection matched less the logic of ruins and monuments and more the logic of rubble, the nonglamorized spaces that once were and now are either something else—a church, kindergarten, mini-mall—or just detritus.

Understanding how things are relived after they are put apart is a great avenue for understanding different paths to attachment, as well to see what were the diverse elements assembled by the bundle "shoe made in Novo Hamburgo." The second part of this short conclusion synthesizes the chapter by highlighting and discussing which categories of things and people were linked and how they were bounded. In the preceding paragraphs I called attention to craft, but one of a particular kind, always described as "German." "German" is a stand-in for "migrant" (on multiple occasions interviewees and informants described themselves as German, Italian, or Portuguese); for the *colono* work ethic that preceded the industrialization of Novo Hamburgo, which resulted in family-run firms and in the domestic unit as the economic form of integration and socialization, as well as in a pastoral understanding of modernity in which—while people were working in factories—farms were repeatedly referenced. (The older generation of skilled workers all lived outside town, and those abroad were building their retirement houses in picturesque nearby Gramado or Canela.)[5]

But German craft was also a stand-in for a set of infrastructural routines, which included the idea of an integrated factory, with everything from design to production being conducted in-house regardless of the scale, from atelier to companies with multiple assembly lines, memorialized in a particular working tool in my fieldwork: the wooden last. Shoemaking also afforded particular lines of self-identification beyond the personal, allowing those involved to claim their non-Brazilian character in two different but complementary ways: through the regional gaucho character of their shoemaking lives, and via the cosmopolitan character (seen in references to countries with artisanal shoemaking traditions, like Portugal, Italy, and Germany) that is memorialized on street signs, at museums, and in everyday life in Novo Hamburgo and is easily reestablished in Dongguan, as seen in the examples of the Brazilian German and Italian eateries and markets in South China I described in the interlude.

If part of the impetus of the chapter was to show the relationship between care work and attachment—as seen at both the individual and the collective level when "shoe people" reflected on how they were morally and personally intertwined with the world of materials they loved and worked with—a second objective was to underscore what happens when we put globalization in the rearview mirror and disarticulate the narrative that thinks of it as only progress and encompassment. While previous chapters played with the idea of scale as something that can be put together (or disentangled), this section unsettled the most common narrative about how the global happens and what consequences it has. It disrupted the linear imaginary of globalization that associates it with progress and modernity by showing that globalization is not something that is happening, or that will happen, but something that *has already happened and is now gone*. What we have witnessed at Novo Hamburgo is, then, a powerful reminder of the *fragility of globalization*.

WHAT DID WE LEARN ABOUT GLOBALIZATION BY LOOKING AT SHOES?

Use-values must therefore never be treated as the immediate aim of the capitalist; nor must the profit on any single transaction. His aim is rather the unceasing movement of profit-making.

Karl Marx, *Capital: A Critique of Political Economy*

THE MULTIPLE SPEEDS OF GLOBALIZATION

The last empirical chapter of this book concluded with bodies and buildings as they were left behind in the search for a cheaper, unskilled workforce, and people struggled to even find ways to make sense of what had just happened. Some workers, recall, were rendered useless, and others were able to stay in place by working for higher-end markets, for which the cost of labor was less of an issue that would determine geographical choice. A few more followed capital to what they thought of as the antipodes of their world, taking advantage of the need for expert knowledge to develop what would later be produced.

US designers, Taiwanese managers, Brazilian technicians and fit models, and their Chinese counterparts had all learned to navigate a shifting world of disjunctures between competing (and sometimes complementary) speeds. *The Perfect Fit* has meandered between two different conversations to explain how and when some things move—be they people, finalized products, parts, templates, forms—or do not move. One conversation focused on the tension between capital and labor; the other one on disaggregating the latter—emphasizing instead the work and routines necessary to put together a shoe with a modicum of quality—and showing the disjuncture (and sometimes felicitous interlock) between the search for skill and the search for cheap labor.

The two different speeds involve very different components: one is composed of elaborate networks of design, development, and coordination, forming clusters along the way of specialized services and aiming to make knowledge "sticky" and, as such, harder to move. The other one—as exemplified by Novo Hamburgo's demise at the hands of national monetary policy—works by abrupt movement, and it becomes heavily dependent on those other, relatively close networks. When craft is made at a global scale, acute problems of delegation and control at a distance arise. The speed of development and of quality control differs from that of production. It's not that, to paraphrase Marshall Berman (1982) quoting Marx, "all that is solid melts into air." Rather, it's that new centers of production over time become secondary centers for command and control. The focus on the little routines, standards, technologies, devices, and infrastructure that take time to set up has been a fruitful if indirect avenue to better explain why capital can't move somewhere with cheaper labor immediately. And even though this book ended on the sad note of bodies trapped in space, unable to go elsewhere, scrutinizing embodied knowledge has been central to show how work and labor don't always go together.

What can be formalized at a distance? What can't be taken out of bodies to travel on its own? What elements from the informal, tacit, and corporeal kind of knowledge I discussed in the first two parts of this book can be moved independently of those whose body it inhabits? The emphasis on work has produced a somewhat different picture of globalization, one complementary to the exploitation of the factory and its surroundings. Rather than investigating the networks of a transnational capital class or the suffering of laborers on the assembly line, or of domestic or sex workers, this ethnography of designers followed the middle tiers creating the sinews of the global value-chain as materialized in the shoe. In looking at what happens next to the factory, we see not only another version of how production is replicated and moved from one place to another, but also the differential speeds at which different parts of the shoe assemblage can leave the tyranny of space behind. The levels of interdependence and integration eventually crystallize into infrastructural inertia (Hamilton and Gereffi 2009; Becker 1995; Deener 2017, 2020; Molotch 2002) that anchors—at least for some time—development, if not production, in place.

The crisis brought by COVID—as discussed in the preface—was another occasion to see infrastructural inertia in place, but on a different scenario. Designers had to work only via screens—since all nonessential travel was suspended—with technicians they did not know well and with whom they had not developed a working rapport, eliminating the co-present, face-to-face moment that was so important for adjusting the details of shoes in development (and for achieving the intimacy necessary to make designer and technician into a tandem). This also made the role of having the same fit model more central, while this actually happened less because of furloughs and people being confined at home. As a result, companies were rushed in their orders by clients, but were less certain about the quality of the final product; materials were shipped constantly to all sites for consultation in an endless exchange of parcels that led to confusion and delays; shipments were stuck for months in ports. On the personnel level, more Taiwanese entrepreneurs left the continent, and a few of my Brazilian informants decided to finally return home as well.

The Perfect Fit studied production beyond (or before) the factory, looking at design and development in the export market for mid-tier women's shoes. I looked at how designers worked on prototypes, imagined how shoes look in discarded materials and correct on paper; when unable to do the same with samples, designers need to make sure fit, look, and materials work perfectly. I also discussed how technicians work to reproduce shoes from other brands, although to do so they need an actual shoe to see how to produce a similar last, to give definitive shape to the shoe. *The Perfect Fit* likewise showed the work of patternmakers, who develop the patterns for the upper part of the shoe from the measurements on a sheet, as well as at the role fit models play in stabilizing the information that goes back and forth *and* how together with technicians they generate—from one body—a standard for shoes that will be followed by the general population. I then examined how that actual foot worked as the known reference among the multiple constituencies in charge of development.

Paying attention to little routines has been also a fruitful avenue to reveal not just the kinds of knowledge that can be moved or mobilized from one context to another but also how, in consequence, the embodied, tacit, and informal kinds of knowledge that Von Hippel (1994) has defined as "sticky"— costly to acquire, transfer, and use in a new location—can be replicated in the lower-value nodes of the chain. Studying the techniques to reproduce hard-to-formalize knowledge has helped us to see how tacit and embodied knowledge can be found in even the most rationalized or streamlined industries, as well as the difficulties for producing when there are no skilled functions close by. The focus on skills—on how they can be settled, black-boxed, and made to travel—also deters excessively teleological accounts of how development and production happen. It shows us how—following the dictum by Everett Hughes—things could have been otherwise. What would have happened if Taiwanese entrepreneurs had not made the jump to the continent? Moreover, what would the global story of shoemaking be if Brazilian factory owners had not joined US buyers in investing in South China, helping to upgrade via the export of skills what had theretofore been mostly an industry that made relatively cheap loafers, sandals, and sneakers?

A lot of studies of globalization have been inspired by the work of Karl Polanyi, the tension produced by marketization between economies, and the societies in which they are embedded, showing the perils of the decoupling between economy and society. This is also a Polanyian study, but I take as a source of ideas the work not of Karl but of his younger brother, Michael, one of the key figures to understand embodiment, tacit knowledge, and the reproduction of skill. While embodiment has been studied in the factory—either looking at the disposable bodies available for production or at the generative practices to make subjects anew as docile, subservient—it has been more of a background, taken-for-granted category, not a central part of the story that would explain how something of the scale of globalization can happen.

The Perfect Fit performs a classic ethnographic trick: it takes what has always and a priori been considered macro and inverts it, centering its explanatory power on the most micro element possible in the social sciences (i.e., embodiment). The intertwined power of infrastructure work and embodied skills means that we need to pay attention to the kinds of abilities that are learned face-to-face via apprenticeship, as well as to how this can happen at a distance. The book has shown how connoisseurship and standardization have a complicated and complementary relationship, unlike the one of opposition under which they are mostly conceptualized; the former is in many cases the condition of possibility of the latter.

THE CENTRALITY OF PERIPHERY

The focus on skill and problem-solving has been a key to helping us understand why Brazilians were hired to replace Taiwanese technicians, quality control, and production managers, opening the subsidiary question of how one craft tradition is replaced by another. It has also helped us to better understand why development has not (yet?) moved out of Novo Hamburgo, even if most local production happens in the Brazilian Northeast, and to forecast that development in China will probably stay in Dongguan for a few more years, even if 75 percent of production has moved into other parts of China and Southeast Asia.

The consequence of this is to rethink what we know about outsourcing, as something that does not operate in a vacuum, underscoring the accumulated embodied knowledge—stored in people, routines, buildings—as the epistemic culture (Knorr Cetina 1999) that makes "disposable" bodies possible. These specialized skills—we could posit—are the condition of possibility by which other "disposable" bodies become key sites of capitalist accumulation. They are also the main road for what commodity-chain scholars call "industrial upgrading," as this is heavily dependent on the development of knowledge, routines and techniques, and, ultimately, physical infrastructure. Instead of positing a separation between outsourcing, where production happens, and industrial atmosphere, where design and command take place, I show how "proximity" is accomplished through a combination of virtual technologies and strategic co-presence, to go beyond our understanding of time as a comparative advantage tied to how development and production are closely intertwined in co-presence (as with the Tuscany story, see Piore and Sabel 1984; Scott 2000; Molotch 2003; Yanagisako 2002).

The Perfect Fit has implied that some of the key components that the globalization literature has pointed at as happening in the center in fact take place on the periphery, in secondary and sometimes temporary clusters made out of partial visits, raids, parachute excursions, and more intense forms of

sociability than what happens, for instance, in New York City. Among those
are two very salient elements: the knowledge spillover that is produced by
the accumulation of specialized services in the same area, and the intense
sociability of face-to-face exchanges, which—according to this research—
actually happen much more fin Dongguan than in New York. Thus, we need
to complicate the distinctions between how idiosyncratic and exclusive the
work done by firms within agglomeration economies is versus that done by
companies that operate by strictly outsourcing production. The literature on
fashion production (Godart 2012; Djelic and Ainamo 1999) presents these as
distinct models, but in what we have observed, when do face-to-face interaction happen? Is it only in New York City, or also in Dongguan?

While the flexible-specialization account of expertise has given us an idea
of the two models' complementarity, interactions and socialization only happen in the "center" region. This ignores the intense work of sociability performed in the many venues where designers abroad come together—from the
breakfast rooms of hotels in Dongguan that cater to the "shoe and apparel
industry"; the area of the city where designers' crews have dinner; as well as
the hotel lounges where they have drinks—sometimes with other designers,
other times with expats who work and live in Dongguan—and exchange war
stories about the exhaustion of their lifestyle, the work other firms perform,
or how sample rooms respond, and the availability of certain materials. Most
cases of companies poaching designers—a really common practice in the US
industry—happen first in South China, thanks to late-night conversations
among designers. The flexible-specialization literature has also ignored the
camaraderie that develops between Taiwanese and Brazilian technicians,
Chinese "office girls" and fit models, and US designers—who tend to work
hand-in-hand on most days together, share lunch at the office, and go out
for dinner together almost daily.

Infrastructure work is less about particular artifacts and more about
relationship-building, but we seldom explore what kind of relationships support infrastructure building. The global intimacies I've described—from ethnic ties to the technician/fit model pairing, from the party-like atmosphere
of shopping in Europe for "proto" ideas to the in-between work and leisure
dinners that happen in Dongguan—are also part of a process of maintenance,
as much as the stabilization of work procedures across contexts, or of the
shoe object itself. All throughout fieldwork I observed the work of lubricat-
ing the social lives of those engaged in the design and development process.
Whether it was checking in when arriving to South China or South Brazil to

see which friends and former colleagues were also there; sending messages from one continent to another asking about each other's personal lives; or the more committed version of it, attending wedding and birthday parties in South China, Hong Kong, and Taiwan; celebrating the end-of-the-year holidays in China after the completion of their work routine there; hanging out in New York City with Chinese and Brazilian agents and traders after and off work. These intimacies are not just a byproduct of globalization but a key element in sustaining it. This is an added way to think about how people become "globalized" beyond the robust contributions offered by scholarship on migration, gender at work, and media.

THE GLOBAL IN MICRO; THE GLOBAL AS MICRO

One of the key issues *The Perfect Fit* has shown is what happens when we study the dynamics of global shoe production through the right feet of the women who work as fit models. One of the consequences of this book is an attempt to generate theory from the ground up to think of and about the global scale. In doing so, I hope to have sensitized the reader to this unexpected match between theory and case, as well as to cast some doubts about our taken-for-granted conceptualization of what counts as micro and macro. While the micro can be thought of as one fruitful avenue to explore empirically large aggregates (Collins 1981), what matters here—as Monika Krause (2012) signaled—is to muddle the easy distinctions between macro and micro. Eliding these taken-for-granted distinctions is a theoretically fruitful avenue to show (1) how face-to-face interactions can have large-scale consequences, (2) how power operates at the micro level, and (3) how interactions are within the realm of improvisation but also mediated and constrained. Moreover, instead of thinking of embodied and disembodied knowledge in opposition, this book has underscored their complementarity and limits, engaging how this knowledge is produced through both mediated and face-to-face interaction.

I've brought a laboratory-studies feel (Latour and Woolgar 1986; Latour 1987; Knorr Cetina 1999) to the study of commodity chains and design, focusing on the machinery deployed in design and showing the construction of an extended lifeworld thanks to the traffic in objects, sketches, boards, designers, and technicians. As I've shown throughout, mood boards, sketches, emails, feet, and even prototypes work as boundary objects, allowing people in diverse locales to work in collaboration. While some of the technologies that enable this are more obvious (and updates of past practices), like email, travel, and the use of "work" English by Chinese and Taiwanese technicians and managers, there are numerous mediating inscription devices that help to de- and rematerialize objects in communication.[1]

I've described some of these in detail: the role of paper, documents, and lasts; the attempts to generate "bridge studies" to translate among standards, making shoes always transposable; the libraries and repositories of templates and designs; the flexible sketches that allow cognition to be distributed; and the multiple inscription devices that make coordination and collaboration possible. The spatial modularity of the design floor points in this direction too. Travel by key agents happens when modularity is not enough and co-presence is necessary for translating between formal and informal kinds of knowledge.

Using concepts from the classic STS literature, this study brings insights from the pragmatist-inspired sociology of work into the sociology of global cultural production—insights that have become common knowledge within the sociologies of knowledge and the arts. Using an unexpected match between case and theory—as low-level commodity production is usually studied either through a global value-chain approach or the shop-floor politics literature—I defamiliarized the work of coordinating tacit and embodied forms of knowing. More to the point, in opening the black box of the input-output of a commodity chain and focusing on the work of producing the standard for women's shoes, I've shown the everyday agency involved in producing a scale. Doing so suggests that the global can fruitfully be studied as something other than a force, flow, or network. It also demonstrates a different kind of agency at the micro level than the "resistance" usually emphasized in studies of globalization. In focusing instead on collaboration and repair—at the level not of elites, financiers (Knorr Cetina and Bruegger 2002), or managers but of craft workers for a low-level, mass-produced commodity—can we bluntly say in consequence "global is as global does"? Moreover, chapter 6 and the coda are powerful reminders of how the scale can be undone, underscoring even more the fragility of global scale-making projects and the importance of understanding its day-by-day maintenance.

What are the consequences for theories in which agency and dynamism are given to the larger scales while the smaller scales—be they of human experience or at the level of interaction—are presented as essentially passive, reproductive, or reactive? Instead of falling into these conceptual traps I've tried to show, as world-systems scholar Georgi Derluguian (2005, 10) wrote, "how comprehensive interpretation of specific micro-interactions necessarily requires articulating their relational position within macro-contexts; but by the same token, an account of global trends will have no force or substance unless its observations and analyses are rooted in empirical situations." The focus on the intersection between objects and agents has been yet another way to counter the "impersonal forces" narrative about how global industries operate. While world-systems theory, commodity-chain analysis, and the "social life of things" approaches have all been great lenses through which to see the work of coordination at in-between levels of aggregation (and sometimes analysis), their shared emphasis on mapping commodities as they move globally has left us with little understanding of the work it takes to put those objects in circulation. Moreover, certain usages of concepts like *flow* (see Rockefeller 2011), given the baggage they carry—as imagining the world within a radical time-space dualism in which time eliminates spatial difference—have made it almost impossible to think in dialectical terms about how globalization happens.[2]

A related meaning of *global* that would result from this pragmatist-friendly approach is to rethink it not as a discrete account of geographical variation in which designs happen in one place and production in another but, rather, as a hybrid realm in which the point at which one stage starts, and when and where it ends, are relatively unclear and absolutely interdependent. This "global all the time" version of the management of time and space is helped by the series of activities I've described in detail; the scale is produced as much as it is productive. These activities point more toward a generative understanding of the "local" pole of the global-local divide, moving us away from a vertical version of how the global operates into one in which the local and the global are always intertwined.

Scholars of financial services (mainly Knorr Cetina and her collaborators) have focused on the synthetic situation as a new way of helping us understand how people coordinate their work mediated by screens and, in doing so, produce some of the same effects that would result from bodily co-presence. There has been less work to show the relative interchangeability of face-to-face interactions and electronically mediated exchanges, especially in the production of tangible goods. The extension of time and space thanks to email, text messages, and phone conversations means that it is unclear where and when things are being designed and developed. What we have learned is that shoes are being designed by a group of people who interact in different locales (sometimes in New York City, or in Dongguan or Europe);

that at every step along the way, they are in touch, regardless of time zone differences, and switch from physical to virtual co-presence depending on the temporal arc of development.

A related implication is that we might need a new vocabulary to describe what we study and how we study it in a case like this one. Is this a multi-sited ethnography? Probably not, since there is little comparison of the three principal sites, and a partial account of their mutual influence. Is it a "global" ethnography (in the Burawoy sense of it)? Not really, since it makes no comparison between my site and previous work on elite design and expertise to assert the historical changes at the level of global forces that have caused connections or disconnections at the local level to happen and be ethnographically manifested. Is it an ethnography of a new synthetic situation, as in the work of Karin Knorr Cetina (2009)? Probably not, since she makes screen-mediated interaction the site of her inquiry, disregarding other potential situations for socialization, interaction, and knowledge-sharing. Has this been a "follow the thing" kind of ethnography? To a certain extent, in its emphasis on many locales, but not really, in the sense that in that kind of ethnographic work we tend to see the work of different agents in different places, but not the work of the same group of people connecting across different time zones and locales as well as in different venues and types of settings (mediated or in co-presence). In this case, on the other hand, we've observed the work of actual people as they engage with each other in a continuum of synthetic and face-to-face interactions, and we've observed those situations in many different places around the world. Shall we call it "highly mobile ethnography"?[3]

STANDARDS ARE NOT STANDARDS; ARE NOT STANDARDS?

The middle part of this book studied how local actors work through frictions in maintaining the global, examining the process of fitting shoes for a US company in both New York and Dongguan. Doing so also underscored the close relationship between the production of scale—how the micro works in producing and "repairing" (Dominguez Rubio 2015; Jackson 2014) the global—and the production of standards—all the background work of calibrating to make sure a size 6 shoe is a size 6 shoe. In observing metrological conflicts and achievements outside the usual suspects (research on experiments, on educational metrics, on the State and social control, on metrology as an autonomous discipline) there are a few gains:

1. We see the processes of re- and decontextualization (as signaled by Timmermans and Epstein 2010) happening not for the constructions of facts with explanatory power but rather for goods made for myriad markets—showing the work to make the fact of the standard be recognized as universal, while pointing at its localized, culturally laden context and at the many devices and tricks used to mobilize them from one place to the next.

2. In making visible the micro work of producing and supporting global standards, we can make more explicit the gendered character of collaboration and production invisibilized in other realms like cultural production or science.

One way to understand this, in classic STS parlance, is to ask: When is a part of an assemblage an agent, and when is it an object? And moreover, when is it—to follow Daston and Gallison (2007)—that an actant replaces other people or nature? This book has pursued a strategy to answer these questions looking at selfhood and the relationships people build as something central to how globalization is done.

An important, related theoretical consequence of this last point is to think what a more humanist STS would look like. In being shamelessly eclectic, *The Perfect Fit* has combined perspectives—from ANT, material and ruination studies, social studies of science and technology, and the sociology of knowledge—that sometimes compete for the right to call a parcel of the world only by the name they have coined. I have taken a classic page from pragmatist-inspired sociology and used some of these ideas as sensitizing concepts to make sense of the world I encountered as I went along. One of the lessons from that body of research is to think how in human and nonhuman collaboration there are still asymmetries and inequalities that match those perceived to happen in society at large (i.e., of gender, class, and race) even if what we are studying is a laboratory-like venue. *The Perfect Fit* has been a window through which to observe in a nuanced fashion the relationship between knowledge, power, and gender—using the STS literature in a field in which, other than in a few studies of how markets are made "global" (see Caliskan 2010 for a great example), the relationship with materials has been absent.

I was interested in scrutinizing how materials are used to relate agents with potentially different—sometimes even competing—definitions of the situation as well as with different capabilities (for a great historical example, see Mukerji 2009). Standardization—as Timmermans and Epstein (2010) have creatively summarized—aspires to a certain order and the production of stability. For that to happen requires the submission of all kinds of actors—but building a small society around standards implies different roles, with different competences, rewards, and obligations. As I have shown in the second part of this book, there are no linear alignments: women who are fit models are both subservient and central to the infrastructure, hard to replace yet tied to the position by their gender, their lower position beforehand in the office and factory structure, the "nature" of their right foot, and the expertise they have acquired from its possession. Fit models are enrolled to be simultaneously things and, at the same time, their own megaphones. In being so, the model paradoxically reinforces her "thing-like" character, becoming—to quote Daston and Gallison (2007) again—just an echo of the technician, with a voice reflected and heard as coming from a speaking foot. But "fit girls" like Linda sometimes resist that process of subsumption, developing their own sense of style, their own expertise in finding technical solutions. When they do, they are valued far above the pay of someone considered "just a foot" while at the same time signaled as "moody," "capricious," "diva-like." These are all categories that point to the fact that—in Latourian parlance—they refuse to be intermediaries, mere objects that just replicate what is being done to them, and act instead as potential mediators, altering the input and modifying the meaning of the elements they are expected to merely reproduce.

Women who fit might be yet another group of allies, but leaving it at that would be a missed occasion to think about the kinds of questions that could connect laboratories of cultural production with the outside; a fit model is not just a particular device with specific uses. While the industry has tried to reduce them to their bodies—allowing ideas to exist physically and disciplining those bodies in order to generate population-wide standards—fit models are also skilled subjects who learn a language, developing rapport with the technician and sometimes with designers. To quote Peter Galison (1997, 2) in his *Image and Logic*, instruments are "not only laden with their direct functions, but also [embody] strategies of demonstration, work relationships in the laboratory and material and symbolic connections to the outside cultures in which these machines have roots." It is our job when studying infrastructure to consider how trajectories like "Chinese fit model" or the position "Brazilian technician" have been made possible, as much as we've studied their somewhat contingent encounter and lash-up in South China—thanks to Taiwanese entrepreneurs and US buyers and designers—and their resulting interdependence.

TASTE AND EXPERTISE

Following the routines behind craft-making resulted in a decentered picture of the process of design and development, one dovetailing with the agents' own definition of their practices, as the challenges around problem-solving make the work of all those involved less routine and almost new every time, even when participating in the creation of a global mass commodity. How do agents think about what they do? Do they know who else is working on a particular project? Do they connect with those other agents? Do they know about their expertise? Trust them? In many interviews and conversations, regardless of the interlocutor or their position in the network, people also remarked on how much shoemaking was something done by a myriad of people, all of them important from beginning to end. A couple of close informants, in fact, suggested for that to be the theme of this book.

At the empirical level, *The Perfect Fit* displayed all the nonmanagerial material care (Star 1995) that takes place within the mass-production process itself. It started with designers, but by now it should be clear they are not the lonely heroes of the story. I now want to come back to them, and to some of the central queries that organized the beginning of the manuscript. Is there alienation in this process? Is there originality? Authorship?

I've treated—in the spirit of Becker (1982), Star (1995), and Mialet (2012), among others—the different members of a team as collaborators, emphasizing how much they put aside whatever they don't have in common as they fully immerse themselves in their work routines. Yet despite the enterprise's collaborative character and the model of distributed cognition (Hutchins 1991, 1995), a design team is still a very asymmetrical and hierarchical system in terms of responsibility, authority, monetary rewards, and internal recognition. It's only logical to then ask (following Menger 2014) which team members are better rewarded for their work, how they are evaluated, who is harder to replace, and what changes if someone makes a mistake or works correctly. Are all laborers interchangeable? A key consequence of asking this is understanding where decision-making resides: in the hands of the head designer.

The head designer is the person who takes responsibility for flukes, hits, and sales *and* who is expected to bring with her the additional value of talent, serving as a multiplier for the skills of the team at large. On the other hand, associates, juniors, and interns do jobs more in line with what Menger has termed guardians or foot soldiers, jobs that matter much more if done improperly than if they are done the right way. So, an associate who insists on designs that are not going to make it to the final cut, or who is too sullen or stuck on how their creativity is stifled, slows down the cycle of sketching-development-production in a costly way. But if they do their work properly, all we see is business as usual. This is even more the case with juniors, who are in charge of developing some of the ideas presented by the head designer and of doing research within the parameters indicated, so their contribution is even more hidden as input within the work cycle and is thus relatively easy to replace.

Despite head designers' authority over their own teams—and the rewards associated with this[4]—the recognition designers receive does not translate into public acclaim. Insiders in the company and the industry recognize the names of head designers for Kenneth Cole, Nine West, Tory Burch, Sam Adelman, Coach, Michael Kors, and other large brands, but even if I had used the real names of the designers I've interviewed or observed at work, readers would have a hard time making sense of who they are. Unlike the fantasy of shoes existing thanks to a signature-like creative gesture by a relatively older male, usually white and European—anonymous women in their late twenties and mid-thirties collectively design most of the shoes other women consume. This should have become even clearer to the reader as we looked, later on in the book, at the work of office and fit "girls" in the China offices.

Beyond recognition and signature, one of the key definitions of artistry has looked at whether the person or group of people generating the object has authorial voice and can produce a particular narrative about the result of their own work (for two fantastic examples, see Mialet 2012 and Wong 2013). In the case of design for the middle-tier US shoe market, what we saw was how the syntax behind one collection was the result of mainly two processes: the translation of products from other market segments—taking into account the material possibilities and copyright limitations; as well as the space saved for a surefire top-seller item to replace what buyers made their money with the year before.

The main process through which the first happened I termed cluttering, in it narrative control comes via retrodiction, making sense of what a collection is about after seeing the internal structure of the "original" objects that were bought to be made into a shoe line. This changes for higher-end brands, which have more narrative and conceptual control over what a collection is supposed to represent, projecting into the future what the consumer will want—in comparison to the mid-tier markets, in which there is a tension between what is prospective versus retrospective, or what line builders for first-cost or black-label collections want, as most of their work is to produce recognizable similes of what customers have already seen in other market segments. There is still variation there, as there are few constructions to work with, so "shoe dogs" have to be skillful in adapting uppers to their existing lasts.

If fashion is the consequence of a collective process of self-selection—as Andy Abbott (2014) puts it, narrowing down abundance—that results in what I have called an "ecology of taste," there is still anxiety about what constitutes originality when designers talk about themselves and their trade. Even though designers know they participate in a craft where everybody copies each other, and they work for firms that systematically poach designers—so much so that by the end of this research, all of the original design team of OM had worked for competitors before or after—they still hold onto the idea of originality. They displace it when discussing items they get from brands in higher market segments—what I've shown they call "originals"—but also (and more importantly) feel a special pride when they are the first designers to translate and successfully transpose items from that segment into their own collections, beating competitors at it. Nobody wants to show their cards to others, even if all designers and line builders are in the business of adapting preexisting objects; originality in this case becomes the word to describe whoever can do an item at their own price point first.

One of my main interests in writing *The Perfect Fit* was exploring how subjective and objective forms of culture intersect, following up on a different-yet-related case of taste, expertise, and cultural materials than the one in *The Opera Fanatic* (Benzecry 2011). Here, I did so by pointing at the career of an object, the collective and invisible work that enabled it, and the paradoxical relationship between replication and creativity. I did this interested less in dethroning the categories of singularity produced by the actors in the field (in this case, "originality") and more in explaining what those categories can generate in terms of routines, relationships, and modes of knowing. Paraphrasing anthropologist Michael Taussig (1980), I hope to have shown the production of magic as well as the magic of production.

Coda

SHOE IS A GIPSY BUSINESS

In the lives of emperors there is a moment which follows pride in the
boundless extension of the territories we have conquered, and the
melancholy and relief of knowing we shall soon give up any thought of
knowing and understanding them.

Italo Calvino, *Invisible Cities*

Dwayne went from OM's sample room and development office to one of the
small factories the company contracts for final production. Unlike with other
technical work discussed in this book, he was not there as things moved
along but rather to make sure the production process was carried out according to the company's instructions and that the final products—shoes to
be shipped ASAP to the United States—were identical to the final approved
samples OM had seen.

As he walked me through the factory, explaining the organization of the
assembly line, Dwayne told me he was on the lookout for two things: who was
in charge of the lasting machine—if it was a different person than the last

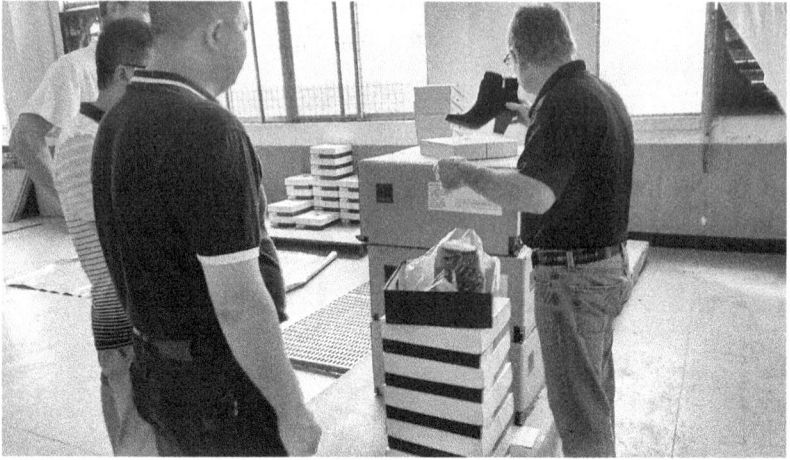

Figure C.1. Dwayne inspecting OM boots at a factory, December 2015.

time he'd visited, he immediately felt that it wasn't a trustworthy operation—and whether the final shoes inside the boxes not only matched the samples but also looked identical to each other. Having been a line builder for most of his life, he had the knowledge to make the call when he thought something didn't seem OK.

As he opened the boxes with boots about to ship, he played with them, making sure they looked and felt identical. When things didn't work out, he called the manager and then went to the end of the assembly line, where female workers did quality control by hand, evening out small details with a cutter. Earlier in our sojourn he had also explored the discarded shoes—all of them marked with a white dot to make sure those pieces were not salvageable. He was there to make sure quality was achieved, as well as to make certain the paying customer wasn't taken advantage of when it came to the cost of the operation.

Dwayne was called "the shoe doctor" among designers at OM and by the rest of the management at the developer where OM did one of its lines. He flew to Dongguan from his home in Texas a few times a year just to control the match between development and production. This almost magical character embodied in his skill the recognition that, as historian Ken Alder (2002) put it, "the price of standards is eternal vigilance."

His tasks also directed our attention to something else: the almost-impossible character of the enterprise given its planetary expansion over

time, the disjuncture between expertise and cheap labor, and the limited capacity for reproducing the conditions to make sure that match was a virtuous
one as development and production become further and further geographically divorced. Much like the Khan Italo Calvino described, shoe production
is trapped between its attempts for controlling and knowing everything that
is going on at a distance *and* the melancholy of understanding the impossibility in the long run of such an endeavor.

Throughout fieldwork I learned of Taiwanese owners who'd closed factories in Huenzhou because of the impossibility of reproducing standards
there; of other compatriot owners, agents, and technicians who had folded
their shops and moved back to the island; and of Brazilians who had moved
to Chengdu, or were offered to move to Ethiopia, where American developers allied with Chinese capitalists had opened factories and needed people
with long-term experience in the industry to supervise the daily operations.
I also met American and Italian designers who refused to keep moving further into China, as Dongguan had finally become a place with an "international" leisure area in which they could all mingle and have fun. Moreover,
I interviewed Brazilian agents who had moved to South China to make their
samples but were considering how to move some of the production back to
Brazil after the currency collapse of 2017.

As I finished fieldwork in 2017, I was learning how much production had
left the Dongguan area, as well as how much of its command-and-control
functions were slowly being passed to (or was it taken away by?) a competing delegation center: Ho Chi Minh City. Closer to factories in Myanmar,
Cambodia, the Philippines, Indonesia, and other parts of Vietnam itself, the
city had a cluster of expert services thanks to the previous establishment of
the sneaker industry in the area. For many of the Brazilians I interviewed
and spent time with, the question about moving there wasn't *whether* but
rather *when*. In a lot of cases my contact with key players in town had become
harder as they were spending more and more time in the former Saigon. Some
of them were opening a leather-supply shop similar to the one they had in
Shenzhen. Others were moving their quality-control operations closer to the
factories there. And yet others were constantly coming and going, sometimes
reuniting in the new context with old acquaintances from the *Vale do Sinos*
area, getting leads on full-time positions.

The potential end of the history of Brazilians in China is part and parcel
of a longer point, the "gipsy business" of shoemaking—as Marcio, a developer who moved to China after twenty years working in Brazil, called it—in

which development follows much later, at a slower pace, after cheap labor has moved. If Ho Chi Minh City appeared as the future, with knowledge and suppliers already there, side by side with cheap labor, what would that say about what I witnessed in Dongguan? Was Novo Hamburgo both the past and the future of Dongguan? The first factory I visited with Grace had since become a kindergarten—much like the one I ventured into in Canudos with Francieli, my Brazilian research assistant. Development rooms were moved farther from the city center in Houjie, as owners closed full-scale factories and instead received the cheapest parts of the process from elsewhere, underscoring the fragility of globalization and how much the geographies that have been settled for a short period of time can be unraveled.

If South China and South Brazil were a study in contrast and comparison, where the bustling craziness of an afternoon of total gridlock resounded like an explosion next to the emptiness and quietness of my walks to visit developers through downtown Novo Hamburgo, then will Ho Chi Minh city turn Dongguan into an empty shell? Will the speed of capital as it passes through places erase the history of the slower pace of a skill that dwells in bodies? Despite its divergent histories of development, would we end up just seeing the seriality of these spectral places in the way of capital? Unfortunately, as social scientists, our answers to this can't be to decry the melancholy brought by the futility of understanding the vastness of the territories we aim to know. This book has been an attempt to make sense of it all.

ACKNOWLEDGMENTS

After years of working writing books, academic articles, and newspaper pieces, as well as being a card-carrying sociologist of culture and knowledge, I've come to learn and inhabit the lesson that what you have just read (or are about to read, if you begin with the acknowledgments) is a collective product I get to sign for. All throughout the process of creation and production, I got invaluable input and help from all kinds of people. From personal friends who offered support; to colleagues who read all or parts of the manuscript; others who came to hear me talk about it; participants in the fieldwork who corrected some of my simplistic early ideas; freelance editors who worked on correcting my English as second language; and the people from the University of Chicago Press who thought writing this book would be a good idea and who shepherded me through the process. The usual disclaimers apply.

The list that follows is relatively capricious; I've been working on this project for a long time, enough to have forgotten sometimes who suggested what and when and where they exactly did it. This book benefited from the free exchange of ideas over the past decade or so with three scholars and friends: Andrew Deener, Fernando Domínguez Rubio, and Pablo Lapegna. They all read parts of this manuscript a different points in time, had conversations with me during research, and always had suggestions on what to do, what to read, what to think beyond the obvious. The book was inspired by the work of three masters who also were kind enough to read sections of it: Chandra Mukerji, Harvey Molotch, and Howie Becker. To all of these people my thanks are probably not enough.

While the research for this book started when I was faculty at the University of Connecticut, I concluded it at Northwestern University. Thanks much to Pablo Boczkowski for his guidance in the transition to the Northwestern School of Communication and for his overall friendship; to Ellen Wartella for her warmth and humanity; and to Michael Rodriguez, Larissa Buchholz, and Hector Carrillo for reading and conversing with me about the book.

Thanks also to the sociology department colloquium, and to the culture and ethnography workshops, where I was able to present and get feedback from Wendy Griswold, Bruce Carruthers, Steven Epstein, and Wendy Espeland; and to my graduate students on campus—Amy Ross, Philip Fang, Nick Bascunan-Wiley, Jabari Evans, and Mora Matassi—who have made my time in Evanston intellectually stimulating.

Parts of this research were presented at colloquiums and workshops at the following institutions and departments: the sociology and Latin American studies departments at the University of Chicago, the sociology department at the University of Wisconsin–Madison Soc, the sociology department at the University of Wisconsin–Milwaukee, Purdue University, Tulane University, the University of Virginia, the University of Colorado at Boulder, the New School, Boston College, Boston University, the University of Michigan, the University of Southern California, and New York University; Columbia University's SKAT workshop; Yale's Center for Cultural Sociology, New York University's Institute for Public Knowledge; the University of Georgia's Wilson Center; NYU Abu Dhabi; the University of Toronto; Central European University; Universidad Nacional Autónoma de México; Universidad de la Plata, Universidad de Buenos Aires, and the Instituto de Desarrollo Económico y Social in Argentina; and Universidade Federal do Rio Grande do Sul in Brazil; as well as meetings of the American Sociological Association, the Social Science History Association, and the Economic Sociology annual conference. In talking at those places I received so much feedback it is hard to do justice to it, but thanks regardless to Marco Garrido, Andy Abbott, John Levi Martin, Liz Clemens, Karin Knorr, and Pablo Palomino; to Mustafa Emirbayer, Jane Collins, Ivan Ermakoff, and Joan Fujimura; to Aneesh Aneesh; to Dan Winchester; to David Smilde, Mariana Craciun, Camilo Leslie, Katie Jensen, and Stephen Ostertag; to Isaac Reed, Fiona Greenland, Simone Polillo, and Jennifer Bair; to Diane Vaughan, Gil Eyal, Luciana de Souza Melo, Hannah Wohl, and Josh Whitford; to David Cook Martin, Rachel Rinaldo, and Mathieu Deflem; to Rachel Sherman, Carlos Forment, and Robin Wagner-Pacifici; to Jeffrey Alexander and Phil Smith; to Gianpaolo Baiocchi and Diana Graizbord; to Kimberly Hoang; to Julian Go, Emily Berman, and Ashley Mears; to Geneviève Zubrzycki and Rob Jansen (who also read the intro and gave me generous feedback); to Paul Lichterman, TJ Billard, and Dan Lanier-Voss; to Vanina Leschziner, Clayton Childress, Erik Schneiderhan, and Dan Silver; to Dorit Geva, Alexandra Kowalski, Daniel Monterescu, and Jean-Louis Fabiani; to Hugo José Suarez, Hector Vera, and Jorge Galindo; to Ezequiel Adamovsky, Sergio Visacovsky, Daniela Lucena,

Isabella Cosse, and Enrique Garguin; to Arlei Sander and Ruben Oliven; and to Juan Pablo Pardo-Guerra, Peggy Levitt, Eviatar Zerubavel, Daniel Menchik, Randy Collins, and Gemma Mangione.

Owen Whooley, Javier Auyero, Pierre-Michel Menger, and Steve Shapin all read chapters of the book and provided me with lots of food for thought, much obliged! Javier has also been a model of what to do as a Latin American scholar in the US. I can't thank him enough for his constant mentoring. I know José Biondi, José Marrone, and Mauricio Borensztein are also thankful for the many virtual times together.

At different points in time Jane Jones, Katie Sobering, Katie Jensen, Amy Ross, and Joseph Fruscione helped in making sure *The Perfect Fit* was a readable experience for English speakers; my gratitude for that. At the University of Chicago Press, I deeply want to thank Elizabeth Branch Dyson, who inherited this project from Doug Mitchell and Kyle Wagner, and who jumped behind it with full force, giving great suggestions for rewrites, choosing reviewers who were challenging but immanent critics, and generating an overall feeling of team excitement about the book. I also want to thank Mollie McFee, who worked with professional zeal to make sure the book would make it on time.

While doing research in South Brazil I was welcomed in Porto Alegre and helped immensely by colleagues like Felipe Comunello, Lorena Fleury, and Rosana Pinheiro Machado. Francieli Ruppenthal was my research assistant and performed with gusto and dedication. In South China my debts are even bigger, so many that I'll probably be unable to repay them by mentioning names (participants have also been guaranteed anonymity, so it would be unfair to reveal who they are). Thanks to the participants in the three sites for making this project possible. *Gracias, Nico!*

I also have many friends who have contributed to this book just by their support. Thanks—in no particular order—to Mariana Heredia, Alejandro Costábile and Jannine Manjarrez, Sebastián Corti, Daniel Fridman, Daniel Sazbón, Nico Kwiatkowski, Ximena Espeche and Gabriel DiMeglio, Javier Uriarte and Fernando Loffredo, Constanza Tabbush and Felicitas Rossi, Victoria Irisarri, Nico Viotti, Pepa Berengan, Fabián Llonch and Gisela Vidallé, Marcelo Guidoli, Sebastián Baña, Nerea Huertas, Cesar Boggiano, Juan Vaggione, Ale Dujovne, Jen Heerwig, Marion Wrenn, María Alci González, Gabi Abend, Mark Healy, Martín Mikulik, and Cristian Paredes for making life more bearable at a strange time.

Alejandra Uslenghi and David Ben-Arie (and Amadeo) have made sure I have a second home in Chicago. They have become my family when away from home; I can't thank them enough for that. In Buenos Aires I have an embarrassment of riches; Eugenio Medina and Angela Natanson (also Pedrito and Lauri!) have become second kin in a place where I'm already grateful for my actual family. Thanks to my parents (Mario and Titina), my cousins (Nora, Liz, and Marina) and my brother Esteban, his partner Fernanda, and my beloved nephew Noah for their constant company from afar.

The Perfect Fit took long enough to complete to see two of my favorite people in the world leave it: my aunt Susana Mide, and the editor of my first two books, Doug Mitchell. This book is dedicated to them in loving memory.

NOTES

CHAPTER ONE

1. Salzinger 2003; Otis 2011; C. K. Lee 1998; Hanser 2006; Hoang 2014; Muñoz 2007; Krause 2018; Collins 2009; Ngai 2005; Parreñas 2001; Knowles 2014; Aneesh 2015; Miraftab 2016, among many others.
2. Aneesh 2006; Knorr Cetina and Bruegger 2002; Knorr Cetina and Preda 2007; Leonardi 2012; Henderson 1991; O'Donnell 2014; Crane 1972.
3. Scott 2000, 2006; Storper 1997; Sabel 1994; Molotch 2002; Amin and Thrift 1992.
4. For more on how Marx's formulation inverted the traditional idea of fetish, see Stallybrass 1998; Pietz 1985; Chin 2016.
5. See for instance Crowston (2013) for a great historiographical study of how fashion operated in the French Old Regime.
6. One of the key scholars in the global value-chains approach, Gary Gereffi, has recently made this point (Hamilton and Gereffi 2009) by using Howard Becker's (Becker 1995) Latourian take on the power of inertia to discuss the levels of interdependence and integration that make it difficult for capital to leave and for industrial upgrade to happen immediately.
7. On this see, among many others: Shapin 1989; Star 1999; Law 1987; Latour 2005; Star and Griesemer 1989; Fujimura 1992; Mukerji 2009.
8. On this see Lee 2017; Otis 2011; Hoang 2014; Paul 2017; Irani 2019; Nadeem 2011.
9. I tried without success to learn Mandarin as I engaged in the project. I spoke English, Portuguese, and Italian, which allowed me to communicate with most of the people at the different field sites I engaged with, but I used key bilingual informants—a sourcing agent, a factory manager, and two shoe technicians—to interview Chinese workers.
10. The advantage of ethnography might be precisely its incomplete and limited character (Candea 2010), an admission of the impossible closure in the business of producing description about otherness. And this happens by design; we don't record the totality of social life in a particular

place. We organize a reality that is multiform, complex, and contradictory, according to (and as such limited by) the questions we want to answer. It is this limitation—the fact that we are limited by theory, language, and selfhood—that actually allows us to produce this kind of knowledge.

CHAPTER TWO

1. At first, fashion weeks happened in central cities for the industry like Milan, London, and Paris—but slowly the format was replicated by other competitors like New York and Tokyo, and more recently by peripheral cities like São Paulo, Shanghai, Mexico City, and Buenos Aires. Even Santiago recently celebrated its first annual fashion week with local designers, brands, and models.

2. A third shop, *Jeffrey*, was located in the Meatpacking District.

3. One of the factory owners OM works with in China knew an OM sales representative who was a friend of his daughter's, and because of that sent Nicole a weekly gift of fifty pictures of what was new at Barney's main shoe floor (the fifth floor) for that week, including the names of the products.

4. Some designers from other companies skip Florence and go to Milan, usually combining their shopping trips with visits to the shoe or leather trade fairs that happen in that city.

5. Much as with the festivals where street pictures are taken, cities actively compete to promote themselves as "design" cities to attract tourism.

6. Trips to "alternative" cities are usually more exploratory than systematic. For instance, when visiting Berlin, the objective of the trip seemed to be to get an idea of what was available in the city. So the time there was spent in one shop strip that included a mall and a department store, where they found the usual higher-end brands. On a second visit to the Mitte neighborhood, the designers went to small boutiques with few items inside, looking for either local products or at least for objects that had been produced somewhere else but happened to be available in Berlin and nowhere else within the travel. In total, OM bought ten pairs of shoes on that trip.

7. I don't have the town's name. The OM team has repeatedly joked that if they gave me the name they "would have to kill me" and that I "could go with [them] only on the condition of not peeking at the name of the town." If I really wanted to, maybe I "could go with a blindfold on."

8. In Hong Kong I witnessed a variation of this while we shopped at some of the larger malls (like the Mira, the Elements, Silvercord, and Harbour

City, all in Tsim Sha Tsui)—spending money on shoes by McQueen, taking pictures of shoes by Toga Pula, and buying jewelry by local craftsmen. We also went to Granville Road, where we were surrounded by young locals instead of the monied foreigners we had seen at the malls; and to the Rise shopping arcade to buy cheap jewelry and studs at two small shops. Trips to Hong Kong usually last a day or two and are undertaken by teams who are already in the Dongguan area working for development or production.

9. The cycle of fashion is such that an accessory bought at River Island was used to develop an ornament in one of OM's shoes, only for the designers to find it on a later trip, reproduced almost to the detail on a River Island shoe.

10. Companies have relatively similar cycles for research, sketching, development, and production, as they all need to have their samples ready for the large fairs where they usually meet face-to-face with their clients.

11. The work of Olaf Velthuis (2005) has also rescued the idea of a tournament of value (via Baudrillard and Appadurai). He shows how, in economic exchanges in the art world, there is a cognitive boundary mobilized between commodity and gift exchange, and how that boundary operates in presenting artists' stipends, salaries, and sold works as gifts, and in dividing the front and the back stages (white rooms, inventory, accounts, Excel sheets, and catalogs) of art galleries. What I'm aiming to show here is less the work of hiding how the final product is a commodity, and more how this happens not just in the circulation phase but within different parts of the production cycle.

12. This scene illustrates, as much as the anecdote about the Italian town, the playful logic behind this phase of design.

13. Moreover, as boundary objects continue to be in play, stakeholders attempt to create measures of standardization to lock in their meaning, and thus aim toward the exclusion of "other" interpretations. The tension between what is tacit and nonformalizable, and what constitutes standardized knowledge, is one that permeates every operation within the design process.

14. The *New York Times* featured the city twice, once in an article entitled "36 Hours in Valencia, Spain" (January 20, 2011) and once before (September 22, 2010), in an article in which the city is described as the next cultural hub and as "waking up from a siesta."

15. I'm excluding the constant checking on Instagram for images posted by designers, stylists, fashion editors, and bloggers, but those images also play a big role in the consolidation of pictures and concepts to anchor a line around.

CHAPTER THREE

1. There is a learning curve to understanding the style of a brand, a collection, what is expected from designers, and the temporality of the operation, but after that period teams tend to work seamlessly.

2. The main issue with machine-made paper patterns is that machines can't take into account small details like the allowance or the fit with a last. While machine-made patterns are cheaper at the outset than having a trained specialist, in the end they cost more money because of fit issues once the upper is developed in the proper materials.

3. I'm using three different shoes for illustration here, but this is the three-step protocol most shoes tend to follow.

4. Calling this the "politics of sight," Pachirat's (2012) blood-soaked experience inside a slaughterhouse spotlights only the most illustrative example of how we've divorced ourselves from the means of producing violence—and how in doing so we have made it psychologically easier to support such brutality. While Nicole, Pepi, and many other US designers travel systematically to cities like Dongguan and interact daily with technicians, managers, office girls, secretaries, and drivers, they never make it past the sample-room floors—where high-skill workers are—and they only see the factory workers from a car, as they are driven from their hotels and apartments to offices and agents' sample rooms.

5. There is one room where most of the work is done by hand, with small scissors and needles; and a second, larger one, where workers use electric sewing machines.

6. For an interesting discussion of the role of tacit and embodied knowledge in fashion, read Entwistle's (2009) discussion of kinesthetic knowledge among fashion buyers for British department stores.

7. A designer who left OM to work for a new company had to correct and develop knockoffs based on her own previous OM designs—because her new brand's director was very much interested in more-casual styles of boots.

CHAPTER FOUR

1. Models are also asked to walk, though that happens less often. Technicians want to see the shoe in dynamic situations as well as to make sure some basic fit and safety issues won't be a problem (e.g., that the heel does not feel wobbly, that the shoe does not slip when the model walks, etc.).

2. On reading traces—and the relationship of that process to the conjectural method and to professions like detective work—see Ginzburg (1980) and, more recently, Boltanski (2015).

3. According to Clint and other veterans of the industry, many of the larger companies in the industry (e.g., Nine West, Brown Shoes, Sam Adelman, and the Camuto Group) had all switched to 7 as the standard size by the 1980s. Once the companies moved development and production from Brazil to Dongguan, they maintained that standard at the new site. Nevertheless, some smaller companies still work with 6 as their base size.

4. There are also specialized machines that measure foot weight, pressure, and force. The ones I observed were located at SENAI, the technical school in Novo Hamburgo, Brazil, which was used by some local companies use to measure feet in greater detail.

5. It was in fact during fitting prototypes that I was told a bizarre-sounding story about how technicians had to apply cream to one model's foot in order to pull on a shoe that had no zipper and was difficult to fit.

6. This convention has been also challenged by the fact that silver pens in China dry easily, so sometimes designers just make do with Sharpies. In a few cases, technicians in China have asked designers to bring silver pen for them from the US.

CHAPTER FIVE

1. I'm bracketing here the fact that Cinderella itself—if we look at it trans-culturally, as Carlo Ginzburg (1991) did—is one of the many guises under which the following myth, which starts with Odysseus and includes the story of Achilles, appears: (1) a shoe or foot is lost or damaged; (2) the bones of dead animals are collected; and (3) the hero journeys to the world of the dead before returning to the world of the living to overcome a great challenge. Ginzburg follows the Warburgian method in order to underscore the similarities about how individuals in diverse cultures have narrated ideas about their own bodies as well as the experience of death.

2. Casting procedures varied in the three field sites. In the US, most casting happens via agencies. Prospective models are either part-timers from the acting and commercial modeling professions, or full-time fit models provided by specialized agencies. In China they are usually "discovered" in factories and offices, though factories and trading companies also post ads on social media. In smaller firms the models are also expected to be "office girls" on top of fitting. In South Brazil, models are cast in response

to ads; they're expected to develop technical expertise over time and to age out into other, specialized roles.

3. On another occasion, models for that company protested having to work on Saturday, something standard in Dongguan, where trading companies—adapting themselves to the temporality of the US—work on the first day of the weekend, usually full time. Their protest underscores once again the power models derive from their unexpected centrality within the infrastructure.

4. I could not reproduce them here because of the low quality of the image, but her feet are indeed identical.

5. I'm following here Andrew Pickering's (1995) idea of *pragmatic realism*, which considers the reference as produced and performative, yet central in organizing the correspondence between models and materials—a correspondence in which the real world helps to stabilize the coherence between the world and its representation precisely via its material resistance.

6. The head designer for OM's higher-end line used to try on shoes herself when working for her previous employer—another US firm—but at OM, because they used 6 as the base size instead of the 7 most large companies use, she was unable to and sometimes used another one of the designers to make sure the boots worked on an "American" leg.

7. While an order from a US client will include anywhere from 30,000 to 200,000 pairs, orders from European buyers can be as small as 2,500.

8. This is further complicated by the fact that the client also has a fit model. Though the model is not present or accounted for during the development process, she usually comes with the buyer during FFaNY—the Fashion Footwear Association of New York's annual international shoe fair—to try on samples for confirmation and production.

9. In this way, the use of "Midwestern" as a catchall category is different from how it has been used to discuss the commercial market for fashion—as in those references (Mears 2011) there is no actual allusion to the body of the consumers but to their taste.

INTERLUDE

1. For a full picture of the trajectories of foreign direct investment in Dongguan, and the role played by Taiwanese and Hong Kongese entrepreneurs, please see Yang 2007; Yeung 2001.

2. The factory became a kindergarten.

3. Because of its recent entry into the industry, not only is there little shoe-making tradition in the region (Chengdu was actually the domestic shoe capital of China) but until very recently there were no technical schools dedicated to shoemaking.

4. I found some of the Brazilians in Dongguan via LinkedIn. The networking site proved a good tool in general, as it allowed me to look at people's CVs and organize some of the information they gave me better, as well as to identify patterns with respect to education, year of arrival in China, and the first companies they worked for.

5. I'll elaborate on the German character of Rio Grande do Sul at large and the Vale do Sinos area in particular in chapter 6.

CHAPTER SIX

1. This underscores one of the classic political problems of the sector: while it employs many workers, its contribution to the GDP is relatively low.

2. About 70 percent of the city's budget derives, directly or indirectly, from shoes, the mayor said in 2010 (Lopez 2010, 9/24).

3. Reinhart Koselleck suggested two categories: *space of experience* and *horizon of expectation*. Both are personal and interpersonal. The space of experience allows one to account for the assimilation of the past into the present: "Experience is present past, whose events have been incorporated and could be remembered." Horizon of expectation reveals one's way of thinking about the future. Expectation "is the future made present; it directs itself to the not-yet, to the non-experienced, to that which is to be revealed."

4. Tellingly enough, one of the key Brazilian line builders I met in Dongguan—who was thinking of retiring back to the Vale do Sinos area—had a similar idea about how and where to go next with shoe production once he was back home.

5. Calling themselves "German" was also a racialized way of distinguishing themselves from the rest of the country, something very much in line with the separatist history of the province, which had rebelled against the federal government and which always had smaller factions agitate the idea of secession.

CONCLUSION

1. The essential characteristics of inscriptions are that they are mobile, presentable, readable, combinable with one another, and immutable. They

are "extracted" from the laboratory and somewhat cleaned, redrawn, and displayed to support a text (though text in this case tends to support the message conveyed by the image).

2. As an example of this, see, for instance, David Harvey (1990) and his discussion of time-space compression as central to understanding the reorganization of capitalism in the post-Fordist era.

3. I owe the impetus to think about this to very helpful and generous comments by Daniel Menchik and further encouragement by Pablo Lapegna.

4. For instance, a head designer makes between US$150,000 and US$250,000 per year, while an associate makes from US$75,000 to US$120,000, and a junior as little as US$35,000.

REFERENCES

Abbott, Andrew. 1998. *The System of Professions: An Essay on the Division of Expert Labor*. Chicago: University of Chicago Press.

Abbott, Andrew. 2014. "The Problem of Excess." *Sociological Theory* 32, no. 1: 1–26.

Adorno, Theodor. 1973. *Negative Dialectics*. New York: Continuum Books.

Alder, Kenneth L. 2002. *The Measure of All Things: The Seven-Year Odyssey and Hidden Error That Transformed the World*. New York: Simon and Schuster.

Amin, Ash, and Nigel Thrift. 1992. "Neo-Marshallian Nodes in Global Networks." *IJURR* 16, no. 4: 571–87.

Aneesh, A. 2006. *Virtual Migration: The Programming of Globalization*. Durham, NC: Duke University Press.

Aneesh, A. 2015. *Neutral Accent: How Language, Labor and Life Become Global*. Durham, NC: Duke University Press.

Appadurai, Arjun. 1986. *The Social Life of Things*. New York: Cambridge University Press.

Aspers, Patrick. 2006. *Markets in Fashion: A Phenomenological Approach*. London: Routledge.

Bair, Jennifer, ed. 2009. *Frontiers of Commodity Chain Research*. Palo Alto, CA: Stanford University Press.

Bank Muñoz, Carolina. 2007. *Transnational Tortillas: Race, Gender, and Shop-Floor Politics in Mexico and the United States*. Ithaca, NY: IRLA Press.

Bazan, Luiza, and Lizbeth Navas-Aleman. 2003. "Upgrading in Global and National Value Chains: Recent Challenges and Opportunities for the Sinos Valley Footwear Cluster, Brazil." In *Local Enterprises in the Global Economy: Issues of Governance and Upgrading, edited by* Hubert Schmitz. Cheltenham: Elgar.

Becker, Howard S. 1982. *Art Worlds*. Berkeley: University of California Press.

Becker, Howard S. 1995. "The Power of Inertia." *Qualitative Sociology* 18, no. 3: 301–9.

Becker, Howard S. 2013. *What About Mozart? What About Murder?* Chicago: University of Chicago Press.

Becker, Howard S., and Robert Faulkner. 2009. *Do You Know? The Jazz Repertory in Action.* Chicago: University of Chicago Press.

Becker, Howard S., Robert Faulkner, and Barbara Kinrshenblatt-Gimblett. 2006. *Art from Start to Finish.* Chicago: University of Chicago Press.

Beckert, Jens. 2013. "Imagined Futures: Fictional Expectations in the Economy." *Theory and Society* 42, no. 3: 219–40.

Beckert, Sven. 2015. *Empire of Cotton: A Global History.* New York: Alfred A. Knopf.

Benjamin, Walter. 1974. "On the Concept of History." *Gesammelte Schriften I:2.* Frankfurt am Main: Suhrkamp Verlag.

Benzecry, Claudio E. 2011. *The Opera Fanatic: Ethnography of an Obsession.* Chicago: University of Chicago Press.

Benzecry, Claudio E. 2015. "Restabilizing Attachment to Cultural Objects: Aesthetics, Emotions and Biography." *British Journal of Sociology* 66, no. 4: 779–800.

Berger, Peter, and Thomas Luckmann. 1966. *The Social Construction of Reality.* New York: Penguin Books.

Berman, Marshall. 1982. *All That is Solid Melts into Air: The Experience of Modernity.* New York: Simon & Schuster.

Bestor, Theodor. 2001. "Supply-Side Sushi: Commodity, Market, and the Global City." *American Anthropologist* 103, no. 1: 76–95.

Bestor, Theodor. 2004. *Tsukiji: The Fish Market at the Center of the World.* Berkeley: University of California Press.

Blumer, Herbert. 1969. "Fashion: From Class Differentiation to Collective Selection." *Sociological Quarterly* 10: 275–91.

Bolker, Jessica. 2009. "Exemplary and Surrogate Models: Two Modes of Representation in Biology." *Perspectives in Biology and Medicine* 52, no. 4: 485–99.

Boltanski, Luc. 2015. *Mysteries and Conspiracies: Detective Stories, Spy Novels and the Making of Modern Societies.* New York: Cambridge University Press.

Boltanski, Luc, and Laurence Thevenot. 2006. *On Justification*: Economies of Worth. Princeton, NJ: Princeton University Press.

Bourdieu, Pierre. 1988. "Flaubert's Point of View." *Critical Inquiry* 14, no. 3: 539–62.

Bowker, Geoffrey C., and Susan Leigh Star. 1999. *Sorting Things Out.* Cambridge: MIT Press.

Brekhus, Wayne H., John F. Galliher, and Jaber F. Gubrium. 2005. "The Need for Thin Description." *Qualitative Inquiry* 11, no. 6: 861–79.

Broughton, Chad. 2015. *Boom, Bust, Exodus: The Rust Belt, the Maquilas, and a Tale of Two Cities*. New York: Oxford University Press.

Burawoy, Michael. 2001. "Manufacturing the Global." *Ethnography* 2, no. 2: 147–59.

Burucúa, Jose Emilio. 2016. Interview by Claudio E. Benzecry. *Public Culture* 28, no. 1:89–111.

Caliskan, Koray. 2010. *Market Threads: How Cotton Farmers and Traders Create a Global Commodity*. Princeton, NJ: Princeton University Press.

Callon, Michel. 1986. "Some Elements of a Sociology of Translation: Domestication of the Scallops and the Fishermen of St Brieuc Bay." In *Power, Action, and Belief: A New Sociology of Knowledge?*, edited by J. Law, 196–233. London: Routledge.

Callon, Michel, Cécile Méadel, and Vololona Rabeharisoa. 2002. "The Economy of Qualities." *Economy and Society* 31, no. 2: 194–217.

Candea, Matei. 2010. *Corsican Fragments: Difference, Knowledge and Fieldwork*. Bloomington: Indiana University Press.

Carrillo, Héctor. 2017. *Pathways of Desire: The Sexual Migration of Mexican Gay Men*. Chicago: University of Chicago Press.

Cheng, Lu Lin. 1996. *Embedded Competitiveness: Taiwan's Shifting Role in International Footwear Sourcing Networks*. PhD diss., Duke University.

Cheng, Peng Cheng. 2007. *The Growth and Transformation of Chinese Footwear Production: The Political Economy of a Global Industry*. PhD diss., Boston University.

Chin, Elizabeth. 2016. *My Life with Things: The Consumer Diaries*. Durham, NC: Duke University Press.

Clifford, James. 1997. *Routes: Travel and Translation in the Late Twentieth Century*. Cambridge, MA: Harvard University Press.

Collins, Jane. 2009. *Threads: Gender, Labor and Power in the Global Apparel Industry*. Chicago: University of Chicago Press.

Collins, Randall. 1981. "On the Microfoundations of Macrosociology." *American Journal of Sociology* 86, no. 5: 984–1014.

Cooley, Charles H. 1902. *Human Nature and the Social Order*. New York: Scribner's.

Crane, Diane. 1972. *Invisible Colleges: Diffusion of Knowledge in Scientific Communities*. Chicago: University of Chicago Press.

Craveri, Benedetta. 2005. *The Age of Conversation*. New York: New York Review of Books.

Crawford, Matthew. 2009. *Shop Class as Soulcraft: An Inquiry into the Value of Work*. New York: Penguin.

Crease, Robert P. 2011. *World in the Balance: The Historic Quest for an Absolute System of Measurement*. New York: W.W. Norton.

Crowston, Clare Haru. 2013. *Credit, Fashion, Sex: Economies of Regard in Old Regime France*. Durham, NC: Duke University Press.

Da Costa, Achyles, and Maria Cristina Passos, eds. 2004. *A Industria Calçadista no Rio Grande do Sul*. Sao Leopoldo: Unisinos.

Darnton, Robert. 1984. *The Great Cat Massacre: And Other Episodes in French Cultural History*. New York: Basic Books.

Daston, Lorraine, ed. 2004. *Things That Talk: Object Lessons from Art and Science*. Cambridge, MA: MIT Press.

Daston, Lorraine, and Peter Galison. 1992. "The Image of Objectivity." *Representations* 40: 81–128.

Daston, Lorraine, and Peter Galison. 2007. *Objectivity*. Brooklyn: Zone Books.

Deener, Andrew. 2017. "The Origins of the Food Desert: Urban Inequality as Infrastructural Exclusion." Social Forces 95, no. 3: 1285–1309.

Deener, Andrew. 2018. "The Architecture of Ethnographic Knowledge: Narrowing Down Data and Contexts in Search of Sociological Cases." *Sociological Perspectives* 61, no. 2: 295–313.

Deener, Andrew. 2020. *The Problem with Feeding Cities: The Social Transformation of Infrastructure, Abundance, and Inequality in America*. Chicago: University of Chicago Press.

DeNora, Tia. 1997. *Beethoven and the Construction of Genius: Musical Politics in Vienna, 1792–1803*. Berkeley: University of California Press.

DeNora, Tia. 2000. *Music in Everyday Life*. Cambridge: Cambridge University Press.

Derluguian, Georgi. 2005. *Bourdieu's Secret Admirer in the Caucasus: A World-System Biography*. Chicago: University of Chicago Press.

Djelic, Marie-Laure and Antti Ainamo. 1999. "The Coevolution of New Organizational Forms in the Fashion Industry: A Historical and Comparative Study of France, Italy, and the United States." *Organization Science* 10, no. 5: 622–37.

Dominguez Rubio, Fernando. 2014. "Preserving the Unpreservable: Docile and Unruly Objects at MoMA." *Theory and Society 43, no.* 6: 617–45.

Dominguez Rubio, Fernando. 2015. "Semiosis beyond Culture: An Ecological Approach." *Culture Section Newsletter* 27, no. 2: 7–8, 11–12, 28–32.

Dominguez Rubio, Fernando. 2016. "On the Discrepancy between Objects and Things: An Ecological Approach." *Journal of Material Culture* 21, no. 1: 59–86.

Dominguez Rubio, Fernando. 2020. *Still Life: Ecologies of the Modern Imagination at the Art Museum*. Chicago: University of Chicago Press.

Douglas, Mary. 1966. *Purity and Danger: An Analysis of Concepts of Pollution and Taboo*. New York: Praeger.

Elias, Norbert. 1993. *Mozart: Portrait of a Genius*. Berkeley: University of California Press.

Entwistle, Joanne. 2009. *The Aesthetic Economy of Fashion: Markets and Value in Clothing and Modelling*. London: Berg Publishers.

Epstein, Steve. 2007. *Inclusion: The Politics of Difference in Medical Research*. Chicago: University of Chicago Press.

Epstein, Steve. 2009. "Beyond the Standard Human." In *Standards and Their Stories: How Quantifying, Classifying, and Formalizing Practices Shape Everyday Life*, edited by Martha Lampland and Susan Leigh Star. *Ithaca, NY*: Cornell University Press.

Espeland, Wendy, and Michael Sauder. 2016. *Engines of Anxiety: Academic Rankings, Reputation, and Accountability*. New York: Russell Sage.

Fourcade, Marion. 2010. "The Problem of Embodiment in the Sociology of Knowledge." *Qualitative Sociology* 33, no. 4: 569–74.

Fourcade, Marion. 2016. "Ordinalization." *Sociological Theory* 34, no. 3: 175–95.

Fourcade, Marion, and Kieran Healey. 2013. "Classification Situations: Life Chances in the Neoliberal Economy." *Accounting, Organizations and Society* 38: 559–72.

Friese, Carrie, and Adele Clarke. 2012. "Transposing Bodies of Knowledge and Technique: Animal Models at Work in Reproductive Sciences." *Social Studies of Science* 42, no. 1: 31–52.

Fujimura, Joan. 1992. "Crafting Science: Standardized Packages, Boundary Objects, and Translation." In *Science as Practice and Culture*, edited by Andrew Pickering, 168–211. Chicago: University of Chicago Press.

Galison, Peter. 1997. *Image and Logic*. Chicago: University of Chicago Press.

Galison, Peter. 2004. "Images of Self." In *Things that Talk: Object Lessons from Art and Science*, edited by Lorraine Daston, 257–96. New York: Zone Books.

Garfinkel, Harold. 1967. *Studies in Ethnomethodology*. Englewood Cliffs, NJ: Prentice Hall.

Gell, Alfred. 1998. *Art and Agency: An Anthropological Theory*. New York: Oxford University Press.

Gibson, James J. 1979. *The Ecological Approach to Visual Perception*. Boston, MA: Houghton Mifflin.

Ginzburg, Carlo. 1980. "Morelli, Freud and Sherlock Holmes: Clues and Scientific Method." *History Workshop* 9, no. 1: 5–36.

Ginzburg, Carlo. 1991. *Ecstasies: Deciphering the Witches' Sabbath*. Chicago: University of Chicago Press.

Godart, Frederic. 2012. *Unveiling Fashion: Business, Culture, and Identity in the Most Glamorous Industry*. New York: Palgrave Macmillan.

Gootenberg, Paul. 2008. *Andean Cocaine: The Making of a Global Drug*. Chapel Hill, NC: University of North Carolina Press.

Gordillo, Gastón. 2013. "The Void: Invisible Ruins on the Edges of Empire." In Imperial Debris, edited by Ann Stoler, 227–51. Durham, NC: Duke University Press.

Gordillo, Gastón. 2014. *Rubble: The Afterlife of Destruction*. Durham, NC: Duke University Press.

Grandin, Greg. 2009. *Fordlandia*. New York: Metropolitan Books.

Greenberg, Miriam. 2008. *Branding New York: How a City in Crisis Was Sold to the World*. London: Routledge.

Gruzinski, Serge. 2001. *Images at War: Mexico from Columbus to Blade Runner*. Durham, NC: Duke University Press.

Gusterson, Hugh. 1997. "Studying Up Revisited." *PoLAR* 20, no. 1: 114–19.

Guthrie, Doug. 1999. *Dragon in a Three-Piece Suit: The Emergence of Capitalism in China*. Princeton, NJ: Princeton University Press.

Habermas, Jurgen. 1981. *The Public Sphere*. Cambridge, MA: MIT Press.

Hall, John. 2009. *Apocalypse: From Antiquity to the Empire of Modernity*. Cambridge: Polity.

Hamilton, Gary G., and Gary Gereffi. 2009. "Global Commodity Chains, Market Makers, and the Rise of Demand-Responsive Economies." In *Frontiers of Commodity Chain Research, edited by* Jennifer Bair. Palo Alto, CA: Stanford University Press.

Hamilton, Gary G., and Cheng-shu Kao. 1990. "The Institutional Foundations of Chinese Business in the Family Firm in Taiwan." Working Paper Series no. 8, Institute of Governmental Affairs, Research Program in East Asian Business and Development, University of California Davis.

Hamilton, Gary G., and Cheng-shu Kao. 2017. *Making Money: How Taiwanese Industrialists Embraced the Global Economy*. Palo Alto, CA: Stanford University Press.

Hannerz, Ulf. 2003. "Being There . . . and There . . . and There! Reflections on Multi-Site Ethnography." *Ethnography* 4, no. 2: 201–16.

Hannerz, Ulf. 2004. *Foreign News: Exploring the World of Foreign Correspondents*. Chicago: University of Chicago Press.

Hansen, Karen. 2000. *Salaula: The World of Secondhand Clothing in Zambia*. Chicago: University of Chicago Press.

Hanser, Amy. 2006. "Sales Floor Trajectories: Distinction and Service in Postsocialist China." *Ethnography* 7, no. 4: 461–91.

Harper, Doug. 1992. *Working Knowledge: Skill and Community in a Small Shop.* Chicago: University of Chicago Press.

Harvey, David. 1995. "Time-Space Compression and the Rise of Modernism as a Cultural Force." In *The Condition of Postmodernity.* Baltimore, MD: John Hopkins University Press.

Harvey, David. 2010. *The Enigma of Capital: And the Crises of Capitalism.* New York: Oxford University Press.

Heidegger, Martin. 1982. *The Basic Problems of Phenomenology.* Bloomington: Indiana University Press.

Heinich, Natalie. 1996. *The Glory of van Gogh: An Anthropology of Admiration.* Princeton, NJ: Princeton University Press.

Hell, Julia. 2018. *The Conquest of Ruins: The Third Reich and the Fall of Rome.* Chicago: University of Chicago Press.

Henare, Amiria, Martin Holbraad, and Sari Wastell. 2007. *Thinking Through Things: Theorising Artefacts Ethnographically.* London: Routledge.

Henderson, Kathryn. 1991. "Flexible Sketches and Inflexible Data Bases: Visual Communication, Conscription Devices, and Boundary Objects in Design Engineering." *Science, Technology & Human Values* 16, no. 4: 448–73.

Henderson, Kathryn. 1995. "The Political Career of a Prototype: Visual Representations in Design Engineering." *Social Problems* 42, no. 2: 274–99.

Henderson, Kathryn. 1999. *On Line and on Paper: Visual Representations, Visual Cultures, and Computer Graphics in Design Engineering.* Cambridge, MA: MIT Press.

Hetherington, Kevin, and John Law. 2000. "Materialities, Globalities, Spatialities," in *Knowledge, Space, Economy, edited by* John Bryson, Peter Daniels, Nick Henry, and Jane Pollard, 34–49. London: Routledge.

Ho, Karen. 2009. *Liquidated: An Ethnography of Wall Street.* Durham, NC: Duke University Press.

Hoang, Kimberly. 2014. *Dealing in Desire: Asian Ascendancy, Western Decline and the Hidden Currencies of Global Sex.* Berkeley: University of California Press.

Holmes, Douglas, and George E. Marcus. 2006. "Fast Capitalism: Para-Ethnography and the Rise of the Symbolic Analyst." In *Frontiers of Capital: Ethnographic Reflections on the New Economy,* edited by Melissa S. Fisher and Greg Downey. Durham, NC: Duke University Press.

Huberman, Georges-Didi. 2003. *Invention of Hysteria: Charcot and the Photographic Iconography of the Salpêtrière.* Cambridge: MIT Press.

Hughes, Everett. 1971. *The Sociological Eye*. New Brunswick, NJ: Transaction Publishers.

Hutchins, Edwin. 1991. "The Social Organization of Distributed Cognition." In *Perspectives on Socially Shared Cognition, edited by* Lauren B. Resnick, John M. Levine, and Stephanie D. Teasley, 283–307. Washington, DC: American Psychological Association.

Hutchins, Edwin. 1995. *Cognition in the Wild*. Cambridge, MA: MIT Press.

Hutchins, Edwin, and Tove Klausen. 1996. "Distributed Cognition in an Airline Cockpit." In *Cognition and Communication at Work*, edited by Y. Engeström and D. Middleton, 15–34. Cambridge: Cambridge University Press.

Ingold, Tim. 1993. "The Temporality of the Landscape." *World Archeology* 25, no. 2: 152–74.

Irani, Lily. 2019. *Chasing Innovation: Making Entrepreneurial Citizens in Modern India*. Princeton, NJ: Princeton University Press.

Jackson, Steven. 2014. "Rethinking Repair." In *Media Technologies: Essays on Communication, Materiality, and Society*, edited by T. Gillespie, P. Boczkowski, and K. Foot, 221–40. Cambridge, MA: MIT Press.

Karpik, Lucien. 2010. *Valuing the Unique. The Economies of Singularities*. Princeton, NJ: Princeton University Press.

Keane, Webb. 2003. "Semiotics and the Social Analysis of Material Things." *Language & Communication* 23, no. 3–4:409–25.

Knorr Cetina, Karin. 1999. *Epistemic Cultures: How the Sciences Make Knowledge*. Cambridge, MA: Harvard University Press.

Knorr Cetina, Karin. 2009. "The Synthetic Situation: Interactionism for a Global World." *Symbolic Interaction* 32, no. 1: 61–87.

Knorr Cetina, Karin, and Urs Bruegger. 2002. "Global Microstructures: The Virtual Societies of Financial Markets." *American Journal of Sociology* 107, no. 4: 905–50.

Knorr Cetina, Karin, and Alex Preda. 2007. "The Temporalization of Financial Markets: From Network to Flow." *Theory, Culture & Society* 24, no. 7–8: 116–38.

Knowles, Caroline. 2014. *Flip Flop: A Journey Through Globalization's Backroads*. London: Pluto Press.

Kopytoff, Igor. 1986. "The Cultural Biography of Things: Commoditization as Process." In *The Social Life of Things: Commodities in Cultural Perspective*, edited by Arjun Appadurai, 64–91. Cambridge: Cambridge University Press.

Koselleck, Reinhart. 2004. *Futures Past: On the Semantics of Historical Time*. New York: Columbia University Press.

Krause, Elizabeth. 2018. *Tight Knit: Global Families and the Social Life of Fast Fashion*. Chicago: University of Chicago Press.

Krause, Monika. 2012. "Recombining Micro/Macro: The Grammar of Theoretical Innovation." *European Journal of Social Theory* 16, no. 2: 139–52.

Kuhn, Norberto, Jr., and Margarete Fagundes Nunes. 2012. "The Role of the New Media in the Migratory Experiences of Brazilian Footwear Industry Workers in the South of China." *Migraciones Internacionales* 66, no. 4: 47–74.

Kusenbach, Margarete. 2003. "Street Phenomenology: The Go-Along as Ethnographic Research Tool." *Ethnography* 4, no. 3: 455–85.

Lampland, Martha, and Susan Leigh Star. 2009. *Standards and Their Stories: How Quantifying, Classifying, and Formalizing Practices Shape Everyday Life*. Ithaca, NY: Cornell University Press.

Lantz, Jenny. 2016. *The Trendmakers*. London: Bloomsbury Academic.

Latour, Bruno. 1984. "The Powers of Association." *Sociological Review* 32, no. 1: 264–80.

Latour, Bruno. 1986. "Visualization and Cognition: Thinking with Eyes and Hands." *Knowledge and Society: Studies in the Sociology of Culture Past and Present* 6:1–40.

Latour, Bruno. 1987. *Science in Action*. Cambridge, MA: Harvard University Press.

Latour, Bruno. 1988. *The Pasteurization of France*. Cambridge, MA: Harvard University Press.

Latour, Bruno. 1999. *Pandora's Hope: Essays on the Reality of Science Studies*. Cambridge, MA: Harvard University Press.

Latour, Bruno. 2005. *Reassembling the Social: An Introduction to Actor-Network-Theory*. New York: Oxford University Press.

Latour, Bruno, and Steven Woolgar. 1986. *Laboratory Life: The Construction of Scientific Facts*. Princeton, NJ: Princeton University Press.

Law, John. 1986. "On the Methods of Long Distance Control: Vessels, Navigation and the Portuguese Route to India," in *Power, Action and Belief: a New Sociology of Knowledge?*, edited by John Law, 231–60. London: Routledge Kegan and Paul.

Law, John. 1987. "Technology and Heterogeneous Engineering: The Case of the Portuguese Expansion," in *The Social Construction of Technological Systems, edited by* Wiebe Bijker, Thomas Hughes, and Trevor Pinch, 111–34. Cambridge, MA: MIT Press.

Lee, Benjamin, and Edward LiPuma. 2002. "Cultures of Circulation: The Imaginations of Modernity." *Public Culture* 14, no. 1: 191–213.

Lee, Ching Kwan. 1998. *Gender and the South China Miracle: Two Worlds of Factory Women*. Berkeley: University of California Press.

Lee, Ching Kwan. 2017. *The Specter of Global China: Politics, Labor, and Foreign Investment in Africa*. Chicago: University of Chicago Press.

Lengwiler, Martin. 2009. "Double Standards: The History of Standardizing Humans in Modern Life Insurance." In *Standards and Their Stories: How Quantifying, Classifying, and Formalizing Practices Shape Everyday Life*, edited by Martha Lampland and Susan Leigh Star, 95–122. *Ithaca*, NY: Cornell University Press.

Leonardi, Paul. 2010. "From Road to Lab to Math: The Co-Evolution of Technological, Regulatory, and Organizational Innovations for Automotive Crash Testing." *Social Studies of Science* 40, no. 2: 243–74.

Leonardi, Paul. 2012. *Car Crashes without Cars: Lessons about Simulation Technology and Organizational Change from Automotive Design*. Cambridge, MA: MIT Press.

Lopez, Luciana. 2010. "Special Report: BRIC Breaking: Brazil's China Syndrome." *Reuters*, September 24.

Lowe, Lisa. 2015. *The Intimacies of Four Continents*. Durham, NC: Duke University Press.

Lowy, Michael. 1992. *Révolte et Mélancolie le Romantisme à Contre-Courant de la Modernité*. Paris: Payot.

Mallard, Alexander. 1998. "Compare, Standardize and Settle Agreement: On Some Usual Metrological Problems." *Social Studies of Science* 28, no. 4: 571–601.

Marcus, George E. 1995. "Ethnography in/of the World System: The Emergence of Multi-Sited Ethnography." *Annual Review of Anthropology* 24: 95–117.

Mears, Ashley. 2011. *Pricing Beauty: The Making of a Fashion Model*. Berkeley: University of California Press.

Menger, Pierre-Michel. 2014. *The Economics of Creativity: Art and Achievement under Uncertainty*. Cambridge, MA: Harvard University Press, 2014.

Mialet, Helene. 2012. *Hawking Incorporated: Stephen Hawking and the Anthropology of the Knowing Subject*. Chicago: University of Chicago Press.

Mintz, Sidney. 1985. *Sweetness and Power: The Place of Sugar in Modern History*. New York: Penguin Books.

Miraftab, Faranak. 2016. *Global Heartland: Displaced Labor, Transnational Lives & Local Placemaking*. Bloomington: Indiana University Press.

Molotch, Harvey. 2002. "Place in Product." *IJURR* 26, no. 4: 665–88.

Molotch, Harvey. 2003. *Where Stuff Comes From: How Toasters, Toilets, Cars, Computers, and Many Other Things Come to Be as They Are*. New York: Routledge.

Moon, Cristina. 2014. "The Secret World of Fast Fashion." *Pacific Standard*, March 17, 2014. https://psmag.com/economics/secret-world-slow-road -korea-los-angeles-behind-fast-fashion-73956.

Mukerji, Chandra. 2009. *Impossible Engineering: Technology and Territoriality on the Canal Du Midi*. Princeton, NJ: Princeton University Press.

Mukerji, Chandra. 2010. "The Territorial State as a Figured World of Power: Strategics, Logistics, and Impersonal Rule." *Sociological Theory* 28, no. 4: 402–24.

Mukerji, Chandra. 2014. "The Cultural Power of Tacit Knowledge: Inarticulacy and Bourdieu's Habitus." *American Journal of Cultural Sociology* 2: 348–75.

Mukerji, Chandra. 2016. *Modernity Reimagined: An Analytic Guide*. London: Routledge.

Nadeem, Shehzad. 2011. *Dead Ringers: How Outsourcing is Changing the Way Indians Understand Themselves*. Princeton, NJ: Princeton University Press.

Nader, Laura. 1972. "Up the Anthropologist: Perspectives Gained from Studying Up." ED065375. *ERIC*. https://eric.ed.gov/?id=ED065375.

Ngai, Pun. 2005. *Made in China: Women Factory Workers in a Global Workplace*. Durham, NC: Duke University Press.

Obrist, Hans. 2014. *Ways of Curating*. New York: FSG.

Ocejo, Richard. 2017. *Masters of Craft: Old Jobs in the New Urban Economy*. Princeton, NJ: Princeton University Press.

O'Connor, Erin. 2005. "Embodied Knowledge. The Experience of Meaning and the Struggle towards Proficiency in Glassblowing." *Ethnography* 6, no. 2: 183–204.

O'Donnell, Casey. 2014. *Developer's Dilemma: The Secret World of Videogame Creators*. Cambridge: MIT Press.

Oliveira, Fernando. 1988. *A Economia Brasileira: A Critica da Razao dualista*. Petrópolis: Vozes.

Oliven, George. 1996. *Tradition Matters: Modern Gaucho Identity in Brazil*. New York: Columbia University Press.

Opazo, Pilar. 2016. *Appetite for Innovation: Creativity and Change at elBulli*. New York: Columbia University Press.

Ortner, Sherry. 2010. "Access: Reflections on Studying Up in Hollywood." *Ethnography* 11, no. 2: 211–33.

Otis, Eileen. 2011. *Markets and Bodies: Women, Service Work, and the Making of Inequality in China*. Stanford, CA: Stanford University Press.

Pachirat, Timothy. 2012. *Every Twelve Seconds: Industrialized Slaughter and the Politics of Sight*. New Haven, CT: Yale University Press.

Parreñas, Rhacel. 2001. *Servants of Globalization: Migration and Domestic Work*. 2nd ed. Stanford, CA: Stanford University Press.

Paul, Anju. 2017. *Multinational Maids: Stepwise Migration in a Global Labor Market*. Cambridge: Cambridge University Press.

Peirce, Charles S. 1894. "What is a Sign?"

Penteado, Adriana. 2011. *Mapeamento e Analise Geomorfológicos como Subsidio para Identificacao e Caracterizacao de Terras Inundaveis*. PhD diss., University of Sao Paulo.

Pickering, Andrew. 1995. *The Mangle of Practice: Time, Agency, and Science*. Chicago: University of Chicago Press.

Pietz, William. 1985. "The Problem of the Fetish." *RES: Anthropology and Aesthetics* 9, no. 1: 5–17.

Piore, Michael J., and Charles F. Sabel. 1984. *The Second Industrial Divide*. New York: Basic Books.

Polanyi, Michael. 1958. *Personal Knowledge: Towards a Post-Critical Philosophy*. Chicago: University of Chicago Press

Polanyi, Michael. 1962. "Tacit Knowing: Its Bearing on Some Problems of Philosophy." *Reviews of Modern Physics* 34, no. 4: 601–16.

Porter, Theodore M. 1995. *Trust in Numbers: The Pursuit of Objectivity in Science and Public Life*. Princeton, NJ: Princeton University Press.

Raustiala, Kal and Christopher John Sprigman. 2012. *The Knockoff Economy: How Imitation Sparks Innovation*. New York: Oxford University Press.

Rockefeller, Stuart. 2011. "Flow." *Current Anthropology* 52, no. 4: 557–78.

Rodrigues Kanaan, Beatriz. 2013. *Homo Faber: Una Etnografia de Praticas de Trabalho na Serra Gaúcha/Rio Grande do Sul*. PhD diss., Universidade Federal do Rio Grande do Sul.

Rofel, Lisa, and Sylvia J. Yanagisako. 2019. *Fabricating Transnational Capitalism: A Collaborative Ethnography of Italian-Chinese Global Fashion*. Durham, NC: Duke University Press.

Rossi, Aldo. 1982. *The Architecture of the City*. Tokyo: A+U.

Sabel, Charles. 1994. "Flexible Specialization and the Re-Emergence of Regional Economies." In *Post-Fordism: A Reader*, edited by Ash Amin, 101–56. Oxford: Blackwell.

Sallaz, Jeffrey. 2009. *The Labor of Luck*. Berkeley: University of California Press.

Sallaz, Jeffrey. 2019. *Lives on the Line: How the Philippines Became the World's Call Center Capital*. New York: Oxford University Press.

Salzinger, Leslie. 2003. *Genders in Production: Making Workers in Mexico's Global Factories*. Berkeley: University of California Press.

Schemes, Claudia, et al. 2005. *Memoria do Setor Coureiro-Calçadista. Pioneros e Emprendedores do Vale do Rios dos Sinos*. Novo Hamburgo: Feevale.

Schmitz, Hubert. 1995. "Small Shoemakers and Fordist Giants: Tale of a Supercluster." *World Development* 23, no. 1: 9–28.

Schneider, Sergio. 1996. "Os Colonos Da Industria Calçadista: expansão industrial e as transformações da agricultura familiar no Rio Grande do Sul." *Revista Ensaios FEE, Porto Alegre,* 17, no. 1: 298–323.

Schneider, Sergio. 1999. *Agricultura Familiar e Industrializacao.* PhD diss., Instituto de Filosofia e Ciências Humanas, Universidade Estadual de Campinas.

Schutz, Alfred. 1959. "Tiresias, or Our Knowledge of Future Events." *Social Research* 26, no. 1: 71–89.

Schutz, Alfred. 1964. *Collected Papers II: Studies in Social Theory,* edited by Arvid Brodersen, 277–93. The Hague: Nijhoff.

Scott, Allen J. 2000. *The Cultural Economy of Cities.* London: Sage.

Scott, Allen J. 2006. "The Changing Global Geography of Low-Technology, Labor-Intensive Industry: Clothing, Footwear and Furniture." *World Development* 34: 1517–36.

Selbech, Jeferson Francisco. 1999. *Novo Hamburgo 1927–1997: Os Espaços de Sociabilidade na Gangorra da Modernidade.* PhD diss., Universidade Federal do Rio Grande do Sul.

Sennett, Richard. 2008. *The Craftsman.* New Haven, CT: Yale University Press.

Sewell, William, Jr. 2010. "The Empire of Fashion and The Rise of Capitalism in Eighteenth Century France." *Past and Present 206: 81–120.*

Shapin, Steven. 1989. "The Invisible Technician." *American Scientist* 77, no. 6: 554–63.

Shapin, Steven. 2012. "The Sciences of Subjectivity." *Social Studies of Science* 42, no. 2: 170–84.

Simmel, Georg. 1957. "Fashion." *American Journal of Sociology* 62, no. 6: 541–58.

Simmel, Georg. 1958. "The Ruin." *Hudson Review* 11, no. 3: 371–85.

Snyder, Benjamin. 2016. *The Disrupted Workplace: Time and the Moral Order of Flexible Capitalism.* New York: Oxford University Press.

Soluri, John. 2005. *Banana Cultures: Agriculture, Consumption, and Environmental Change in Honduras and the United States.* Austin: University of Texas Press.

Stallybrass, Peter. 1998. "Marx's Coat." In *Border Fetishisms: Material Objects in Unstable Spaces,* edited by Patricia Spyer. New York: Routledge.

Star, Susan Leigh. 1990. "Power, Technology and the Phenomenology of Conventions: On Being Allergic to Onions." *The Sociological Review* 38, no. 1: 26–56.

Star, Susan Leigh. 1991. "The Sociology of the Invisible: The Primacy of Work in the Writings of Anselm Strauss." In *Social Organization and Social Process:*

Essays in Honor of Anselm Strauss, edited by Anselm Leonard Strauss and
  David R. Maines. Hawthorne, NY: Aldine de Gruyter.

Star, Susan Leigh. 1995. "Introduction." In *Ecologies of Knowledge*, edited by S. L.
  Star, 1–35. Albany: SUNY Press.

Star, Susan Leigh. 1995. "The Ethnography of Infrastructure." *American
  Behavioral Scientist* 43, no. 3: 377–91.

Star, Susan Leigh. 2010. "This is Not a Boundary Object: Reflections on the
  Origin of a Concept." *Science, Technology & Human Values* 35, no. 5:
  601–17.

Star, Susan Leigh, and James R. Griesemer. 1989. "Institutional Ecology,
  'Translations' and Boundary Objects: Amateurs and Professionals in
  Berkeley's Museum of Vertebrate Zoology, 1907–39." *Social Studies of
  Science* 19, no. 3: 387–420.

Star, Susan Leigh, and Anselm Strauss. 1999. "Layers of Silence, Arenas of
  Voice: The Ecology of Visible and Invisible Work." *Computer Supported
  Cooperative Work* 8, no. 1–2: 9–30.

Stark, David. 2009. *The Sense of Dissonance: Accounts of Worth in Economic Life.*
  Princeton, NJ: Princeton University Press.

Steinmetz, George. 2008. "Harrowed Landscapes: White Ruingazers in Namibia
  and Detroit and the Cultivation of Memory." *Visual Studies* 23, no. 3:
  211–37.

Sterne, Jonathan. 2003. *The Audible Past: Cultural Origins of Sound
  Reproduction.* Durham, NC: Duke University Press.

Stoller, Ann Laura. 2008. "Imperial Debris: Reflection on Ruins and Ruination."
  Cultural Anthropology 23, no. 3: 191–219.

Stoller, Ann Laura. 2013. *Imperial Debris: On Ruins and Ruination.* Durham, NC:
  Duke University Press.

Storper, Michael. 1997. *The Regional World: Territorial Development in a Global
  Economy.* New York: Guilford Press.

Strauss, Anselm L. 1978. "A Social World Perspective." *Studies in Symbolic
  Interaction* 1: 119–28.

Strauss, Anselm L. 2001. *Professions, Work and Careers.* New Brunswick, NJ:
  Transaction.

Sudnow, David. 1978. *Ways of the Hand: The Organization of Improvised
  Conduct.* Cambridge, MA: MIT Press.

Taussig, Michael. 1980. *The Devil and Commodity Fetishism in South America.*
  Chapel Hill: University of North Carolina Press.

Taussig, Michael. 1993. *Mimesis and Alterity: A Particular History of the Senses.*
  London: Routledge.

Thayer, Millie. 2001. "Transnational Feminism: Reading Joan Scott in the Brazilian Sertão." *Ethnography* 2, no. 2: 243–71.

Thevenot, Laurent. 1984. "Rules and Implements: Investment in Forms." *Social Science Information* 23, no. 1: 1–45.

Thevenot, Laurent. 2009. "Governing Life by Standards. A View from Engagements." *Social Studies of Science* 39, no. 5: 793–813.

Timmermans, Stefan, and Steven Epstein. 2010. "A World of Standards but Not a Standard World: Toward a Sociology of Standards and Standardization." *Annual Review of Sociology* 36, no. 1: 69–89.

Tsing, Anna. 2005. *Friction: An Ethnography of Global Connection*. Princeton, NJ: Princeton University Press.

Tsing, Anna. 2013. "Sorting Out Commodities: How Capitalist Value Is Made Through Gifts." *HAU: Journal of Ethnographic Theory* 3, no. 1: 21–43.

Vaughan, Diane. 1996. *The Challenger Launch Decision: Risky Technology, Culture and Deviance at NASA*. Chicago: University of Chicago Press.

Velthuis, Olav. 2003. "Symbolic Meanings of Prices: Constructing the Value of Contemporary Art in Amsterdam and New York." *Theory and Society* 32, no. 2: 181–215.

Velthuis, Olav. 2005. *Talking Prices: Symbolic Meaning of Prices for Contemporary Art*. Princeton, NJ: Princeton University Press.

Vera, Héctor. 2015. "The Social Construction of Units of Measurement: Institutionalization, Legitimation and Maintenance in Metrology." In *Standardization in Measurement: Philosophical, Historical and Sociological Issues*, edited by Oliver Schlaudt and Lara Huber. London: Pickering and Chatto.

Veron, Eliseo. 1998. *La Semiosis Social*. Buenos Aires: Nueva Visión.

Von Hippel, Eric. 1994. "'Sticky Information' and the Locus of Problem Solving: Implications for Innovation." *Management Science* 40, no. 4: 429–39.

Wacquant, Loic. 2004. *Body and Soul: Notebooks of an Apprentice Boxer*. New York: Oxford University Press.

Wagner-Pacifici, Robin. 2011. "The Cultural Sociological Experience of Cultural Objects." In *Routledge Handbook of Cultural Sociology*, edited by Laura Grindstaff, Ming-Cheng M. Lo, and John R. Hal. New York: Routledge.

Wang, Junmin. 2009. "Global-Market Building as State Building: China's Entry into the WTO and Market Reforms of China's Tobacco Industry." *Theory and Society* 38, no. 2: 165–94.

Weber, Max. 1905. *The Protestant Ethic and the Spirit of Capitalism*. London: Unwin Hyman.

Wissinger, Elizabeth. 2015. *This Year's Model: Fashion, Media, and the Making of Glamour*. New York: NYU Press.

Wong, Winnie Won Yin. 2013. *Van Gogh on Demand*. Chicago: University of Chicago Press.

Wynn, Jonathan R. 2015. *Music/City: American Festivals and Placemaking in Austin, Nashville and Newport*. Chicago: University of Chicago Press.

Yanagisako, Sylvia. 2002. *Producing Culture and Capital: Family Firms in Italy*. Princeton, NJ: Princeton University Press.

Yang, Chung. 2007. "Divergent Hybrid Capitalisms in China: Hong Kong and Taiwanese Electronics Clusters in Dongguan." *Economic Geography* 83, no. 4: 395–420.

Yang, Mayfair Mei-hui. 2011. *Gifts, Favors, and Banquets: The Art of Social Relationships in China*. Ithaca, NY: Cornell University Press.

Yeung, Godfrey. 2001. *Foreign Investment and Socio-Economic Development in China: The Case of Dongguan*. Houndmills: Palgrave.

Zerubavel, Eviatar. 2003. *Time Maps: Collective Memory and the Social Shape of the Past*. Chicago: University of Chicago Press.

Zubrzycki, Geneviève. 2011. "History and the National Sensorium: Making Sense of Polish Mythology." *Qualitative Sociology* 34, no. 1: 21–57.

Zukin, Sharon. 1993. *Landscapes of Power from Detroit to Disney World*. Berkeley: University of California Press.

INDEX

www.ingramcontent.com/pod-product-compliance
Lightning Source LLC
Chambersburg PA
CBHW060031030426
42334CB00019B/2280